# Backroom Boys

Edward Smithies was born in Daventry, Northamptonshire, in 1941. He spent his earliest years surrounded by the aircraft parts, models of fuselages and wings, and blueprints that his father brought home from the aircraft factory where he worked. He lived in London for many years and taught history.

# Backroom Boys

### Personal stories of
### Britain's air war 1939–45

**EDWARD SMITHIES**

**CASSELL**

A CASSELL MILITARY PAPERBACK

First published as *War in the Air* by Viking in 1990
This paperback edition published in 2002
by Cassell,
an imprint of Orion Books Ltd,
Orion House, 5 Upper Saint Martin's Lane,
London WC2H 9EA

An Hachette UK company

3 5 7 9 10 8 6 4 2

Reissued 2012

British Library Cataloguing-in-Publication Data.
A catalogue record for this book is available
from the British Library.

ISBN 978-0-3043-5927-1

Printed and bound by CPI Group (UK) Ltd
Croydon, CR0 4YY

The Orion Publishing Group's policy is to use papers
that are natural, renewable and recyclable products and
made from wood grown in sustainable forests. The logging
and manufacturing processes are expected to conform to
the environmental regulations of the country of origin.

www.orionbooks.co.uk

# CONTENTS

# LIST OF PLATES

## ILLUSTRATION CREDITS

Hampshire County Libraries, 9; Imperial War Museum, 11, 14, 16, 18, 26, 29; Popperfoto, 1, 7, 8, 13, 15, 17, 25, 30; R.A.F. Museum, 2, 12, 19, 23, 27, 28; Topham Picture Source, 3, 4, 5, 6, 10, 20, 21; Ullstein Bilderdienst, 22, 24

# INTRODUCTION

THIS BOOK IS ABOUT THE PEOPLE WHO DESIGNED, BUILT, serviced and flew the aircraft that were so crucial to Great Britain's role in the Second World War. It seeks to see this war from their point of view, through their eyes, and in their words. It presents what they remember about the war in Europe and North Africa, and asks what they think of it all now. My interest in them and their war derives from the distant memories I have of the Second World War, which took place during my earliest years, and from the powerful and romantic picture that was presented to teenagers in the 1950s of the RAF's achievements and heroism ten years before.

I was born at the end of 1941, in the small English country town of Daventry, in Northamptonshire. This was the third winter of the war, which wasn't going well for Britain. Over two years of fighting had produced few results beyond defeats. A few days before I was born the British Army suffered a heavy reverse in North Africa and it looked for a time as though the whole of the Middle East might fall to Rommel's Panzer Army. In Russia the Red Army was being thrown back by the Wehrmacht along a front of 2,000 miles. The capture of Moscow and Leningrad was expected at any time. The United States was still neutral but in a few days the Japanese would bomb Pearl Harbor. That attack followed by a series of defeats culminating in the fall of

Singapore shattered the position of the Western powers in the Far East, and enabled Japan to threaten India, Australia and the Pacific shores of the USA.

Only in the air had the war gone at all successfully for the Allies. The RAF had defeated the Luftwaffe in the Battle of Britain, after a hard struggle. The Germans would not now risk an invasion of Britain. Indeed, the RAF was increasingly going on to the offensive, and Bomber Command had begun attacking German industrial centres. Huge British resources were diverted to the provision of planes, armaments, scientific and technological equipment, airfields, and so on. People drawn from a wide range of peacetime occupations – or none – joined the war effort, designing, building and servicing aircraft, the equipment that went into them, and the facilities that supported them. Many others flew war-planes, repaired them, or worked as administrative staff in the various headquarters and operational stations. Among this vast wartime army was my father.

Both my parents were Northerners, my father from Halifax in Yorkshire and my mother from Lancaster. They told me proudly as soon as I was old enough to appreciate the fact that their home towns were also the names of the two most famous British bombers of the Second World War. Among my earliest memories are the names of great German cities that were the targets of those bombers in the big aerial offensives during the later stages of the war. From news reports on the radio Berlin, Düsseldorf, Stuttgart, Essen, Hamburg, Dortmund, and others became familiar to me much earlier than the names of British towns of equivalent size.

My father, like many engineering apprentices of his generation, decided to get into a drawing office as soon as he could. This was the hub of most engineering factories where new products were designed, and where ambitious young men could attract the attention of their superiors. In the mid-1930s, one of the more promising industries was aircraft engineering.

In 1933 Hitler became Chancellor of Germany and soon embarked on a substantial programme of rearmament. The Luftwaffe was marked out for massive expansion. The British were reluctantly obliged to follow and began to build up the RAF and provide it with modern planes. In the 1920s the aircraft industry had barely survived, as it struggled desperately from meagre contract to meagre contract, too many firms competing for too little work. The Air Ministry doled out just enough orders to keep them alive. But after 1933 the aircraft industry was urgently needed. Orders began to flow and the industry to expand. Like many other young men, my father believed this was the industry of the future and he took jobs at several airframe and aero-engine firms: the Blackburn Aircraft Company at Brough, Rolls-Royce at Derby, and Bristol Aircraft, large and important concerns.

The outbreak of war provided new opportunities for ambitious young men: my father joined a recently established firm of sub-contractors to the aircraft industry called Westbourne Engineering. This company, eventually based in Daventry, rapidly colonized the small town and its surrounding villages. Several hundred people were employed, many, if not most of them, women. The local economy, previously a mix of boot and shoe manufacture and unemployment, was transformed into one based on general aircraft engineering.

My father and mother moved into a house opposite the factory. I became aware of a world which seemed to be filled with huge blueprints – photographic prints, white upon blue – which had a peculiar chemical smell. They were the preliminary sketches or plans in the days before computers did this kind of work. They lay on tables and chairs, sometimes spread out, sometimes folded neatly into piles. You had to shove them out of the way to sit down. One was usually available for study in the lavatory and more littered the floor in the garage. Balsa-wood models of the interiors of wings and airframes, smelling strongly of glue, contested for place as ornaments with the metal models of the aircraft the firm was working on. I first became familiar with the shapes of the Swordfish and Mosquito, Lancaster and Wellington, from seeing these miniatures round the house.

The lightness and intricacy of the wooden wings was a marvel, you could hardly feel their weight when you held them in your hand. Masses of multicoloured discs, each representing some part of the work process, were piled up in boxes, and the ones not yet printed on made excellent tiddly-winks. Books and pamphlets, distributed by the Air Ministry and the Ministry of Information for propaganda purposes, filled the bookshelves. I was too young to read them, but the photographs fascinated me. They showed aircraft, their crews posed in front of the wheels, arms round one another, smiling at the camera. Aerial shots presented broken dams, smashed railway lines with trains lying on their sides, blasted factories, endless rows of streets with not a house or block of flats intact, stretching away it seemed for ever. And there was one booklet with photographs which I didn't understand, showing what seemed to be vast heaps of broken dolls, lying still or being pushed by dumpers into huge craters.

Sometimes visitors stayed in the house, some from the world of show business, invited up to entertain the workers in the factory. Others were RAF pilots on morale-boosting tours, travelling round the country telling aircraft workers 'to keep at it', keep the planes moving, so we could smash the Third Reich. These dashing young men were a great draw and local girls would gather outside the house hoping to catch a glimpse, an autograph or even a date. Sometimes, a few weeks or months later, we'd get the news that the young hero had been killed, shot down over Germany or France, and gloom would settle on the factory and our household for a time.

Those war years made a deep impression on my parents. They felt that they were lived at a different pitch or level compared to the years before and after the war. They remembered it as a wonderful and terrible time, a period of great camaraderie, when class barriers for once seemed to fall, and everyone felt that they belonged to the national community. At the same time there was always the fear, even in a remote spot like Daventry, that you could lose your life, and that friends and relatives, especially those in the services, were in great danger.

Shortages were severe, discomfort general. But women could

walk home at night, even in London itself, and not give a thought to the danger of assault. Girls would hitch lifts and arrive safely at their destinations. A new and better world was being fought for, one that would contrast completely with the bad old days of unemployment, poverty and futility. Jobs for all, good wages, equality: that was what they believed the future would be, both were quite convinced of it. They were also convinced, once the war was over and receding into the past, that somehow it had all 'gone wrong'.

When my father talked of Westbourne Engineering during the war, he made it sound an unusual firm. A small nucleus of skilled workers had started production in Daventry and provided the basic engineering knowledge: they were supplemented by hundreds of local people, few of them skilled, many of them from agriculture, most of them women. Groups of workers arrived from Belgium, France and Holland, some of whom fled at the time of the defeat of France, others escaping later. One of the managers had slipped away from the Channel Islands in a boat with friends after they were occupied by the Germans.

The factory produced parts for a number of aircraft firms, and my father was particularly proud of the work they did on two aeroplanes. These were the superbly versatile Mosquito and the Lancaster, the best heavy bomber of the war. I have very distant memories of being taken into the factory when it was working at full stretch on these aircraft: the men in brown overalls setting the machine tools, the women working on lathes and drills, wearing turbans and pinafores, the peculiar smell of the slurry, the mess of swarf on the floor, and the deafening noise! Towards the end of the war parties of work people were taken to a nearby airfield to look at the planes they had helped to make, and were even taken up to sit in the controls. It was with the idea of finding out how accurate my distant memories were, and how typical the experience of Westbourne Engineering, that I began to trace people who had worked there and in other aircraft firms during the war. I soon found that many were anxious to talk about their memories: the feeling that the war had been an exceptional experience in their lives, and that the years after represented a period of anti-climax and disappointment, turned out to be very common. They put me in touch with their relatives and friends, some of whom had flown or serviced the aircraft they themselves had worked on.

I was very impressed by the great care and trouble people went to to prepare for our conversations. They invariably traced and brought out mementoes from the period: photographs of themselves and workmates on the shop floor, copies of works' magazines, posters and newsletters. Aircrews and airmen showed me their log-books and medals. Often memorabilia were beautifully arranged in albums, put together for children and grandchildren. Pride in the achievement of parents is pronounced: I have heard from many sons and daughters wishing to tell me about the experiences of their fathers or mothers, in the air force perhaps, or the WAAF, the Women's Auxiliary Air Force.

Their generation was particularly 'air-minded'. Former workers in the aircraft industry frequently told me that they were attracted to it, even though it was not especially well paid, because their imaginations had been caught by the romance of flight. The air circuses of the time, the achievements of pioneers like Amy Johnson or Charles Lindbergh, films about the aerial battles of the First World War like *Hell's Angels*, were formidable propagandists.

Several of the men I spoke to had worked in the aircraft industry for forty or fifty years, 'from stringbags to Concorde' they would say. They showed me photographs to illustrate how the technology of the industry had been transformed, and how primitive aircraft factories had been in pre-war days:

'Short Brothers' factory at Rochester – which built the first heavy bomber of the war, the Stirling – was built and extended in a rather hotch-potch system along the bank of the Medway. There was nothing uniform about it. They built shops as and when they could. Nothing was laid out from the production point of view. As the factory extended it spanned some of the small creeks that came in from the river. Old lighters were sunk in those creeks, filled up with chalk. Eventually the creeks were filled in, the factory floor built right across it, and that floor *moved* in the different conditions of the tide! It wasn't any good trying to maintain accuracy under those conditions, if the floor's floating about a bit.' (*Mr Chinery*)

'Handley Page's was quite a small firm which was suddenly blossoming out into a big production. But they didn't have the know-how at all. They didn't have the labour to call on. There was very little control. If you got fed up, and it was boring, laborious, you put a bit of metal under your arm and walked briskly as though you were entitled to. The charge-hand was down the bottom of the section. Unless you were working under his nose he couldn't see you. Handley Page didn't have much organization. And it didn't seem to get much better. I didn't notice it getting any better.' (*Mr Dury*)

Nor were workers treated well, even by firms with a good managerial reputation. Skilled workers, the core of the work-force of a successful firm, were hired and fired ruthlessly:

'De Havilland's was a happy place. We all knew each other so well. We were a happy family, the directors all knew us, called us by our names which was nice, wasn't it? There were a lot of ups and downs. It was almost frightening in those days – shortage of work and so on.'

'*Redundancies?*'

'Didn't use that word in those days, just used the word "sack". Got the sack. Friends and neighbours were hit. It was awful there then, whole batches of people being put out. Almost every night they used to walk around the factory, you put your head down so they wouldn't see you. We used to look out of the window and see old so-and-so walking along the road. My God, he's got the sack, I wonder what he's going to do.' (*Mr W. Phillips*)

'The manager at Vickers was a right bastard. He'd sack a man for eating, through the works' time, just like that, go and get your cards. And then he had a particular friend, a half-crippled, very short bloke. Used to stand on a box to work. After sacking one bloke, he'd give *him* an apple.

'You were allowed two minutes late, at the gate. After that you were stopped and they'd phone through to the foreman and say do you want so-and-so, and he'd say yes or no. Very often he'd say no. There were people waiting for jobs. It certainly had an effect on me – the fear of losing my job kept with me from then right through. I'm amazed even now at the levity with which people can treat their jobs.' (*Mr R. Phillips*)

'At Handley Page – Happy and Peaceful by the way – they used to come down with the money in boxes, money and cards, at four o'clock, or five o'clock and say, "Right, you're leaving at six o'clock!" The chap had been working all day long and wouldn't know until that time that he was going at the end of that day, or at the end of that shift. They would just do it.

'In those days safety was not really a thing. Compensation was very small, if you managed to get it. You could tell a tradesman by the number of fingers that he'd lost, part of a finger or some fingers. If you're on bonus you don't use guards on machines or strictly to the letter, do you? You also had people who were favourites to the foreman and what-have-you. One foreman never bought a cigarette in his life! He would come out of his office, walk up to one of the chaps and say, "How are you doing?" The first thing the chap would do is take out his packet of cigarettes and say, "Have a cigarette." He would have a couple of puffs of it, warm his hands by the fire, and walk back in the office. When he wanted another cigarette he'd come out and speak to somebody else. And you weren't allowed to smoke! If you were caught, say, in the toilet smoking, you were fired.' (*Mr Moreton*)

Photographs of pre-war aircraft factories usually show that only men were employed. The exception was the dope [varnish] shop. But after 1940 women arrived in all departments in large numbers. This was the most startling aspect that many men remembered about the war:

'I was about the last one to have any female labour – I was very much against it. Wrongly so as it happened. In fact they were better on some jobs than men. They didn't mind carrying on with the same job all the time, they got down to it. Most of them were very meticulous about it too, the women. Most of them. Very good. I couldn't speak too highly of them. They did a very good job.' (*Mr Rayner, Hawker's*)

'The women! We brought women in there, straight off the fields! You can't imagine what some of them looked like! Oh raw, real raw they were! And you know, by the time the war ended and they were on the way out, they were like ladies of leisure – real ladies! Because they'd earned good money during the war and they could buy anything they wanted. It was something that never happened to them before. They came in and worked with the men – in fact I thought some of them worked better than the men!' (*Mr Patrick*)

After the initial shock the wartime factory could be an enjoyable and even exciting place, especially for girls and women who had previously been in domestic service or had not worked at all. Many found engineering to their taste, and discovered unsuspected pleasures in an aircraft factory:

'You really felt you were doing something better because it was to do with planes. I enjoyed the work. There's lots of times I've been about places and I've thought, oh, look, there's a centre lathe, I'd give anything to still have the know-how to work a lathe! In the beginning I used to think I'll never be able to stand that noise but you grew to be able to switch it off, though I did lose my hearing a bit.

'It was interesting because there was lots of perks on there –

you had fun! You had more fun with a mixed community than with a whole class of women sitting icing cakes. There was an air of excitement, agitation, because I'm thrown in among a lot of men that are going to watch me, whereas when you're with women you don't have to be noticed. I used to walk around in the flight shed to see the men welding. I knew I was nice to look at, and all the old men wanted me.

'You had to leave a note for your night-shift man to say what your machine was doing during the daytime, and he would leave one back. These little notes would go on from the machinery and gradually it was, will you meet me somewhere? Make a date with him. I remember this particular night there was a man rushed in on nights so he could see me before I went home, and I said cheerio to the inspector, then I walk out to the gates and have a kiss and cuddle with the one that's on night shift, and I get on the bus and there's another one there! We go to town and I kiss him good-night. I get on the trolleybus to go home and meet another one, and when I open the door my Mum says, "You seem happy after twelve hours' work!"' (*Mrs East*)

Women with husbands or boy-friends in the forces found that work in an aircraft factory gave added purpose to their lives:

'I heard that he'd been taken a prisoner of war, he got captured before Dunkirk. When the Belgians stopped he was one of the first to be caught. From 1940 to 1946 he was a prisoner of war. For nine months we didn't know whether he was alive, dead, wounded, or otherwise, then he sent us a letter from Germany. We didn't get them very often. They were all censored, you see. In between time I used to be making socks and balaclavas and helmets and all the rest of it. That's why I loved my job. I'm helping my future husband get out a bit quicker, that was my way of looking at it. So I worked extremely hard.' (*Mrs Brown*)

The men working in the factories were mostly in reserved occupations:

'I'll be quite candid about it, in common with every other able-bodied man at the time I had to go to the labour exchange to be recorded, and I was very relieved to find I was in a reserved occupation. Talking to some old soldiers from the war, I think that we were probably in as much danger and sometimes more danger than they were – with the exception of Dunkirk and things like that. They told me I was more important to the country working on the bench at de Havilland's than I would be going overseas. So I was relieved – well, I was only just married anyway. I don't particularly think it was cowardice – it was just I felt I would be more use ...' (*Mr Orran*)

'I must admit I was lucky in not having to go and kill anybody or fight. We had to stop there and get on with our work. If we hadn't none of our aeroplanes would have been produced. If you wanted to join the forces you had to disappear. You know, just not come in! Go and tell some story to the RAF and reappear at the end of the war. Which a number of people did but they were very unpopular.' (*Mr Snow*)

'We could all dance but there was one chap there who couldn't. He used to say to me, "Would you come to a dance with me one night and teach me?" I turned round and said, "It's a pity you weren't in the war like my boy-friend!" He went up and told the foreman, and he came to me and said, "You want to watch your mouth saying things like that to the blokes in here because they've been exempt, they're all doing their bit!" Yes, OK, just a slip of the tongue, nasty little bit of violent temper. But, but, a short while after he was called up and he was killed. And that stuck, and it stuck with the rest too. And I had to live with it.' (*Mrs East*)

The photographs I was shown of servicemen surprised me. I

had not realized how young the men who flew against the Axis powers were. Many were still teenagers when they flew fighters in action, or completed a tour of operations in bombers. A twenty-five-year-old in the RAF in 1943 or 1944 was an old man – often nicknamed 'uncle' or 'grandad'!

'Invariably you went out two crews to one truck, fourteen people sitting on each side, very rough old trucks, invariably driven by a Waaf, the last female face and figure one saw. I was sitting there and the guy opposite me, he'd done about twenty-three trips. I'd only done my first eight. He was a little bit older than me, not too much, but five or six years, and that was really old – I was twenty and he was twenty-five, twenty-six, and we called him grandad! I said, "What's wrong, grandad?" I remember he had this beautiful dolly, soft dolly, sticking out of his Mae West flying suit. He said, "He's on the booze! We're gonna catch it, we're gonna chop it, they're gonna get us!" And that night they did. But that's just one of these things, anyone on the booze would catch it. You didn't drink and survive.' (*Mr Durran*)

They were lucky to survive so long. The casualty rates were appalling. The dangers of combat and bombing are well known, those of training, air-tests and transport less so. Yet everyone I spoke to who had flown or worked as ground crew during the war had stories of crash-landings, balings out and narrow brushes with death to describe:

'The aircraft had been tested for forty-five minutes by a test pilot, but it had no radio – it hadn't been fitted. I asked for a weather report and I was told that the aerodrome was clear, and it would stay that way during the hour it would take me to get there.

'It was deemed necessary always to take a fitter with you to check the aircraft and he had checked it and it was a hundred per cent. Off we went. The fitter was enjoying a very pleasant afternoon – I was flying above cloud. I knew the aerodrome like the back of my hand and when I got there I was above it but I was still in cloud, so I circled round knowing that they would hear this and sure enough up came the maroons from the ground. If they fire three reds in a row that means it's down to ground level – there's no chance. Three reds came up. So I pushed off, couldn't find anything that was open at all, circled round the other way, and got back.

'Still three reds so I thought that's it. Run out of juice. This poor old fellow at the back, what the hell do I do with him? He'd never been in a plane in his life. So I told him the position. I said, "You'll just have to trust me. We'll roll the aircraft upside down, count three after you've left and pull the ring. But don't touch it till you're out of the aircraft!"

'I rolled the aircraft over, hopefully somewhere over the aerodrome and out he went. I watched his chute open before he hit clouds. I circled round again. Pushed the stick forward, it's working because I'm falling out. Well, there's a lot of bullshit about how it's just like jumping off a six-foot wall, it felt like a fifteen-foot wall. It's a horrible feeling – I was buried by the parachute. I struggled out in my stockinged soles and the one good thing about it was I knew within a mile where the aircraft had gone down – I pointed it out to sea and it did eventually go in the drink. To my great delight there was a pub only three hundred yards away! Although it wasn't opening time I knocked on the door, the chap took one look at me and said, "Come on in!"

'By the time the blood company got there looking for me I was paralytic, but not with injuries!' (*Mr Landels*)

'It was a target in the Ruhr, Wuppertal I think. We went in without any problems, other than flak, dropped the bombs, but we were stragglers. We were coming back across Holland at about eighteen thousand feet. The rear gunner called up and said he could see a plane. He was firing at it and meanwhile the plane's fired at us. A lot of the bullets and incendiaries went into the wings, but we thought we were quite safe. The pilot's gone on for home.

'Then the rear gunner called up and said he could see a lot of sparks flying past his turret. Me being the odd Joe, I had to investigate. I pulled back a curtain over one of the fuselage windows, looked out and the whole of the upper surface of the wing was on fire – the metal cover was peeling up and flying past. I said to the pilot, "We're on fire, what you gonna do?"

' "Bale out!"

'I'd got as far as the end of the bomb bay when there's an almighty bang and next minute I'm flying through the air by myself. I just pulled the strap and floated down gracefully to earth! When I landed in the wheat field I broke my leg, broke it there, so I was lucky really. The pilot had his neck broken, he *landed* with a broken neck, but he was all right, he lived. The engineer was killed – he landed but he didn't get a chance to open his parachute. Poor old Joe, the rear gunner, as he baled out he was smothered in petrol and he burned like a torch. This was three weeks after my twenty-first birthday.' (*Mr Towers*)

RAF squadrons included men from all over the world. Crews were often made up of several nationalities:

'My pilot was Canadian, we had a Canadian wireless operator, Rhodesian mid-upper gunner, and a Jamaican rear gunner, a Harvard man. Biggest man ever to fly in a rear turret – he was six foot three. We had to get him in and then shut the doors on him – he'd never have got out. This white Rhodesian – "I'm not going to fly with that black bastard!" But we solved it. The rear gunner put him in a static water tank, cooled him off! They agreed to fly after that. They were a remarkable bunch. Cat's-eyes Lindsay in the rear turret, strange man who stammered like mad on the ground but never in the air.' (*Mr Power*)

Photographs often show ground crew as well as aircrew, all mixed together, arms round one another, part of the same team.

Affection between those who flew and those who kept the aircraft in good repair and armed was very strong:

'We always had the same ground crew – the thing in the air force was that it was the ground crew's aeroplane and we only borrowed it. "Bring it back in good condition, don't bring it back full of holes!" Our lives depended on them. We thought far more of them than the air force apparently did. We knew that if the bloke had said, "Right, that engine's good!", then that engine *was* good. That was where the discipline was, in his skill in applying it when he could easily have stepped down and said, "Well, it's bloody cold up here, let's give it a rest." They didn't, they stayed there and they finished it.' (*Mr Pring*)

Aircrew have huge affection for the planes they flew, even those that have questionable reputations, like the Stirling or the Beaufighter. Photographs or paintings of them – sometimes huge romanticized action scenes done by a professional, occasionally amateur labours of love with precise technical detail and questionable perspective, done by themselves or members of their families – adorn the walls of their homes. Wives seem to approve of this, though occasionally the enthusiasm for memorabilia goes a little too far. 'We had part of a cockpit in the loo! That was just too much! I threw it out when he was at one of his reunions.'

'I flew Spitfires and I was as happy as a sandboy! They are beautiful aircraft, absolutely beautiful. There's nothing wrong with them at all. Our squadron life really was out of this world. Quite honestly, if we could have stayed at Biggin Hill doing sweeps, the war could have gone on for ever because it was ideal. You were doing a job you enjoyed, you had everything you wanted, nice little room, the food was excellent, you got time off and it was really absolute heaven! The Spitfire's the plane for me! I was never worried about having holes shot in me, that never seemed to cross my mind. What used to worry the life out of me was the fact that I might get shot down and become a prisoner of war and then I couldn't fly again. That was the big thing that used to worry most people.' (*Mr Robertson*)

'You've got to remember we were all young men and we were all flying mad, so most of our conversation was on what happened to him and how he coped with it, and it was very largely talk among each other. We'd all volunteered and for most of us this was all we ever wanted to do. Believe it or not we thought ourselves fairly fortunate to be doing it, and getting paid for doing it. As for the chop, it was never going to be me. Even now when I go flying if the aeroplane crashes I'm going to walk away from it.' (*Mr Pring*)

Difficult and dangerous operations, on fighters in 1940 and 1941 in France and England, in Malta and North Africa, and in Italy, or during the bomber offensive against Germany, produced high casualties:

'I've seen people arrive in the morning, go on ops that night, and they'd be gone! We used to go out to dispersal three crews to a coach. When we came back we'd be the only crew left. The rates of losses were terrible. The day we arrived on 35 Squadron they tried to put us on ops but fortunately we sent our kit by train so we had none. The previous night they'd been to Kassel, and they'd lost six aircraft out of eighteen! We wondered what we'd come to. How did they keep morale up? The thing was people expected it. It wasn't a shock. You knew what your chances of survival were – very little. I think there was more a sense of relief if you came back – you knew you had to go anyway. I can't recall any lack of morale.' (*Mr Gill*)

'Twenty-one of us went on this operation, and seven got back. The other two planes never came back. A lot of the chaps did four or five trips and then they were shot down. That was it. Four or five trips and finish! Oh, they'll never get me! Never get me! You always thought that they'd never get you! I was twenty-one, I suppose. The blokes used to look at themselves, oh they couldn't get me! That's how it was, yet all around him – it was silly, because you just didn't have any sense. I never realized how high the casualty rate was. You see, when you went to a squadron you met all the boys, then, oh! (*a raid*) and you'd lost two or three, just two or three, oh we've just lost two or three, and then another two or three, and then they were all gone! They were all passing through! And I never thought about it, never! What a silly fool I was!' (*Mr Jarvis*)

A bad operation was doubly horrifying. If you survived, it was to know that you might have to go through the same trauma tomorrow night. You'd got away with it once, but would you be so fortunate a second time? The agonies suffered by many young men will never be known because they did not survive that next operation. The longer trips, to cities like Berlin and Leipzig, or to north Italy, could take up to eight hours, or even longer. Several in a week could produce a state of exhaustion. This situation was perhaps slightly easier for the pilot and navigator who had plenty to do and were kept busy. But the gunners, who were in effect extra eyes, watching out at the rear of the aircraft, staring into the night sky hour after hour, had a hard time of it.

The odds against them made many superstitious. Young men at the peak of their powers, who in peacetime could expect to have most of their lives in front of them, had to contemplate the possibility, even the probability, that they might be killed any day. Many became believers in premonitions, good-luck charms and ill omens:

'I flew from the ninth of July 1943 until the second of December 1944, and in that time I did thirty-five operational trips over Germany with fourteen different crews! Fourteen! This chappie, Flying Officer Steele, said to me once, "Junior" – they used to call me Junior – "would you care to fly with me tonight?"

'I said, "Oh yes, fair enough, anything to get an operation in!" Once you start a tour, you're anxious to do the lot and say you're finished. I suppose it's nerves and everything. I flew with him twelve times, and on the thirteenth time that I was going to fly with him, just to test the aircraft, another pilot that I flew with said, "Junior, my wireless operator's gone sick, would you care to fly with me?"

'I said, "Yeah, too true!" So I yelled to Rusty Steele, "All right?"

'He said, "All right!"

'When I got back somebody told me Rusty had crashed! He'd gone into a hill and the whole lot was killed. That would have been my thirteenth trip with him. Right from that day I've always said thirteen was my lucky number!' (*Mr Emery*)

'This sounds stupid, and I'm not the least bit one who thinks of ghosts or psychics or anything like that but I had Mac's shoebrush with me. It was on the shelf, you could see it. I woke up one morning after we'd done a trip and the shoebrush was missing, so I said who's got the shoebrush? And this is where superstition comes in – Trevor said, "Wasn't that Mac's shoe-brush?" Yes. "I wonder if he's gone for a shit?" That's what we used to say for shot down.

'I went up to the flights and looked for the crews that were missing, and there's Mac's crew missing. About eight or nine weeks later the shoebrush is back on the shelf, nobody will admit to having taken it. I woke up, "The shoebrush is back!" Trevor said, "I wonder if Mac's back?" I got a telegram from Mac that day. Apparently the rest of his crew were killed and he was the only survivor. I know for a fact that somebody brought the brush back but the coincidence is so strange. I often go to see him, and I said to him one day, "Look here, 1333453!"

'He said, "What a memory you've got!" Little did he know that I've still got his brush and it's inscribed 1333453! Every time I clean my shoes I see his number!' (*Mr Miller*)

It required the strongest nerves, very considerable deter-mination and great courage to go repeatedly on these eight-hour operations over Germany and occupied Europe, or to get back into a fighter after you had crash-landed. Many men were wounded, sometimes severely, managed to survive a bad crash, baled out, or saw friends killed right beside them. Yet they were expected to go on and finish their tour. Getting back into the aircraft knowing from experience what might happen put the greatest demands on them. Hardly surprisingly, the pressures proved to be too much for some, and their nerve went:

'Everything lit up all of a sudden, searchlights and everything, like day, and there were these dots below. All of a sudden the ack-ack opened up! The astrodome vanished, holes all over us, but we got out of it. The next thing was we haven't got much fuel. We just about got into Tangmere which was a fighter aerodrome, not really equipped for bombers. We came off the runway and even then got one wing-tip stuck in a tree. When I went down the fuselage to get out of the aircraft, sitting on the lavatory, just inside the main doors, sitting on there with his head in his hands was our wireless operator. I said, "Open the doors, Bob!"

'He said, "I'm not opening them! A bloody German'll poke his head in!"

'I said, "No, we're all right, we're at Tangmere."

' "I've had enough of this," he said. And he never flew again. He was married. We used to come up to London when we weren't flying and the next morning get the early train back from King's Cross. He and his wife would be there with their arms wrapped round each other. He'd get back to Gravely often, the station, cross the platform and go back to London! They brought him back three times and he wouldn't fly so they took his rank away. Lack of Moral Fibre. But as a lot of them said, he may have done the right thing. He may have been a live LAC as opposed to a dead flight sergeant.' (*Mr Gill*)

The disgrace and punishment of people who could no longer fly still upsets many former aircrew:

'I don't remember any problems of LMF on the squadron. We met them before we got to the squadron oddly enough. One or two people found they couldn't cope. You see, I found this very difficult. They were degraded and it was very tricky to get round it. Far better for a man to say, "Look I can't cope with this!" than to go on and kill six other chaps.' (*Mr Power*)

'This crew I knew were hit over Germany and finished up in the English Channel. The dinghy was punctured but they got back to England and three of them refused to fly again. They were brought up for Lack of Moral Fibre, stripped and everything. One of them was shovelling coal among the coal dumps. We thought this was terrible because they'd done about sixteen ops. The strange thing about aircrew was that you volunteered for it, but it was a job to get out of it once you'd got in.' (*Mr Poulter*)

Nevertheless, many people feel still that they had a 'good war', that they were lucky not to have missed it:

'I crash-landed three times altogether. Well, I was lucky in that I always did it on our own airfield. I managed to get back that far. The odds were always against you, but of course being twenty years old it's always the other fellow who's going to get it. You're immortal, aren't you? It really was the high point of my life – it's never going to get that intense – you're never going to live on the edge like that again! I couldn't do it now anyway, at this age, so there's no point in trying to recapture it. You've had it, you were very lucky – you've had something that thousands and thousands of people would like and never will have. You've survived it and that's it.' (*Mr Pring*)

This book is a collection of some of the conversations I had with only a proportion of those people who were good enough to give me their time and tell me their memories. There were nearly three hundred in all, together with many more who wrote to me or answered my letters. I am greatly in their debt. I promised my correspondents anonymity and have in most cases used pseudonyms in the text. There is not space to acknowledge everyone who gave me their time, but I would like to thank the following without whom this book could not have been written:

Messrs T. J. Arbuthnot and L. Armandias, Mrs V. Arnold, Messrs S. Atkins, H. Banyard, A. Barton, W. Bentley, J. Bisdee and G. Blunt, Mr and Mrs S. Bostridge, Mr W. Bowens, Mrs D. Brown, Mr and Mrs L. Cardall, Messrs J. Carroll, H. Chaplin, H. Chapman, J. Chatfield and I. Clar, Mrs D. Cockle, Messrs M. Collis, E. Crosswell, R. Davey and S. David, Mrs M. Day, Mrs Doyle, Messrs E. Draper and H. Dury, Mrs B. East, Messrs B. Edwards, F. Emery, H. Evans, E. Fantle, E. Fawcett and S. Fincham, Mrs D. Fishwick, Miss P. Forbes, Messrs R. Gill and V. Grayston, Mrs A. Groom, Mr E. Handyside, Mrs W. Hart, Messrs H. Hawkins, G. Henderson, W. Herrington and G. Hill, Mrs I. Holmes and Mrs E. Humphries, Messrs M. Hyett, J. Jarvis, C. Jordan, R. Kelly, D. King, W. Landels, C. Leach, H. Lewis and G. Lord, Mr and Mrs E. Lovell-Cooper, Miss N. McVicar, Messrs J. Millard, G. Miller, E. Moreton, G. Munro, T. Ninam, J. Northrop and H. Old, Mr and Mrs R. Page, Messrs H. Park, H. Patrick, S. Pearce, M. Phillips, R. Phillips, W. Phillips, L. Port, A. Porter, L. Poulter and H. Powell, Mrs F. Quarry, Messrs W. Randle, D. Raynes, L. Rayner, R. Robertson and K. Schuck, Mrs M. Schuylemann, Messrs P. Sharpe, L. Skipper and D. Snow, Mr W. Spreadborough, Mrs V. Stagg, Mr A. Stephenson, Mrs E. Stevens, Mrs M. Stutter, Mrs J. Swale, Mrs R. Symons, Messrs A. Taylor, T. Thackray; R. Thew, R. Thirsk, W. Tomlinson, D. Towers and W. Toynbee, Miss J. Truman, Messrs P. Twist, L. Unwin, M. Van Cleemput, N. Waite and L. Watford, Mrs V. West, Mr R. Whitehorn, Miss E. Wilson, and Mr and Mrs L. York.

By its nature an oral history gives the personal experiences and opinions of individuals, their interpretation of their own lives; it cannot provide an overview of the war as a whole. Several excellent texts which do are available, such as: John Terraine, *A Time for Courage: The Royal Air Force in the European War, 1939–1945* (1985); R. J. Overy, *The Air War 1939–1945* (1980); Max Hastings, *Bomber Command* (1979); and on phases of the bombing war, Martin Middlebrook, *The Battle of Hamburg* (1980), and *The Nuremberg Raid* (1973).

I also owe a considerable obligation to the local newspapers, aircraft industry, air force and squadron associations who agreed to publicize my request for contacts and who often went to a great deal of trouble to put me in touch with participants in the air war. A work of this kind would not be possible without such generous and painstaking helpers.

# 1

# 1940

Two aircraft were crucial in winning the Battle of Britain, the Hurricane and the Spitfire. The design teams led by R. J. Mitchell at Vickers Supermarine and Sidney Camm at Hawker's created aeroplanes which have achieved legendary status. It is difficult to imagine how the War in the Air could have been fought without them, or the Battle of Britain won.

With hindsight the process of creating the Spitfire, which flew throughout the war and in all theatres of combat, is seen as having a kind of inevitability. 'The hour will find the man and the machine!' The reality was very different. Victory in the Battle of Britain depended on a number of small private aircraft firms developing the best planes in the world. If they had got it wrong the RAF would have lost. Yet these firms had been neglected by the Air Ministry, and starved of capital and investment. The Supermarine factory, when Eric Lovell-Cooper first went there in 1924, was not impressive:

'Oh, gosh, it was awful! I thought, what have I let myself in for! It was a row of derelict houses with a gateway. The house next door had an empty room full of derelict bicycles – that's what it looked like through the window. They weren't broken, they'd just been left there by the people at Supermarine's who rode to work. Above were the offices where all the girls worked.

1

The bedrooms of the houses, you see. The drawing office was lit half by gas and half by electricity, and some of the gas was just jets, open fish-tail jets. Mitchell's office wasn't as big as this room. I thought, what the hell have I let myself in for? Is it worth while staying here?'

*Eric Lovell-Cooper* had trained at the important Norwich aircraft firm of Boulton & Paul. He first worked there in 1918 making parts for an aircraft which was going to fly the Atlantic. He must have been an impressive sight as a teenager, standing well over six feet tall. As a promising youngster he was advised to try for a job at Supermarine's. 'They were supposed to have a pretty bright chap there!' This was R. J. Mitchell.

'Mitchell took me on because he knew wood was going out. He wanted somebody that knew about metalwork. He didn't appear till I'd been in the firm three days. I said to myself I'm duty bound to stay a week.

'The first job he gave me to do was a radiator for the Southampton flying boat. He expanded a bit on what he wanted and I began to realize he broke all the cardinal rules of what I knew about aircraft design. He knew how simple they were provided you did them the right way. People like to think of him watching the seagulls fly, well he probably did, everybody did. You couldn't help it down there – blooming seagulls all over the place. But one thing about it, we knew that seagulls couldn't ever be a satisfactory flying boat. Although they'd got the perfectly formed hull for the job, their wings were in the wrong place!

'Mitchell wanted his designs to be the best of course, but not too much the best otherwise we wouldn't get the plane produced in time. He'd got the right idea about aircraft. Super-accuracy wasn't necessary in those days. None of us knew enough about aircraft to be super-accurate. We weren't going at speeds that were suicidal then. When we were having guesses how fast the Southampton would go we had a sweepstake on it and the boy that put in the lowest estimate won the prize.'

When Eric arrived, Supermarine's was managed by an eccentric businessman named Scott-Paine. 'He put the works on its feet and it became a name in the aircraft industry. He was a showman, that was all, but he was a jolly good one. Supermarine's was his idea – they used to write *another* Supermarine product! Big letters across. It could have been an empty crate – advertisement you see. His way of demonstrating the strength of a Supermarine product was to jump on it or try and put his fist through it. Sometimes the specimen he was jumping on broke up and he'd say, "Well, it's not as strong as I thought it was!"

'Everybody would laugh and he'd say, "Here! Stop your bloody laughing! I'll give you the sack!"

'They'd all shut up of course, laughing inwardly. You can imagine what sort of a ragtime outfit it was.'

The great armaments firm of Vickers bought Supermarine in 1928, mainly to secure the talents of R. J. Mitchell, and began to modernize the company.

'Sir Robert McLean was the chairman and he had his finger on every aspect of the job. I remember him telling Mitchell, "The Schneider Trophy things bring a lot of credit to the firm but they don't fill the coffers! We've got to produce some aeroplanes that pay their way and fill up the money-bags!" So we had to start on a new line.

'He was a pretty fearsome chap to have to deal with – he made you feel about that high! He began by sacking most of the bosses, and those they didn't sack left of their own accord. Vickers had a whole stock of up-and-coming management people and some were drafted down to our place, including Trevor Westbrook. Most of our people were woodworkers. That didn't go down too well with Westbrook. Anyone who worked in wood was a back number. They were all sacked, apart from the very young ones. I will say this for him, he knocked the firm into shape. Sir Robert also wanted to put Barnes Wallis in charge of us – that was a row, I can tell you!

'Wallis'd just done the R100, the big airship, and come back with flying colours, the wonder man of the air! He turned up immediately after the Christmas holidays, took over Mitchell's office and went and sat in his chair, but we were an independent crowd – we didn't like it!

'Mitchell came to me and said, "You might put a desk up in the loft for Wallis!" There was a V-shaped roof to our place and you reached it by a sloping gangway. It was a most precarious thing to walk up – sheer drop of about forty feet down below with no railing! If you got near the edge and suffered from vertigo I should think you'd have had it.

' "Oh," Mitchell said, "you can put a desk and a chair up there for Mr Wallis but don't make him too comfortable!"

'To cut the story short, Barnes Wallis realized the game was up. That was the last we saw of him! He went back to Vickers. Mitchell said, "It's either him or me!" I heard him say that. "You can make your own choice!" But Vickers had bought the firm because of Mitchell! He was in charge. But can you imagine what it would have been like if we'd lost him!'

Mitchell and his team began design work in 1930 on the aeroplane that became the Spitfire; the prototype flew in 1936 shortly before Mitchell's death. This brilliant design with its famous elliptical wings was years ahead of its time, but even so Mitchell's successors at Supermarine led by Joe Smith had to fight to preserve the plane. Eric Lovell-Cooper remembered one traumatic incident:

'Beaverbrook came down the office one day. "Smith!" he said. "We've got to stop production on the Spitfire, we've got the Beaufighter!" His son Max Aitken was a pilot in the air force at that time and he came back with glowing accounts of this twin-engined fighter machine that Bristol's was producing – it was absolutely the cat's whisker! Poppa Aitken came down. "We'll stop production on the Spitfire tomorrow and we'll start building Beaufighters!"

'Beaverbrook only stayed about five minutes. You could never reason or argue with him, he just came down, delivered his ultimatum and cleared off.

'Poor old Joe looked at me and said, "What's going to happen now?"

'I said, "He can't do a thing like that!"

' "Yes he can! He's got Churchill's ear! Anything he says goes!"

' "He can't be so damn silly as to do that!"

' "Well, what shall we do?"

'I said "Ring Freeman!" He was the only man I could think of who *could* do anything. Sir Wilfrid Freeman was the man responsible to the Ministry for the procurement of aircraft, a very level-headed chap. In fact he kept his job all the way through the war so he must have been pretty bright. "Ring him and he'll do something. No good sitting here."

'So Joe did and came back into my office. "I think we'll be all right after all!" Life went on, and of course everything was all right. But it shows you how it was just like that!' (*Snaps his finger.*) 'You can imagine what a mess we'd have been in if we'd have relied on the Beaufighter!

'You see, you never could judge how far these people would go – you knew that they could do it and you were always afraid they might, that was the snag. If you'd got enough faith in your own judgement you didn't worry very much but it was a bit hard at times, I can tell you, carrying on under those conditions.

'Beaverbrook absolutely dominated everything. Some of the Air Ministry officials who were supposed to be working with him seemed to spend most of their time chasing round after him. That was his method of doing things. I think in a way he stirred the country up and made us realize we'd got to get our backs into the job or go under and in that respect he was probably a very useful man.

'From then onwards the Spitfire was sort of my machine, I didn't have any option. It meant a twenty-four hour day as far as I was concerned. I was never off the job. People said, "Oh, it's all right for you, you've only got to sit on your arse!" Well, you try and do that for twenty-four hours a day! But they were happy days really.

'When the air raids started on Southampton the whole place shook. The worst of it was the smell. It's the sewage I suppose. Oh, it's terrible! And the gas of course. Wet everywhere. Running with blood and dirt, oh, it was shocking! The devastation was terrible! There were the usual people trying to clear up, and it looked as if the best thing you could do was blow the whole thing up and start again.

'The air raids didn't devastate our works, they were almost intact. Where the Germans made a mistake was they didn't come back and bomb us again! If they'd done that they'd have done some damage. All they did was to smash up one or two Spitfire aircraft and make the place uninhabitable, or unworkable, or whatever you like to call it. We all had to shift out quickly, but the actual material damage was nil.

'You always think of bombs dropping down nose first, but even the best bombs don't do that. They go like a diver going off a diving board, out flatways first, slightly nose down, and gradually turn into the vertical and go down absolutely straight. If they're not a well-designed bomb they go down like a rotating arrow with the back end whizzing round at a rate of knots and the front end trying to do its stuff going down straight.

'I watched one or two of 'em from my window. They used to fly in so low that you could see the pilots waving to you as they went by. The bomb doors would open and the bombs would fall out – it was almost as if someone was emptying a load of rubbish out from a dustbin. The bombs would take up all sorts of funny attitudes before they hit the ground.

'I must tell you about a rather curious arrangement we had at the Supermarine works before the war started. The Europa firm run by the Baltic Trust, I think it was, transatlantic liners, started a scheme to launch a seaplane from the liner when it was about three or four hundred miles west of England. The idea was it would land in Southampton at least a day before the ship would normally get there. It would bring mail from the ship to their

Southampton office, and that funnily enough was in the base of our design office!

'There were only a couple of Germans there but it always struck me as being very absurd – there were we busy building Spitfires to fight the Germans and they'd got a couple of their people on the spot! Whether they did any actual spying or not I don't know. But I always thought it was through their office being there that our place was singled out for an attack when the bombing did start.'*

Hawker's aircraft factory at Kingston did not make a very favourable impression either when *Tom Clare* joined the firm as a metalworker in 1928.

'Conditions in the factory in those days were pretty rough. The tooling was very bad. All these young lads were doing their little jobs, bits and pieces, and there was no planning as we know it today, no paperwork. There was nobody to show you anything unless you had a word with the chap next to you. *If* he knew anything about it. *If* he would tell you! Nothing big about it at all. At one point they had a clear-out and there was only eight people left on the plane floor!

'When I went there, the only aircraft was rag and string. That was the pattern of it. I remember Tommy Sopwith with a blooming great cigar come round smoking, overcoat and mac on, asking us why we were cold! Ooh yes, Tommy Sopwith! They had an old car. When Sir Frank Spriggs and H. K. Jones, who came in when Tommy Sopwith went into liquidation, wanted to go out, up to town, fitters off the bench used to have to rush downstairs, put their chauffeur's hat on and drive them up. No vehicles! That was how poor it was.

'The machine shop was nothing but belt-driven machines. No automatics. If you was within range when a belt broke you caught

* For Eric Lovell-Cooper's recollections of Supermarine's role during the later stages of the war, see pp. 95–105.

it. Old Sawbone Nightingale was the bloke who came round with the adhesive to stick on the belts when they broke. I've never seen hands like it. He didn't clean 'em, he just put them on the grindstone. I've seen him go up to the forge, upstairs where the blacksmith was, and he's got the old coke fire like a blacksmith would have, the old bellows. Sawbone'd come in there and pick a bit of red hot coke out and light a fag, his fingers smoking with all the grease on his fingers – they were black with thick callouses.

'No craft distinction then – you did what you were bloody well told, unless you wanted the sack! Because plenty of people outside wanted your job. That was the big incentive – the sack! They didn't want to over-labour at all. In the early days it was nothing for them to come round on the Friday afternoon, give a couple of dozen people an hour's notice or two hours' notice. I was looking at that one time. We were very shy of work. Charge-hand hadn't got a job for me for a couple of days.

'In 1935 we started building the Hurricane. I made the first rib for it. They put it in the first test rig that was ever made. And that was a funny old thing. None of the paraphernalia that there is today of gauges and God-knows-what, it was just weights and stuff stretched on it, loads put on it. Very elementary.

'When I first went there there was no smoking allowed in any shop. They used to go down in the toilet. You were booked in. Archie was a one-armed bloke in there, and if you slipped him a fag through the window when you gave your number – he had to write it in a book – he'd let you smoke. They were stable doors, half doors. Later on when I became an assistant foreman, you were allowed to use three other toilets. They were locked, with full doors, and you had a key. That was class distinction!

'There was always somebody up to a lark, always a bit of devilry among them. If you got caught you'd have got the sack. But today they lack, I dunno, the spirit that was there. Anybody would have helped the other one. If a bloke was in trouble, somebody would help him out. There was always a lark going on, a joke, somebody was playing a trick on somebody, putting spurs on the back of their heels, or a notice on their back. Painting

8

their heels. Some blokes would go up the road and find their heels were painted bright yellow. But there was always a good spirit among us! It was always friendly. Nothing vicious about it.

'You weren't allowed any breaks in the mornings, you weren't even supposed to have a drink, though we used to take flasks and they knew we did. We used to keep it out of sight, and perhaps a jam sandwich, or marmalade, or whatever you could afford, and you had that somewhere about tennish on the quiet. Look round and make sure – put it in the drawer away somewhere, put the cup down there and hide something over it, and that's the way it went.

'Then they agreed that you could have a tea break for ten minutes and they came round with barrows. Of course the milk cartons on there were handy things to roll up and throw.

'When I had a five-pound note in my pay packet it was out of this world. That was for working weekends and two nights' overtime a week and Saturday and Sunday.'

Hire and fire, penny-pinching, and shabby treatment of staff prevailed through much of the aircraft industry before the war. *Viv Prince* began his working career as a dockyard apprentice during the Great War. In 1925, the dockyard at Rosyth closed and like a lot of redundant dockyard workers he found a new job in an aircraft firm. After the Second World War he had a distinguished career in the industry, but his experience as a young man in some of the leading concerns had its 'ups and downs. In all I worked in seven different firms!'

'I was offered a job at Fairey's at Hayes. I transferred from a very nice comfortable job in the dockyard where I was more or less my own boss with my own office to the workshops at Fairey's. But they were very good and they had a very interesting programme then. But you'd be sacked on the spot. Marcel Lobelle (*the chief designer*) would come out and say, "I sack you! Out!" He would pay people a month's wages and of course he'd be sorry the next minute. But he was a very clever man. He had inspired thought. Do you know that he said in my interview, "You are not English, I am not English, I hate the English, we will be friends!" '

When promotion failed to materialize, Viv gave up his job and moved to Blackburn's at Brough in Yorkshire.

'I got this job as a foreman. Blackburn's had a contract for fifty wing-tip floats for the Stranraer flying boat and they had nobody who knew anything about Duralumin construction so I started this thing off. Honestly, the conditions under which we worked there were terrible, terrible!

'I didn't like the way they treated the work-force. If you wanted to go and spend a penny they had a man timing you! The other thing was that they promised us things and didn't keep their promises. The day we finished this rushed job was the day they broke up for a week's *unpaid* summer holiday – in 1927. There was no paid holidays for the works. I was tipped off that something was going to happen in the afternoon, and it did. They sacked every one of the people who had worked on those floats except myself – two hours' notice, that's all they got.

'I'd already discovered that the works manager was a corkhead – that's a boat-builder – from Cowes. He couldn't read a drawing! He needed somebody to read a blueprint! He was a very good bully. I'd worked my blokes very hard to get those fifty floats finished in the time and then to sack them on the night of their holiday – !'

So he quit.

'When I got on my motorbike with the little box with my paraphernalia strapped on the back, the manager was watching for me. He'd heard I'd been in the cashier's. He tried to stop me going! I drove off with him hanging on to my bike! I dragged him a third of the way across the aerodrome. He was saying, "Come back! come back!"

'But it was valuable experience from this point of view that when I went to Cowes, I knew all about corkheads, I was a way ahead of them.'

He secured a new job at Short Brothers, at Rochester, working on the flying boat they were designing for the Japanese navy. 'Most interesting job, and I did all the wing structure and detailed it – may I say that I was looked upon as being a very good and accurate draughtsman. That must have helped along the line somewhere.

'Short's had a big staff then. They were doing the sea class flying boats, and also the Singapore, and so forth. They were extremely busy and they had a big design office. Then suddenly the slump, you know, 1930–31, and the outcome of that was that my brother-in-law, an assistant designer, told me that it was all on a hire-and-fire basis and that unfortunately I stood a good chance of losing my job.

'However, the chief draughtsman at Short's sent for me and said, "I have a letter here from Handley Page's. They say that they want to take on three draughtsmen – they hear that we're getting rid of some." So we went up to Cricklewood. The other two chaps got sacked at the end of the three months with a lot of others, but I was rooted in Handley Page's until this aeroplane flew. It only flew once I think, it was a shocker, the HP46. However that was nothing to do with me.

'Handley Page was hire and fire too and I've seen a whole section who were working on the Hannibal being fired.'

*'For what?'*

'For shortage of work! They were all on a two-hour basis. Not a week's notice, or even a day's notice. Conditions were very very very poor.'

Viv's peripatetic career continued. From Handley Page to Saunders-Roe at Cowes ('I had a little office with a drawing board all to myself with a beautiful view of the Cowes Roads'); however the firm were working a system that turned out to deprive the staff of their bonus, so Viv returned to Handley Page. 'I was anxious to get back to London because Cowes in the wintertime was pretty foul. But I had a row with Sir Frederick himself. He said they were paying me far too much money!' He quit once again, this time going to the new firm of Airspeed. 'To show you how versatile you had to be – I did the flying controls! Complete! From the cockpit right the way through on to all the control surfaces!'

Finally, in 1936, he moved to Supermarine. 'When I got there I found that I had been chosen to become the weapon installation designer on the B12/36. I worked on it right from the start and was with it when R. J. Mitchell died, and the little bit I had to do with him, I got on extremely well. He used to have terrible tempers as you can imagine – he was in shocking distress a lot of the time.

'It would have been a wonderful aeroplane if it had been allowed to continue. We made a prototype. It never flew and it was destroyed in a hangar a few hundred yards away from the Woolston works in a German air raid, which seemed poetic in a way. It was far ahead of the four-engined bombers of that era that were being built for two main reasons. One was Mitchell's natural flair for a good line and other was he said, "We'll make the wings do some of the work carrying the bombs!" So we fixed it that we carried nine bombs in each wing and nine in the fuselage whereas the Stirling carried all its bombs in a very *long* fuselage. Supermarine had to stop production because Beaverbrook said you cannot produce bombers and Spitfires. So B12/36 had to go and go it went, but it had a design top speed of 365 m.p.h.'

Even at Supermarine in the mid-1930s conditions left much to be desired. 'They built a magnificent new office block at Woolston, and do you know, the staff lavatories in there, when you sat down on the seat you couldn't shut the door! A chap said to me the first day I was at the firm, "Viv, there's only two people you've got to keep in with here to get on!"

'Who's that?

' "Joe Smith, the chief draughtsman, and the chap who takes the time when you go to the bog!" '

From there, shortly after the start of the war, he moved to de Havilland at Hatfield. 'I was pitchforked, there was no arguing about it, off to Salisbury Hall (*where the Mosquito was designed*). I took the first Mosquito down to Boscombe Down. I was sent to watch it landing on this horrible grass surface – they didn't have two- or three-thousand-metre runways there, they only had bumpy grass – fourteen bumps across – I counted. And do you know it broke its back? This was the prototype. It had a loading carriage in the rear fuselage on the port side, and the fuselage cracked right around. The point of greatest stress! It was cured very simply – all they did was to glue on a strip of spruce along the outside on the bottom edge to get over this sharp change in section.'

*'How did you go about designing an aircraft?'*

'It's very simple. The de Havilland method – you design under strength to get the maximum possible lightness. You test and if it breaks you redesign. You design a particular part, a component, anything, and then you test it to destruction. You'd be amazed how much gets into aircraft which is far too strong. The effective cruising altitude of a Mosquito – every pound overweight meant one mile difference in range and a foot difference in altitude. It could be fatal not to have that capability.'

*'Why were some companies so much more successful in producing good aircraft than others?'*

'I can tell you the outstanding firm and that was de Havilland's, there's no doubt about that. It came from the top and Sir Geoffrey was a man who knew who you were and he would stop and speak to you, and he did it without any patronage. And Bishop (*the designer of the Mosquito*) was a genius – I was going to say this all the way through – Bishop was an absolute genius.

'Then it was very pleasant to go to Supermarine and be in on a new thing. R. J. Mitchell, like Camm, Bishop – they could *see* a design – and by the way, they were all terribly bad draughtsmen! But they could paint a picture and you could see what they were trying to get at. It's amazing the facility all those top people had.

'De Havilland's were poor payers! Don't think that they paid big money because they didn't. None of the aircraft industry were big payers, of the old established companies.'

After the war, in 1953, Viv spent some time in the USA. I asked him how the American firms compared with British ones.

'The biggest single thing you notice is that in one project that we looked at – only one aspect of one project, they had a *hundred* designers! Now in this country I think the most prolific, most populated design I ever saw was the Comet and even then it was only six designers with a few senior draughtsmen, one to do the wings, one the fuselage, one the undercarriage, etc.

'The aircraft industry in America only exists by the amount of money that *we* put into it from 1938 and 1939 and through the war. We bankrupted ourselves with the money. I first saw this at Martins at Baltimore. They had three factories there and I would say that any one of them would have swallowed up the whole of Vickers at Weybridge or de Havilland's at Hatfield or Handley Page's at Radlett. I was taken for a walk round the production line of the F104 and I was exhausted! And I was a very fit man at the time. I was exhausted! The damn thing stretched away into the distance! They told me we've got you British people to thank for this!'

In May 1940 the RAF was caught up in the Battle of France. A separate command for France had been set up in January 1940 and several squadrons sent out. *Geoff Dale* joined a squadron of Westland Lysanders doing tactical reconnaissance over northern France and, after 10 May, when the Germans invaded, Belgium.

'I joined the RAF immediately I left school. There were large

14

adverts in the press for short-service commissions because of the hasty rearmament at this time. I went to Ad Astral House with a number of other enthusiastic young individuals. The board was headed by an air commodore. They asked the usual questions – where I went to school, what I was interested in, what my hobbies were. When I was about sixteen or seventeen I built a three-wheeler car and that took their fancy!

'Outside, a large hairy flight sergeant said, "Medical at two o'clock!" I hadn't expected that for a moment, but they put me through the full aircrew medical which was pretty thorough in those days. Apart from physical fitness, they did quite a lot on co-ordination, a great deal on eye tests, and a kind of centrifuge test where they spun you round. At the end the medico said, "Sit down, read that!" It was a sheet of paper with very small print on it, and I started to read it aloud thinking it was still part of the eye test. I was in a rather nervous state so I didn't really appreciate what it was saying. He said, "All right?" and I said yes. "Well, sign it!" I didn't realize that what I was signing was the actual agreement for a short-service commission. Didn't realize it until they sent me instructions to report!

'The qualities they were looking for in flying were delicacy of touch, a really smooth take-off, no sudden movements, a very careful controlled kind of approach to flying, and when we were landing no messing about. As smooth as you possibly could. They separated you off. One channel went on to single-engined aircraft and the other – the ham-handed people – to multi-engined. Instrument flying was important and so was the general behaviour of the individual, the way he went about things. Not too volatile and not too dull!

'I was posted to the School of Army Co-operation at Old Sarum, and converted on to Lysanders. Most of the instruction was by army officers who expected you as an air force pilot to be interested in artillery, how to range a gun and how to organize the infantry in certain attacks, which was something we didn't want to know. We wanted to fly. We didn't mind co-operating with the army at the flying stage, but there was a general feeling that we hadn't joined the air force to do this. It seemed much more glamorous to get into Fighter Command.

'At the beginning of 1940 I was posted to France. We went to a big flat airfield near Amiens. I didn't know at the time that there was another army co-operation squadron on the other side so you can see how large it was. We requisitioned a number of houses in the town. There was a little café quite near and I and one other chap moved in there. I learned a lot of French from the girl and her husband but it was a bit of a patois. Later I moved up to Lille and some of the expressions weren't understood up there.

'At first it was all training. Navigation, cross-country flying, practising dropping and picking up messages, doing a bit of practice bomb dropping, bit of air firing –'

*'When the action started did the training turn out to be the right sort?'*

'Oh yes, yes. It did. Apart from the work we had to do, there was general reconnaissance when they sent you out and said have a look at that particular area or those people. We operated the radio with the morse key in the front cockpit. You had to be able to send morse without thinking, fly the aeroplane, look at the ground and look behind you all at the same time. Another job was to ferry the army commanders around so that they could see how they could dispose their troops along the borders. We used to fly freely over Germany. They wanted to have a look at it from the air because their boys were down in the trenches. We weren't allowed to go over Belgium at that time. Generally we had a wonderful time until things broke in May when we were whistled up into Belgium.

'It wasn't an airfield, just a few cornfields filled with stubble, but it was flat. We stayed there for five or six days, until the German shells were able to reach us. Then we cleared off back to Lille. It was a bit of a hectic time because we were suffering quite a lot of losses – our new pilots got shot down very quickly. They didn't have enough experience. I had an air gunner who had extraordinarily good eyesight. He could see things normal

16

people couldn't. He was very quick and very loyal, terribly reticent about jumping out and leaving me to it. (*Laughs.*) All the pilots were very young – I suppose the oldest was not more than twenty-two. The airmen tended to be somewhat older and we got a lot of strength from the way they handled themselves. They were always pretty cheerful, never despondent about what was going on.

'It was a very confused situation. We were beleaguered by refugees, by indiscriminate bombing of the towns around by the Germans. They got one of their Panzer divisions round behind us and there was a problem with protecting the airfield. I got myself a little two-five Browning. You could buy them in the shops: it was something to protect yourself with. When we came back to Lille I and a buddy of mine were billeted quite near the airfield. We dragged our bags in there, and the good lady, the owner of the house, said, "I'm leaving, I'm going south to my daughter. Here's the key to the door. If you have to leave, give it to the lady next door!" And off she went. We had a complete house to ourselves, fully furnished and everything. Even a barrel of beer in the cellar. Next day he got shot down so then I was alone, in this big house. You could hear these shells whistling about, and the odd bit of shooting at night which was presumably fifth column. It was a bit of an awesome situation.

'I was detailed to do a reconnaissance to try and find this German armoured division. I found them in some woods near an escarpment. It was very quiet – they were a very cunning lot! They put all this hardware under the trees and in the woods and put up a road-block which aroused my suspicions. I was flying very low because they told me to. If you came up against any opposition you got right down on the ground and flew round in great tight circles, and it worked reasonably well. I got away twice with such tactics, but you didn't really have much of a defence. Generally speaking if you did meet any opposition the only thing to do was to run hard and pray to the good Lord.

'When I found the Panzers I made two passes. All the vehicles were a dark blue colour. I thought that's strange, they're all the same colour and I haven't seen anything quite like it before, so I went back to have another look! The first time I got over them without anything but the second they opened up. It's a question of judgement, of either using other people's experience or learning the hard way yourself and getting away with it. I was very low, couldn't have been more than about two hundred feet at the most. They put a burst right through the top of the cockpit but I didn't know that until I got back. They hit the engine. I looked down and there was a bloody great point-five machine-gun blowing straight at me! About a hundred feet below. Quite a horrifying sight. And with all the right equipment. I thought we'd had it. But fortunately neither my gunner nor myself were injured.'

*'Can you remember at what point you realized how badly things were going in France?'*

'Very early. Even when we got up into Belgium the main roads coming south were starting to be crowded with refugees. Then various Belgian troops on bicycles came back, while the Germans strafed the refugees. Everything was going the wrong way: things were happening so quickly that within three or four days they were shelling us. One of the astonishing things was we were sent out to do general reconnaissance, and there was hardly anything to see! You couldn't discover where the fighting was going on. Occasionally you'd see a burning vehicle. We were fortunate in that we were hopping from airfield to airfield so we didn't have the aggravation of having to work our way through refugees like some of our ground people did. When we left Lille there were seven of us left – we started off with about fifteen and then we got about five reinforcements. They got themselves shot down at Lille when I was up in Belgium, but seven of us actually managed to fly out.

'When we left Lille we sent all the airmen off. One of the corporals commandeered a Rolls-Royce and he and the other boys just cleared off in it. They were heading towards Dunkirk, but we never saw them again.'

*'Did the possibility that we might lose the war cross people's minds at this time?'*

'No. I don't think so – people didn't really know the true situation. All we wanted to do when the organization started to break down was to get back to England.

'At one stage the army pulled out and left us. We had no rations at all. The boss went off to corps headquarters, came back and said, "We're getting out!" We flew down to Saint-Omer but I didn't get there. They'd damaged my aircraft quite considerably. When we got airborne everybody opened the throttles wide including myself and headed for Saint-Omer but they were much faster than I was, so they disappeared. I ran into some Dorniers bombing one of the towns *en route*. By this time I was pretty well lost, so I landed in a field and was picked up by an army patrol and looked after for that particular night.

'They were an RAOC unit – I think their total armament was two heavy Vickers machine-guns and here they were with a division of Panzers just up the road! You must remember I was still only eighteen or nineteen, and to see senior officers not knowing what was going on or what they should do next was a bit demoralizing. Those few days, from the tenth of May till about the third or fourth of June, were very confusing and frightening. You didn't know what was going on. But as long as I had the aeroplane I was quite happy.

'They had quite a nice little set-up. A mess by a stream near the little villa where they had their headquarters. We had something to eat, and the colonel said, "Do you want to try and get in touch with your boys?" The headquarters were just along the road, I suppose about a quarter of a mile. By this time it was dark. One of the officers and I set out. We'd been going for about three or four minutes when someone fired at us. Bullets were bouncing off the road! We ducked into the headquarters to try and make this telephone call, but they'd already cut the wires so we didn't get through.

'The following morning I came down. They gave me a good

breakfast, and then the chap said the Germans are just up the road (*laughs*) – the tanks are half a mile away. What do you want to do? Come with us or go back to your aeroplane? I collected my gunner who was rowing himself in a boat on the river. They took us back to the aeroplane, dropped us there and rushed off at high speed. We eventually managed to get it started and I flew on to Saint-Omer which was burning by that time. There weren't any aircraft on the runway so I thought it's best not to land because the Germans are probably already there. We had no cross-Channel maps so the gunner and I had a bit of a confab and decided we would come out from Calais and Dunkirk. The only airfield I knew then was Shoreham so I flew down there.

'When I landed, I phoned up the Air Ministry and found out where the squadron was. They tried to get me to go back across the Channel with a load of bombs (*laughs*). I'd only just come back.

'Now we did routine patrols up and down the east coast with the idea of spotting any invasion craft that might be coming across the North Sea. We used to patrol at dawn every day from somewhere up near Newcastle down as far as Hull. I did two stints of air–sea rescue down at Manston, one just after the Battle of Britain. We had two Lysanders down there: we'd load them up with smoke floats and dinghies and when they got information that somebody was down in the Channel they'd call us, give us a rough bearing and distance and we used to go and try and find them.'

'*Did you manage to find them?*'

'Rarely. We did find a few. Two Spitfire pilots on one occasion. It's extraordinarily difficult to spot them in the water. Somebody in a Mae West is terribly difficult to see. We used to find mines and all kinds of things. If it was a big aircraft there was always wreckage but we didn't have a high degree of success. We used to work with the high-speed launches out of Ramsgate, Deal, and if we found anything we dropped smoke floats to lead the launches on to them. If there was anybody in the water we'd drop dinghies.

It wasn't a very pleasant job, largely because the weather was too good. People could see for miles. It wasn't until we lost two aircraft that they gave us fighter cover. I had two people shot down when I was there – we only had two pilots and two aircraft. We'd take it in turns, and on both occasions the chap I was with got shot down, one just off Dover, one a bit farther out – one when we actually had a fighter escort! They came straight through the escort, shot the Lysander down and then went off!

'Later we did photographic work for the Second Front. We used to take strings of photographs every few days. I remember we wondered what on earth we were taking all these pictures for. We didn't really twig that we'd invade France. I suppose if we'd thought about it we would have appreciated what it was all in aid of but it just didn't seem to ring a bell at the time. They mixed it up with other things. I was flying the Mustang then and you'd go flat out across the Channel about ten feet above – perhaps twenty feet – lowish – you always operated in pairs. You'd just scream along the coast, break out and come back again.

'We lost one or two people, I don't know why. It's one of these things that are difficult to determine. One of the main rules with our type of operation was you always kept down on the ground because it was difficult to see you from above, and the radar had difficulty detecting you. Also you were not so much at risk from ground fire because you were too fast. To illustrate that, we sent some guy to photograph a radar unit somewhere in Normandy, and this chap hadn't long been with the squadron. He found it all right and photographed it, but he thought he'd missed it, so he turned round and went back! He pulled a very tight turn and went straight back over it. The first photograph showed all the anti-aircraft guns unmanned. In the second they were all firing at him, and this was a typical illustration of what you should not do. You made one pass and that was it. You never came back.

'Towards the end of '43 I was posted to Hawarden in North Wales. I had a Mustang flight up there trying to teach people how to shoot straight. That was the last of my continuous flying career because I went down with some trouble with my neck. This (*a photograph of a crashed aeroplane*) is the remains of a Lysander when a chap hit me when I was flying in formation. He put his wing-tip right through the fuselage.'

'*You managed to get this down?*'

'It came straight down!'

'*You wonder how anybody came out of that alive!*'

'I had an airman in the back. It's always the way. I was giving him a lift! They'd say, come on boss, take me up for a trip! When I came round I was hanging down like that because I hit my head on the reflector sight up here, and I can remember seeing my legs and thinking, you know, wonderful! (*Laughs.*) Some woman came running across and I thought what's she shouting about? What's wrong? It was this crack I'd had on the head. I broke an oil pipe and it dumped about half a gallon of oil on the exhausts and the engine momentarily caught fire. It was the last time I smoked in the cockpit.'

*John Bisdee* had not been trained to fly a Spitfire when, in December 1939, he was posted to 609 Squadron at Drem in Scotland. 'When I arrived I'd never flown a monoplane in my life. We got hold of a Harvard, the American trainer with flaps and an undercarriage which went up and down, and I did about two hours on that, practising landings and that kind of thing. Then I went off solo on a Spitfire. Luckily I didn't make any major error, such as landing with your wheels up which was very easy to do.

'The pilots already there were Auxiliaries. There was a slight difference between the Auxiliary Air Force and the Volunteer Reserve. In the first you went in as an officer and gentleman and it was a bit of a rich man's occupation. You had to buy your own uniform – you probably got an allowance for it – but then you had an officers' mess which entailed officers' mess bills and so on. The Auxiliaries had volunteer pilots plus one RAF flight

22

lieutenant who combined the job of adjutant and chief instructor to the squadron. The airmen were partly volunteers like garage mechanics from Yorkshire, the salt of the earth, and there was a basic collection of regular RAF airmen with each flight in charge of a flight sergeant.

'In the VR we used to fly every other weekend, and you got paid one and sixpence an hour for being in the air, and a shilling an hour for sitting on the ground. We used to go to lectures in Store Street, in London, at least one night a week, and there you learnt all kinds of useful things like WT (*wireless telegraphy*), meteorology, the theory of flight, and about engines. We flew in civvies, and wherever you went you could join one of these reserve centres, and you automatically met a whole lot of very nice chaps who were in the same position. We were all sergeant pilots, and it was a great thing and kept us out of mischief.

'When I got there, the main body of the squadron was right up in northern Scotland. Nobody seemed to know quite what they were doing but there was an enormous amount of enemy reconnaissance activity, such as this business of Scapa Flow when the *Royal Oak* was sunk by Lieutenant Prien's submarine. Then they came back and we were very lucky because we got a lot of practice flying round convoys, which gave you flying experience. You always managed to do a few aerobatics on the way there or back. We had a lot of sightings of German aircraft trying to attack convoys and reconnaissance aircraft. During the phoney war we were fairly active. I think we had a larger score of German twin-engined aircraft than the whole of the British Expeditionary Force up till the time of the German blitz.

'When we were up in Scotland a flying officer called George Proudman, known as Cannon George in the squadron, came up with the prototype cannon Spitfire. It had two cannons, but unfortunately while he was with us, though he flew on every available sortie and practically wore out his aeroplane he flew so much, he didn't ever meet an enemy. He also had the misfortune to crash on landing, on top of another aircraft!

'If we'd had cannons in the Battle of Britain I believe the

defeat of the German air force would have been very much more complete than it was. A number of aircraft got back across the Channel with leaking glycol and so on from bullet wounds which would undoubtedly have been destroyed if we'd had cannons. Even one or two, given to the people who were the best shots, would have had an enormous effect. Whether we didn't have them because George Proudman's efforts came to a rather abrupt end I don't know. But the effect of cannon on a Messerschmitt 109 was catastrophic.

'During the campaign in France we were sent to Northolt to cover the retreat from Dunkirk, and we had very bad losses, about half the squadron. Lost probably through lack of training more than anything else. I don't think a lot of them ever saw what hit them.

'A number of chaps dived down on the German bombers below and were clobbered from behind by the Messerschmitts who were protecting them. In those days you were very liable to get separated from your mates – I'm certain that a lot of them got picked off one by one. My flight commander used to fly with an Irving flying jacket which had a large fur collar which completely prevented him looking behind! In those days the Spitfire did not have a rear-view mirror. We heard about the idea and our maintenance airmen went out and bought mirrors from the local garages and made a beautiful fairing to fit in actually much better than the Air Ministry model. By the time of the Battle of Britain we had them just above here and you could get some idea of what was on your tail.

'The 109 had one cannon firing through the airscrew, and they did a lot of damage. We had .303s in the Battle of Britain. I believe some of the dead-eyed shots had them harmonized so they concentrated at two hundred or three hundred yards. It was remarkable how well they did. By that time the German bombers already had – what we hadn't got – self-sealing petrol tanks. We felt that the Air Ministry and the industry generally were not entirely with it. It was only after Dunkirk that our squadron got armour-plating behind the pilot's body, and even then it was only held on by sort of thumbscrews. I imagine that if a cannon had hit it, it would have made an awful mess. You would have received the full benefit of the chunk of armour plate as well as the cannon shell.

'At Dunkirk you had a hell of a long flight across from places like Northolt. I remember very well being harangued by old Boom Trenchard, the father of the Royal Air Force, standing there with his enormous moustaches, and about six inches deep of medals! We felt after that we couldn't be shot down but of course we were! The times I went over we flew fairly high up, at about eighteen thousand or so, but there were Germans everywhere. You could only stay for about an hour if you weren't engaged, but if as always happened you *were* engaged, if you stayed in the battle for more than a quarter of an hour at the very most you would never have got home.

'When you disengaged you didn't know where you were, but I always jolly well looked around a bit before I finally dived out of the battle. That generally meant you hadn't got any ammunition left so you flew down as fast as you could, out over the sea and weaved like mad to see that nobody was behind you.

'We were also detailed to fly down to Warmwell near Weymouth where we did two escorts with Winston Churchill. He was trying to catch up with the ever-retreating French government. We finally caught up with Prime Minister Reynaud near Tours, and I was on one of the escort flights. We landed on an appallingly bumpy grassy aerodrome, his nibs in a de Havilland Flamingo, very nice high-wing monoplane. We waited the whole day to escort him back over the Channel.

'After that we got a really good regular air force CO called George Darley who pulled the squadron together. Previously we practised the standard pilot command attacks which were totally useless. They involved approaching the enemy from behind, from miles away, and it took you hours to catch them up, forfeiting any form of surprise. Darley's great contribution was that he flew as a target and trained us to attack from out of the sun, to do quarter attacks, and head-on attacks. He bore a charmed life because I'm quite certain we were very dangerous, even from the collision point of view.

'People who were lost over Dunkirk lacked training in cohesion. The Vic formation didn't really lend itself to breaking into combat. Afterwards we would generally fly either in pairs with one chap more or less level with you, or as 609 Squadron did in the sweeps over France, a sort of zigzag formation which enabled everybody to look behind them at one stage or another. We used to fly in four sections, two flights each of two, and sections would be either three or four people. It was very much more flexible. You could see the chap in front of you and also see the people behind. The better the training the more chance there was you wouldn't be left entirely on your own, though really it happened over and over again. One moment umpteen aircraft were milling round, the next the sky was absolutely clear and you couldn't make out where everybody had got to! I can't remember in the Battle of Britain ever coming back from a heavy battle with anybody else. Probably met somebody over the circuit.

'There was quite a gap between Dunkirk and the Battle of Britain, a very good thing to have had. We received the first four Poles to join the RAF and the first three American volunteers. All the Poles and Americans managed to last out the battle. I was lucky because I was never actually shot down in the Battle of Britain, but some people were, and I've got a picture here of one of our American pilots with his foot through the wing! (*The photo shows him, a small dark character with a wry expression on his face, looking at the camera, actually standing in the wing where a piece of it has been shot away.*) Unfortunately the Americans were killed when they were sent to Eagle squadrons. It was a great loss of three very fine chaps.

'My first encounter with the Luftwaffe in strength was from Middle Wallop. We were vectored in the direction of Weymouth, Portland naval base, and over the RT the control said, "Hundred plus bandits!" Then, "Two hundred plus bandits!", then "Very many bandits!" They gave us a fairly good height for them, and sure enough when we got there, we found an absolute beehive of

German aircraft. I suppose there were bombers underneath dive-bombing the naval installations but I never saw them. Up above a collection of Messerschmitt 110s and 109s was going round and round in a left-hand circle. Very much like a hive of bees, and an awful lot of them!

'Unfortunately I was flying one of the oldest and slowest Spitfires in the squadron, so I got a bit left behind. When I finally struggled into this battle these aircraft were just in front of me with all these bloody black crosses, letting out condensation trails round the back. The only thing I could do was to get up a bit of speed by diving down. I flew right through the middle of the beehive to attack aircraft on the other side – that way you were less likely to be clobbered! The other Germans couldn't tighten up their turn enough to shoot at you. I can't remember much about it now except that I used up all my ammunition.

'At that time 609 was literally the only squadron attacking this enormous number of enemy aircraft. I think others may have followed afterwards, but in the Middle Wallop sector there were only two fighter squadrons, us and 252 and I don't think 252 joined in that particular battle. One day we were sent in the other direction, over London, and I got a photograph of the German formations. We had an arrangement on our gun-sights that if you fired, a cinema camera took a picture of what you were shooting at, but you could also press a button which set off the camera without wasting ammunition. It took a picture of this enormous long formation of Dornier 17s, Heinkel 111s and JU88s parading along in front of a beautiful cloud formation, and then I somehow got lost, or separated from the rest of the squadron. I dived in and did manage to do a lot of damage to a Heinkel 111.

'I remember one German attack on the aerodrome at Filton at Bristol. The bombers had an escort of Messerschmitt 110s which went two-thirds of the way to the target and then started to do this circling business. On that occasion we hadn't been very well directed – we found the escort and didn't find the bombers, but I shot down a 110. It turned over, one engine thoroughly kaput, and disappeared into a cloud. Well, in those days you had to watch out a bit because you were quite liable to find that somebody from another squadron might be round there claiming your aeroplane so on this particular occasion, since I hadn't got any more ammo, I turned over and went down. Through the cloud came (a) a Messerschmitt 110 and (b) two parachutes, so the German crew got out. The 110 crash-landed in Dorset somewhere near the Long Man of Cerne Abbas which was a bit of a landmark. When I got there a whole lot of yokels were dancing round the flames waving pitchforks! I flew round them once and confirmed it was a German, the one I'd shot down, and I then flew home.

'If you had a good controller, he would be able to tell you how many angels the enemy was at, you know, angels ten meant ten thousand feet – they were generally more like angels fifteen – and roughly where they were and where they were going. He gave you a vector which had been worked out on the ground as a likely ideal interception point, but it didn't mean, at the beginning, that it gave you the opportunity of pouncing on the Germans out of the sun! Directly you saw the enemy your leader would call out "Bounty Squadron, tally-ho!" and from that moment onwards it was generally left to the commander of the formation to decide what to do. A first reaction was practically always to shout "Buster!" which meant put the engine through the gate. If you were lucky and they were below, you could swoop round a bit from the sun, but if as very often happened they were about level you had no hope of surprising them. You just hoped when you got into the battle you were more manoeuvrable than they were. Practically always there was another gaggle of Messerschmitts above you, so you had to watch out, as they said, for the Hun in the sun, because they'd had the time to position themselves up sun of the people they were trying to protect.

'Their fighters were suffering from the constraints of petrol and a stage came where the German bombers were entirely unescorted, which is when they got most of their losses. At the end of the Battle of Britain, they fitted bombs on to Messerschmitts, and they did a lot of nuisance raiding. You'd get a collection of Messerschmitts coming over very high up which would go into a dive and hope that they hit Dover harbour or Folkestone or one of the aerodromes.

'Really, the Battle of Britain never struck me as ever coming to an end! The supply of German aircraft seemed never-ending. Now there is a set of dates when the Battle of Britain started and was considered to finish. It was very unfair because fellows like John Dundas who'd been right through the Battle, were killed literally about a week or so after it was deemed to have finished. As far as we were concerned the Battle was very much still on! These collections of Messerschmitts were dashing across the Channel and flexing their muscles.

'I remember we were called up to intercept a German fighter sweep over the Isle of Wight. They were all Messerschmitts with yellow noses – obviously rather an élite collection because they had all the clues, they were right up sun, and they came down at us. We broke and went round and during the battle John Dundas was heard to say, "Whoopee! I've got a Hun!", and that's the last we ever heard of him. It turned out he had shot down Major Helmut Wick, who was the top-scoring German ace at that time, and it must have been Wick's number two who shot down John. The Germans actually sent a broadcast on the international distress wave asking for news of Major Wick. He must have been a thoroughly unpleasant Nazi. During that night our air–sea rescue launches went out, and some motor gunboats, and the Germans sent out a flotilla of E-boats, and quite a naval battle developed, but nothing was ever found of John. Yet his name is not on the roll of honour of the Battle of Britain. I've brought it up several times, but nothing very much seems to happen. There were several other famous people too.

'In February 1942 I was posted to command 601 Squadron which had been "the millionaire squadron". For some unknown reason it had been given the doubtful pleasure of trying out an American fighter called the Airacobra. The squadron was then at a pretty ghastly place in Yorkshire called Acaster Malbis, which was somewhat below the level of the Yorkshire Ouse and distinctly muddy, particularly for all-electric-controlled aircraft, with tiny little nose wheels which dug into the mud. When I got there only one aircraft was serviceable. So I went off to see the AOC of 12 Group, known as King Saul, a very good friend to us. I said, "Look, these Airacobras are an absolute dead loss! The sooner somebody tows them away, the better!"

'He said, "I quite agree. Don't worry, you're going to get Typhoons!"

'I said, "My airmen wouldn't really recognize a serviceable aeroplane if they saw one, can I please have some Spitfires?" We were given Spitfires, and within about a month we were back operational both day and night. Although I was the only person who had ever fired his guns we were sent off by some quirk of the Air Ministry to Malta. I'd have thought they could have found a better experienced squadron.

'We flew to Malta off an American aircraft-carrier, the USS *Wasp*. We'd been equipped with Spitfires with four cannons and we did a tour of ops which was normally three months in Malta at that time. It was fairly hard work! I was shot down on my second day! Over Malta there was a terrific amount of bomb dust which was sand, really, because Malta is sandstone. If you tried to clean your perspex hood you got a whole lot of minute scratches caused by bits of sand on the rag cloth that the airmen used for polishing it. For this reason we always used to fly with our hoods open. I'd attacked a JU88 and I hung around a bit too long. I thought I saw in my mirror an aircraft behind me, my number two. It wasn't, it was a Messerschmitt! I was only about a thousand or twelve hundred feet up, and luckily had my hood open. The aircraft was totally out of control, going round like a whirligig, and I was more or less blown out of the cockpit. I pulled the ring and found myself hanging in my harness upside down by one leg! I only had about ten seconds on the parachute, before splosh, I was in the water. I was very lucky to get away with it. If I'd had to open the hood I wouldn't have made it.

'I don't think we had much trouble with the hoods. Latterly the hood had a jettison ring device, but it didn't at the beginning.

It was difficult to get out of a Spitfire cockpit because of the airstream directly you got up. Under your bottom you had this bulky pack of your dinghy and your parachute – the dinghy was folded in the form of a cushion, so you sat on that, and underneath that was the parachute. You could catch on an awful lot of things on the way out. The airstream was pushing you backwards against the top of the cockpit, where the hood was, so it wasn't all that easy, but it's remarkable what you can do if you know you bloody well must!

'The situation when we got to Malta was really very much the same as the Battle of Britain. We were on the whole in a minority. When we got there the arrangements for meeting us were not very satisfactory, and the aircraft were more or less in a line being refuelled which was emphatically not a good idea. But when the second collection of aircraft came off the *Wasp* our very good AOC Hugh Pugh Lloyd had organized with the army an enormous dispersal area. It had taxi tracks all over the place which were named after the various regiments – Gunner Lane and Queen's Own Road, et cetera, and the pens for the aircraft were built out of the flimsy metal petrol tanks brought in by submarine. You knocked the top off, filled it with sand or bomb rubble and built up the pens using these things as sandbags, as bricks really, and it cut down our losses on the ground enormously. I can't remember 601 Squadron losing a single aircraft, although the bombing was pretty concentrated. They calculated that in our first month at Luqa we'd received about three thousand tons of bombs! They all seemed to be pointed at *you* but luckily they missed. We had one roller to roll the bomb craters on the aerodrome, and that was kept in a very secure bomb-proof shelter. It was the only thing we had for repairing the aerodrome.

'Once we had everything well organized the Germans took an awful caning. I remember looking up at a Heinkel 111 with part of one wing shot off, coming down spinning like a sycamore seed and landing plonk on a bit of Malta. One of the crew had fallen out and was burning on the wing by an engine, and I must say that by that stage it didn't really put me off my lunch! The next day they came over again and they got the same treatment, and after that more or less they gave up. That didn't mean they stopped altogether, but Kesselring was ordered by Hitler to take his air force away having failed to take the island, and a large amount of them went off to Russia. So we'd won that battle.

'I had an experience over Grand Harbour in Malta with a cannon Spitfire, and a Vic of five Italian aircraft. They'd come over to bomb Grand Harbour and I dived on the leader with my cannons going. Although my aircraft had four cannons all but one had stoppages, but the result on the Italian bomber was fantastic. The thing caught fire, one wing dropped off completely, and the wreckage landed on the naval hospital at Bighi. I went to have a look the next day to check the effect of my cannon fire on it, and also to establish the fact that I'd shot it down and not the ack-ack. It was peppered with cannon shells, and being wood like a Mosquito it was a mass of wreckage. I've never seen anything like it.

'From March to June 1943 I was Wing Commander day fighters in a new allied air force called the North West African Coastal Air Force. During that time I wrote the Fighter Cover Plan for the convoys going into Sicily on Operation Husky, and my AOC had me up one day and said, "Well, you've written the damn plan, you can go and see whether it works!" I found myself commanding a small RAF wing on the ex-Italian island of Lampedusa! I was the first allied governor of occupied Axis territory, so there I was called Eccellenza by the Italians, and various other unprintable names no doubt by my little wing. We stuffed the island with radar and I had the marvellous experience of standing on the cliffs at Lampedusa, which were very high at one side, and on the evening before the invasion of Sicily, the tug aircraft and their gliders actually passed below me, between the top of the cliff and the sea, on their way to Sicily. It turned out to be a very tragic affair because a lot of them were dropped in the sea by their tow aircraft.

'While I was waiting to go over to Lampedusa, an army colonel appeared. He said, "I must get to Pantellaria as I've got the

Allied surrender terms for the Italian admiral commanding the place. How am I going to get there?"

'"If you don't mind coming with me I'll take you." I had a little unarmed trainer.

'"But what about my kit and my batman?"

'"They'll have to go by sea, I'm very sorry!" He immediately was very crestfallen because nobody wanted to be separated from their kit. However, we flew over and we just managed to dodge the various bomb craters in Pantellaria, and I found one little strip where I could land this aircraft. We got out, managed to find a troop carrier and cantered off to the headquarters of the Italian admiral. He gave it out that he was prostrate with nervous strain and grief, but we announced ourselves and said, "Right, sign this!"

'He said, "I wish to say that I'm only doing this because there's a shortage of water on the island, and my respect for the civilian population."

'We said, "Well, we really don't mind what your reasons are, but there is another load of American bombers on the mainland ready to take off, do you want another pasting?" He then realized that signature was the best policy, so he signed it.

'By this time we were flying the later Marks of Spitfire. The Mark IX had a supercharger with two gears, and that used to go up like a lift, a very good aircraft. You could go very high up indeed, let's say about thirty thousand, but at that time we were living on unadulterated oxygen up there. A lot of us got awful trouble because the oxygen was totally dry, the method of making it left no water vapour at all, and it was very scarifying to the tissues in the nose. I'm still suffering from it. Every morning an enormous quantity of mucus comes out of your nose and it makes you feel quite sick!

'Later, I went off to Italy and commanded a wing as what the Americans called Air Defence Commander. Foggia was being built up as a bomber base for attacking places like Schweinfurt and Romanian oil wells. We had squadrons of rocket Beaufighters which were deadly at sinking German coastal shipping, and radar-equipped Wimpeys. We also ran what turned out to be a very successful air–sea rescue operation. We had Walrus and Catalina amphibians, and even had three squadrons of the newly recruited Italian air force, with Savoia Marchetti float planes, and two flotillas of air–sea rescue launches. The casualties of the 15th Air Force were pretty great, but we managed to pull four hundred and fifty of them out of the drink in six months!

'I began in the Royal Air Force as a sergeant pilot and finished as a group captain. At the end of the war I went to see a senior officer at the Air Ministry who tried to persuade me to stay in. I asked what rank I would be. He said, "We'll look after you."

'I said, "That's what they told my father at the end of the First World War. He was an acting brigadier and when his post-war rank came through, he was made a captain. It broke his heart." So I came out then and went back into business.'

*Frank Baker* flew both the Hurricane and the Spitfire in 1940. He is now a plump jovial man in his late sixties. His living room is full of mementoes of his long service in the RAF: on the walls there are eye-catching paintings of both planes in action, and from time to time he demonstrates their assets and disadvantages as fighting machines by pointing out details. 'The Hurricane was an idiot's aeroplane, very forgiving. If you couldn't fly it you really shouldn't be in the air. The undercarriage was so strong, so well constructed, that you could drop them in very carelessly and get away with it. They would bounce and bounce.

'If you did that in a Spitfire the undercarriage would have poked up through the wing! The Hurricane's also much stronger. From the cockpit back it was wood covered with fabric. You could shoot away great lumps without affecting its performance too badly. Do the same with a Spitfire – the monocoque metal construction wouldn't take the punishment. The Hurricane could turn very very tightly and in dogfights it all comes down to who can out-turn the other. The pilot who's got the smallest turning circle will get inside and shoot the other down. Because it has a lower wing loading I found I could turn a Hurricane more tightly than I could a Spitfire, so that if a 109 or a 190 stopped to play with me, I could turn inside him. You've got to shoot ahead of him, which means you've to turn tighter.

'The first Spit I flew was a Mark I. It didn't impress me. It seemed tinny. Thinner wing. Looked very much more delicate than the sturdy solid Hurricane. It looked like an aircraft that wouldn't take a lot of beating. In fact it *would* take a lot of beating! It certainly wasn't a case of love at first flight. The undercarriage was pumped up manually, it wasn't automatic. When you're taking off you went across the airfield doing this (*imitates the pilot pumping up the undercarriage*), trying to hold it level with one hand and pump up the undercarriage with the other! I preferred my Hurricane. I didn't fall in love with the Spitfire until I'd flown the Mark IX.

'The public's imagination was caught about the Spitfire because it was capable of tremendous development. When you consider that it virtually spanned from fighter biplanes up to jet fighters – there's no way the Hurricane could have done that because the airframe couldn't absorb the additional power that was available. The Spitfire was such a clever design that it could.

'When war started, as I had already been through all the selection boards, I went along on the *eighth* of September and was immediately accepted. I got my wings in mid-1940 so that that's how I started flying. Why I was selected to fly fighters as opposed to bombers I don't really know.

'If you were going on to Fighter Command you went to an Operational Training Unit. The first time you flew a Hurricane or a Spitfire was the first time you flew it! We had no twin-seat models, although a twin-seat Spitfire was built for the Irish air force. Quite a daunting experience because you've got a thousand horsepower! It's a lot to let loose! I can clearly recall my first take-off in a Hurricane – I was up at about two thousand odd feet still trying to find the lever to get the undercarriage up!

'You would do an oxygen climb. First one you'd done. You'd get used to flying at altitude with oxygen, probably going up to twenty-five thousand feet. The higher you get the thinner the air gets. You reach a point, the absolute ceiling of the aircraft, where it really has only one airspeed it will fly at, that's its maximum speed, its stalling speed, everything! If you try and get above that height you'll just fall out of the sky until she hits a point where she picks up sufficient speed.

'When I joined the RAF we were very short of fighter pilots, screaming out for them. Many left the training unit with anything from fourteen to twenty hours on a fighter. It meant that you really didn't fly it, it flew you. But you arrived at a squadron supposedly competent (*laughs*). If you were lucky you survived long enough to get the skill and experience to help you survive a bit longer. If you weren't, if you were unlucky, you popped off on your first or second flight, simply because you never saw the person who shot you down. The first thing you knew was cannon shells were exploding round about and bits were falling off your aircraft!

'We were all aware that we were going against pilots whose training was probably much lengthier than ours. Some of the German pilots took part in the Spanish civil war, so they had been preparing for the war for a lot longer than we had. Essentially I was a civilian in uniform. I can only assume that I survived because Him and him (*points up and down*) had been having an argument and they hadn't decided yet who was going to have me!

'Can I put it this way? Being young I thought I was indestructible. Maybe someone else is going to die but I wasn't going to die. So the thought that I'm going off into the air and someone's going to blow me to bits never really rang a bell. Then there's the day you look in your rear mirror and see somebody on your tail shooting at you! You suddenly realize this is dangerous! You can get killed! When you're shooting at another aircraft it never occurred to you that there were people in it. It was an *aircraft* you were shooting at. You don't have time to be afraid. You're afraid later. Perhaps if you'd been in a tight spot when somebody has been shooting at you, the next time you get into that spot you're afraid.

'The Germans were a very formidable enemy. We had the greatest respect for their aircraft and air force. The Messerschmitt 110 for instance. Unusual aircraft in that it had slots on the leading edge of its wings and the advantage of this is it could turn very tightly, gave it a much lower stalling speed. Flown by a good pilot you had your time cut out. Where an aircraft can't turn inside the other one, the practice is not to stay with it, but to peel off from him and then use your speed and your height to attack him at an angle.

'We did a lot of formation work. At that time, the RAF squadrons tended to fly in three Vics of three with one in a box, one above, and one below weaving, as look-outs. Useless formation! The only people that could really keep look-out were the people weaving above and below so the others were very dependent on them. The mistake they made was they always put the new boys on these weaving positions when they should have gone to the most experienced. Because we were flying into the sun, which was always on the south of us, Jerry could attack us from out of the sun. He could nip in and if he was clever cut off the two weavers, which left the rest of the boys unaware we'd lost them!

'Towards the end of '40–41, we developed the finger four, which became the standard formation. The squadron, instead of flying behind one another, would fly in three lots of four. There were actually two pairs flying as a group. Flying in that way you covered an immense range of the sky. These four were looking to the left here, and these four on the left were looking to the right, so they all covered one another's tails. Also a very fluid formation because you could do a rapid turn-around, whereas if you've got three lots of three trying to turn tightly, it's just not on. But it was the pre-war idea. This tends to happen in wars, they fight the last war all over again. It takes time for them to realize conditions – and the vehicles they're flying in – have changed.

'Funnily enough, with formation flying the closer you get the easier it is because you can see any relative movement of the wings. If you're far away it is difficult to judge the distance so it's more difficult to fly in wide formation than it is to fly in tight formation.

'In '40, '41 we had a lot of Czechs and Poles came to join the British squadrons. Having flown many different aircraft, they found the Hurricane terribly easy. (*Imitating accent*) "This is a lovely little pet!" We didn't develop the hate for the German air force – or should I say *I personally* didn't – that the Poles and the Czechs generally did. They really hated the Germans with an intensity. The treatment they got in Poland was quite frightful. They had a habit if a German baled out of shooting them. I think that's on record. This of course wasn't considered quite cricket. I don't think it occurred to some of our people that it wasn't cricket we were playing! So the Polish boys said, "OK, we'll not shoot them down." If someone baled out, they would fly straight at the chute and then turn away at the last minute. The slipstream would hit the chute and cause it to cannon.

'At that time a very large proportion of the pilots in the RAF were NCO pilots. I see so many Battle of Britain films with a lot of blokes with wings on their arms – you don't see so many for sergeant pilots, but that's what a great many of them were!

'When I joined I was an AC2 earning fourteen shillings a week. Now that may not sound a lot but I came from a civilian job where I was only getting ten shillings a week! This was in a laboratory as a rubber technician. I can't remember what I got as a sergeant pilot but I know that at that time it was *to me* a princely sum. We never said, is that all I'm getting for going doing this job? We didn't think of it in those terms. Most of us would have done it for nothing, if we'd had the money to spend on beer. If I'd been commissioned I would have had a lot of expense, but as a warrant officer I didn't because the service paid for my uniform. I had all the advantages of being an officer with virtually none of the responsibilities. My NCO's mess fees were almost non-existent – everything was provided for me, so I was relatively well off.

'I was in a reserved occupation, but I got away in the first week of war. Things were so disorganized that it took my company a couple of weeks to realize that I was in a reserved occupation. They then applied to get me out of the RAF but the RAF said we've got him, you've lost him, we need him! So that was that.

'Later in the war, in '41, I went back to the company that I worked with to visit the people there. A number of them hadn't got into the services. They were terribly guilty about this. But none of us in the services would ever have dreamed of saying to them – or thinking! – you shouldn't be there! What's the good of a gun if it's got no ammunition, what's the good of an aeroplane if it hasn't got an engine? The part they were playing was every bit as vital. We were having a high old time anyway. When you've got a pair of wings on your chest, the women just flock for you! You could walk into any Palais de Danse, look about and say right!

'One change I remember. Ferry pilots would deliver aircraft to the squadrons. It was a wonderful sight to see a Spitfire come in, draw up to the dispersal and out pop a beautiful shapely young thing. She'd take out her mirror and compact which reduced us to the level of not being quite as good as we thought we were! These girls would fly something like ten or twelve different aircraft in one day!

'The aircraft were looked after splendidly. Usually a fitter and a rigger were allocated to each one. They were very good – the ground crew took great pride in their aircraft. I remember once in North Africa I felt the aircraft was a little bit dirty so I got a bucket of water and sponge, and some beeswax. I went out and started washing, and I hadn't been there more than four or five minutes when a couple of airmen came out and said, "What do you think you're doing?"

' "I'm washing it."

' "Do you think it's dirty? That's our job, we'll wash it. You lay off."

' "I'm going to polish it too, with beeswax!" That would give you the extra two or three knots. Make a difference between existing and not.

' "We'll do that for you! So off you get!"

'This was very much their attitude. It was their aircraft and we were graciously being allowed to fly it for 'em. And when the aircraft was finished you could almost see your face in it it was so polished.

'I didn't consider I had a tough time during the war at all. Although I did two complete tours of operations, in which I was shot at and one thing and another, I consider I had a very easy war. The bomber boys – I could *not* have got in an aircraft realizing that I had to be in there for six hours and for most of that time I'm going to be shot at! Then to come back and realize I've got to do this another twenty-nine times! I'm afraid I would have been in a mental home. I joined with fifty-nine other people. Of the fifty-nine, about forty went to Bomber Command. Of the remaining twenty, ten went to Coastal Command, Transport Command, other commands; ten of us went to Fighter Command. By the end of the war there were four of us left, all from Fighter Command. Many of the bomber boys would be lost in their first operations because early in the war the odds against you surviving an operational bomber tour were very high. So Fighter Command was really a relatively safer occupation than some of the others.'

*George Lord* also flew the Hurricane in 1940. 'The first one had a two-bladed wooden airscrew and a ring-of-beads sight – the old steam method. They were all old aircraft, and Sutton Bridge was a very small aerodrome below sea-level. It was like being in a basin. Coming down you had to be ever so careful – you couldn't have a low approach because of the banks. You had a job to get down because you didn't have enough airfield.

'Nice aircraft to fly in but the chap who shared a room with me said, "I'm terrified of Hurricanes! I won't last five minutes!" He was killed within a month. And a Pole there. He said, "I want to fly bombers. I'm not afraid to fly but I don't want to fly Hurricanes, I'm afraid of them!" He was bending all the aircraft he got into, hoping that he'll be posted. But they kept him there and in the end he was killed.

'I went into the RAF VR August 1937. I spent all my time at

40

the aerodrome flying, I never went anywhere. There were so many crashes even before the war had started! A crash a day. Before the war you had the cream of the country, but the daft things they used to do! And in 1940 when I was working with the army people. Hospital at the end of the airfield was full of them – they kept crashing in the grounds!

'I went to Number 1 Squadron and when I got there the scramble bell went within five minutes. I went and jumped in this aircraft – it had a reflector sight. I'd never seen one before! I didn't know what to do with it! I knew it was a gun sight but I didn't know what to do with it. We learned!

'They always wanted you. In the course of a day, if I look in my log-book, there were four or five sorties! There were always enough people around to allow somebody off for a day or half a day. But never any more. I don't remember having any leave as such, not like in other parts of the air force, when I was on other duties.

'When war broke out I had done about three hundred hours' flying, which was a lot for a part-timer, and it stood me in good stead. But a lot of them hadn't got that, very little indeed. They joined up in 1940 and before they knew where they were, they were in Fighter Command. Even so, a good knowledge of flying – how to do aerobatics properly and so on – isn't always the answer. There were people killed in mid-air collisions which you can't avoid – or shot down by your own people – you can't watch everybody at once.'

*'Did people get superstitious?'*

'Well, if they did they never said so, but I'll tell you a thing about being afraid, everybody's frightened, it doesn't matter who they are. You're young in those days, and you think you've got all your life ahead of you, and you think, God! this time tomorrow I might be dead! It wasn't a fear of what you're going to do, it's a fear of the fact that this time tomorrow you might not be there! Friend of mine had been shot down and badly hurt. He couldn't jump out because the runners of his hood had been damaged, so he had to sit in the aircraft. You're sitting there and you think, I've another four thousand feet to go before I hit the ground! He said to me, "I just cannot cope any more! I can't go on operational flying!" He went to see the doctor and told him how he felt about it, and the doctor said, "Have a word with the station commander."

' "No," he said, "there's a war on, he's got to fly!" He was shot down on his first sortie after he came out of hospital! If people lose their nerve I never hold it against them. People aren't all made the same, some conceal it better than others, some overcome it. I used to find it's the hanging around waiting – suddenly the scramble bell would go and break the silence. Oh, what's next?

'After October 1940, the air activity lessened a little bit but you always had these odd Germans coming over. They didn't come over in packs like they had, they kept popping out with unexpected attacks on you! I always felt that when we went on sweeps, there was such a mass of aircraft, psychologically it was comforting. We all took our turn to do weaving. As the squadron goes along you had a couple of weavers to keep an eye on the rest. But there again you can always get picked off by an odd aircraft. Even in formation flying people bump into one another. We lost two, one sat on top of the other. The unforeseen was the hazard. You know what can happen, it's the things that you don't know –

'In January '41, we started these rhubarb raids, flying over enemy territory. Very dangerous. They had to be carried out in certain conditions. No cloud base, or a very low cloud base, very bad weather, and at least three aircraft at a time from one station.

'They decided they couldn't very well say we'll detail people because the chap could always pick on somebody he didn't like. They weren't prepared to ask for volunteers because it made people feel a bit awkward, so they said we'll have a draw for it, which was fair. They drew for a morning sortie and an afternoon sortie, and for the afternoon sortie there's myself and the wing commander.

'I don't know where everybody else went, but I remember they had the old tortoise stoves, with big pipes going through them, and I sat there thinking to hell with this. I had all sorts of visions – on a rhubarb raid you had to go across the Channel, and the coast was so heavily defended! The outcome was, the morning sortie went off, and by lunchtime the clouds had started to break which was good for us but bad for the sortie. Then we heard old Haw-Haw on the radio saying three Hurricanes had been shot down off the coast of Belgium. We learnt later one of them had been taken prisoner.

'The wing commander, incidentally, was most unfortunate. His flight was jumped on by a whole crowd of Messerschmitts and they were all shot down, the lot of them. The wing commander baled out and fell out of his parachute, at thirty thousand feet. Dreadful death, dreadful death!

'At his funeral, when we were at the grave side, the dispatch rider came down to say the scramble bell had gone for the squadron. We all tore back to the aerodrome. They had to go on escort duty, but a posting had come through for me. The flight commander said, "You can either come with us or get cracking with your posting." I'd been in Fighter Command, what, seven months, I got to the point where I thought if I stay I won't live much longer! This is the feeling you get with people coming and going, so I said, "I'll get my things ready for posting."

'I learned later on they escorted these Blenheim boys over to the Continent to bomb a petrol dump and they had heavy losses, because the Blenheims flew at such a low level. They really took a pasting. The coasts were very heavily defended.

'When we talk about the Battle of Britain, it was just a stage of the war for us. I don't think we ever realized till Churchill's words that it had become the thing it has. I think if Hitler had known how tired people were, if he'd kept it up a bit longer, we couldn't have kept on for much longer. We were losing pilots and planes! People were inexperienced and panic-stricken. The training was a great help. When you don't know from second to second what the situation's going to be, you keep your eyes and your wits about you and just do what you think is necessary. It's said the Germans were only doing a job. I don't agree with that. We had a reason for fighting, I don't think they had. We were fighting for existence, they were fighting for world domination.

'Discipline was lax! Nobody tied you down. We used to exchange tunic buttons with different people and I had an RAF button, a Free French, a Czech and a Polish one! The AOC came round one day and he stood there looking me up and down, he said, "Would you mind telling me which air force you belong to?" We all wore our top button undone, fighters always did – we were always known as glamour boys, and Bomber Command as Brylcreem boys!

'I used to suffer agony at high altitude, the aircraft was so cold that my hands got numb. At about twenty-five thousand feet you're all frosted up, as you came down the pain was absolutely incredible! I've been in tears lots of times. It was just as if somebody had hit you on the fingers and crushed them, that sort of pain, absolute agony. We'd no heating whatever, none at all. There was no room to wear your tunic, your flying jacket and a Mae West. I just had my tunic, sometimes overalls, and a scarf, but I never had an Irving jacket. I don't know how people sat in the aircraft with the Mae West on, and straps on top of that!

'So much was luck! Before the war we asked about parachute training. They said we don't have it because you may never need to jump out. One day we went up, climbing through all this dreadful murk, got to the top of the cloud, and we were flying all over the place. Well, the next thing I knew was the aircraft was shaking like mad, the dust was coming up, all the instruments were rolling around, the gyro was spinning, the altimeter was unwinding like a broken clock – what the hell's happening?

'I'd got into a high-speed stall. I was watching these instruments here and they were unwinding so rapidly I couldn't read 'em! I juggled with the rudder and all this vibration stopped. I'd come out of the stall position and was now gathering air speed.

'I thought, I'll jump out, and this is as true as I sit here, I opened the hood to jump and was just undoing my strap when I saw a couple of motor cars going along in front of the aircraft!

I'd come out on the main street of Peterborough! I couldn't read my altimeter. We were at eighteen thousand feet, and I'd lost all that altitude in a matter of seconds. If it hadn't been for that hole in the cloud at that instant I should have jumped out! At fifty or sixty feet! This is what makes your flying career, this sort of thing. If you had a flying career where nothing happened, you hadn't lived, so to speak.

'When I went to Central Flying School at Upavon, I really learnt about flying. People get complacent. You go on for so long, nothing ever happens, you take things for granted, but I never did. Every time I took off, I did my cockpit check in full, always, always! When I was an examining officer, when I did a check on a pupil, I always knew who his instructors were because he made the same fault as the instructor did. Being a flying instructor is hard work. It's often been said, to do an hour's flying instruction, as instructor, has the same strain on you as six hours of operational flying! You're talking all the time, you're correcting people all the time, and they're all different, you can't teach one pupil the same way you treat another.

'The amazing thing was, in most cases half the course didn't want to be pilots. They didn't mind flying, or being navigators, they did not want to be pilots. They didn't want the responsibility. In the end the wastage rate got so high that Flying Training Command were getting worried about it. They said, we're bringing all these people over to Canada, and you're chucking them all out. It's a waste of money. In future you will not suspend more than ten per cent of one course. If you had sixty people on the course, you could safely say that you would suspend ten before the first stage, another ten might just scrape through but never progress, and in the end you could whittle them down to ten who would stay on the course. In many cases you could suspend the whole of a course for one reason or another. Now we could suspend only ten per cent. That's six people out of sixty. It's no wonder that there was an enormous loss in 1942, 1943, 1944 – many of these people didn't want to be pilots, they were *made* to be pilots! That was wrong.

45

'When I look back on it now I'm proud to have done it but I wouldn't like to have to do it all over again! The horrors of war don't sort of penetrate when you're that age, as they do in hindsight. The best way to ensure survival is not to take off unless you have to! On operational flying, keep a good look out! Even before the war people were having mid-air collisions. And caution in every respect. Treat your aeroplane with respect because they'll always turn round and bite you, especially if you don't know them very well. It's important when you learn to fly you learn all about aerodynamics, why aircraft do things, what happens when you do certain things. So if you get into trouble you know exactly what to do. Don't try to be the best pilot in the air force, try to be the oldest!'

# 2

# RETALIATING

$A$T THE START OF THE WAR THE RAF had only a small and largely outdated bomber force to attack the enemy and it was not sure how even that could be best employed. The aircraft were slow, unreliable, poorly defended, and their crews had little knowledge of modern navigational techniques. They had a very poor record in actually hitting the target, and losses were extremely serious. The Luftwaffe and ack-ack were great hazards but so were the distance, the weather and night.

But the RAF was determined to carry the war to the Germans by raiding their cities. RAF bombers in 1940 included the Hampden, made by Handley Page, the Armstrong Whitworth Whitley and the Vickers Wellington. Short Brothers were bringing the Stirling into production – this four-engined heavy bomber reached the air force in November 1941. These aircraft varied in quality: airmen still speak highly of the Wellington and even the Stirling, but the Whitley appears to have had few friends. Yet it was an important part of the bomber force sent to raid Germany in 1939 and 1940.

*Bill Beverley* had joined Royal Air Force Volunteer Reserve before the war when he was nineteen. 'On 1 September 1939 we were stopped from coming out until we'd signed on in the RAF. There were two burly sergeants on the door – "No, you can't go out, you've got to go in there!" You *were* in the RAF VR, you'd already signed up for that, so you really had no choice. I don't think anybody hesitated.'

He was sent to air training school where he was offered the choice of fighters or bombers. 'For me at that time big was beautiful so I chose to go on bombers.'

He joined his squadron in August 1940. 'The first twenty-four hours I spent in shelters – we were bombed by some thirty JU88s and a lot of aircraft were destroyed.' He flew the Whitley bomber, which had a crew of five. Crews called it 'the flying coffin', because of its shape and its peculiar flying attitude, nose down. When it was flown in action the losses it suffered gave the nickname a bitter flavour.

Bill was captain of one of these aircraft. At this early stage of the war pilots had no communication or radio, but only dead reckoning by map and watch. The concept of the bomber stream had not yet been developed. Navigators made their own routes to the target, and pilots set out individually. Finding their way there was hard enough, but getting back posed some real problems, as Bill recalls:

'On one op I had the acting CO of the squadron flying with me. We completed the trip but when we arrived back in this country, there was a thick fog, something like two hundred feet of it. Above it you could see quite clearly and looking down straight through it you could occasionally see the ground. We even found the aerodrome but as soon as I made an attempt to come down into this fog, the whole thing disappeared! It was impossible to land.

'We couldn't communicate with the ground although we could hear them talking to other aircraft. So we had to fly around and try and find some other place to land. It was unfortunate because in 1940 any field of any size had ditches dug in it or poles sticking up – anti-invasion measures.

'Then I remembered that in my lectures somebody had told me that if I flew over an English ack-ack battery and gave a certain signal, they would lay down their searchlights in a line with an aerodrome which would be clear and would receive me. I flew over this battery and gave this signal. It didn't seem to work at first but after a while it did.

'All the lights came down and pointed in one direction. Fine! I'm going to get down now and I flew along the beams right out to sea! What happened I don't know, whether they thought, this is a German intruder! Maybe they were trying to deceive us.

'Anyway, out to sea. Well, that was no good. And then I suddenly remembered Flamborough Head, maybe I can get down there? I tried and actually touched the ground but then I saw something looming up in front, out of the fog, so I had to pull up again, right over the cliff and out to sea. I started climbing, thinking hard what am I going to do next? By this time I'd been in the air eleven hours twenty-five minutes!

'Finally, the fuel ran out so I had to ditch in the sea. The aircraft manufacturer said they would float for five minutes. By the time I got out, the last one, the tail was under water. The dinghy was in the tail so I had to decide if we should dive in and get it or not, but the plane was going down. Better try and hang on together. We were under water to the shoulders. Every now and again I sent off a Verey pistol – we must have been about two or three miles out to sea.

'Eventually we heard the sound of an engine coming towards us – I don't know how long we'd been there – maybe two and a half, three hours? Suddenly everything went silent (*laughs*) and we thought, oh hell, they can't find us in the fog! Later on we heard the splash of oars. We hailed and they found us. As we were getting aboard, the plane's aerial snapped, wound itself round the navigator, and we had a heck of a struggle getting him unwound! He nearly drowned.

'When we landed we were sent off to hospital to check we were OK. We'd been in the water for several hours. That was about the eighteenth of December 1940. On Christmas Day morning we were walking down Bridlington promenade and lo and behold there was my aircraft on the beach – it hadn't sunk!

'That was just one trip and altogether I did thirteen. There were problems on all of them but one.'

But Bill's skill as a pilot which brought his crew through several very near shaves caught the attention of senior staff and he was sent for special training. As a result he became a test pilot.

'The instructors really put me through it. I'd be taking off, and suddenly my instructor would shoot his hand out, pull the throttle back and leave me with one engine! I would have to decide whether I'm going to stop or take off, but usually they did it when it was too late to stop, so I'd have to take off on one engine. Or I'd be landing – I'm just about to land – and they'd whip up the undercarriage and say, "Your undercarriage has failed!" I'd to make all these quick decisions – they keyed you right up.'

He tested hundreds of aircraft, sharing in the admiration for the Spitfire, Hurricane and Lancaster, but horrified at some of the other aircraft the Air Ministry had ordered.

'The Beaufort! A reconnaissance torpedo fighter. The test pilots hated flying them because they were quite vicious. Whenever one came up for testing we used to draw straws. My turn came. We'd only got about seven hundred feet up when the port engine exploded, caught fire and the aircraft turned on its back! I found it very hard to get it over and just saw the ground spinning up. I managed to flatten out when I hit the ground. I jumped out and ran – I was expecting the thing to blow up. When I crashed the petrol tanks burst and I was saturated!

'I got a hundred yards away and suddenly remembered I had a passenger! I rarely had one on test flying but an armourer had been pestering me for weeks, could he have a flight? On this occasion I said yes and he was in the turret!

'I had to run back and he was still sitting there! I banged on the door and got him out – "Run!"

'We found we were within fifty yards of a house, at the end of a cul de sac. I felt the blood running down my leg from a gash there, but they'd rung up an ambulance already. They bandaged me up and then, within half an hour, like falling off a horse, you must get back on again, so I had to get in an aircraft and go up!'

At the end of the war he was seconded to Frank Whittle's company Power Jets. 'It was my first experience of flying a jet and they warned me that on take-off I'd probably black out – no such thing as a pressure suit then! It was nearly true. I didn't actually black out, I greyed out, with red spots in front of my eyes. Each time I took off I still greyed out but it gradually faded. I got used to it.

'But I'd reached a point where I thought I'd had enough, so I gave up flying, at the end of March 1946. I think the main reason was the lack of communication, it caused all sorts of problems. In fact on my operational sorties on Whitley aircraft I only had one trip that worked perfectly, where I had no problems at all. At Power Jets I was flying at thirty thousand feet at times and I had to find my way down again when I didn't know where I was. It was getting me down. I haven't flown since – as a pilot. Of course I've been on holiday now and again when I've had to fly. That frightens me to death because I'm scared of flying.

'One story I must tell you. The target one night in 1940 was Cologne. Over the target it was brilliant moonlight, no clouds, and I saw Cologne and the Cathedral as plain as anything. I went and found the target and I was sure we *had* found it, but we noticed there were fires burning about five miles east. I flew round again, no that wasn't it, I *had* found the place.

'We thought righto, we'll go round and bomb it. The intelligence had been telling us, as the Berlin raids had been stepping up, the Germans had been pulling guns away from Cologne to Berlin and there were hardly any searchlights at all. I thought OK, I was flying at about fifteen thousand feet, come down to about twelve thousand. I ignored the fires because I was the first one taking off so I should have been the first one there.

'I got down to twelve thousand and aimed the bombs and as

soon as those bombs hit the ground you've never seen such a change! The colours of searchlights swung up, the guns started out, banging like mad, you could see the tracer coming up and banging round you, all sorts of types.

'I dived to try and get out of these searchlights, but I was in them for twenty-five minutes! When I got home I had a look at the aircraft – it was shot through with holes! Some as big as a clenched fist! There were a hundred and thirty of them.

'Well, obviously, it was a set-up, they knew we were coming. Our people set things in motion and we heard a month or so later they'd tracked it down. What had happened, the mechanics on the far side of the airfield – airfields were quite massive, perhaps a mile or two round – instead of coming back for lunch broke a hole in the fence and went to a local pub. They more or less knew where we were going and there were fifth columnists in this pub. They got to know and that's why they were ready for us. So that's my spy story.'

*Norman Cookson* also flew the Whitley bomber in 1941. Like Bill, he joined the RAF via the Volunteer Reserve. 'We learnt to fly free of charge! The first time I went up was fantastic! You can't keep up with it! I was all over the place but the feeling is marvellous.

'I learnt to fly on the Tiger Moth which was very nice. It had no vices. It landed very nicely, quite a low landing speed. We had to start them up ourselves by turning the prop, swinging it, so you had to be a bit careful to keep out of the way or you might get hit.

'Later on they introduced Hurricanes to give us a bit of experience. They had manually operated undercarriages. You had to pump a lever but taking off needs all your attention, and trying to pump up this flipping undercarriage at the same time was a bit hairy!

'The hard parts were aerobatics, rolls and loops and formation flying. That brings you out in a cold sweat, keeping your eye on the bloke there, on your right. All the time you're throttle and stick, trying to keep a position just here, keeping your eyes glued on his wing.

'The Spitfire was good too, it had a nice strong undercarriage, but we never did any dual flying on them. We just got cockpit drill, learnt about flying the aircraft and off we went! The runways were very small and bumpy and the undercarriages weren't nearly as strong as the Hurricane ones. If you messed up a landing the undercarriage collapsed and you did a ground loop on one wing! Which happened to me.

'Before I got to the end of the Spitfire conversion they had a rush on bomber pilots and they wanted some of us to transfer. I wasn't too keen to stop on Spitfires so I transferred to a bomber OTU, Whitley OTU, in Scotland. I started flying the old Whitley around. It was completely different, much more stable so you'd got more time to think. The only trouble was there were too many mountains sticking up and we lost a few aircraft running into them. Visibility wasn't always very good.

'From there we went on to the squadron. I had to do six raids as second pilot on the Halifax to learn how to do things and what went on. I must say I didn't particularly enjoy it – I can't profess to be one of these brave types for whom it was all a great adventure. I think that went for most of us – actually, we were all scared stiff.

'We used to get a briefing and do a night-flying test to see if the aircraft was all right. Then the navigator worked out the course and you took off at the appointed time and made your way. My first raid was Berlin – it shook me up a bit. As soon as we got over the French Channel coast, the flak opened up. That gave you your first taste of it.

'When you got within reach of Berlin they had a hell of a defence, guns and searchlights – searchlights everywhere. Particularly a blue one which searched till it found an aircraft: when it got you about twelve others coned you! You tried evasive action but you felt like you were walking into a public place without any clothes on, that's the feeling – completely naked and defenceless.

Luckily we were never attacked by a fighter but I saw others of the squadron shot down by fighters, go down in flames there. The flak was very heavy – it came in and ricocheted through the plane – I've got a bit upstairs.

'The pilot used to scare me a bit. He'd have a few drinks in the mess before we went and keep dropping off to sleep, leaving it on George (*the automatic pilot*). We flew long distances on George. It saved a lot of strain, but he was dozing there and I thought suppose a fighter comes up? They gave us tablets to keep us awake – we used to take handfuls and hope for the best.

'We also had to do a trip to Italy to bomb Turin. We flew down to Stradishall to refuel and bomb up, because with that long journey, we wanted to make sure we'd got enough petrol to get back. They hadn't seen four-engined planes before so everybody turned out to have a look. We were quite the little heroes strutting in with our Halifaxes. We had a meal in the mess and everybody was asking us what they were like.

'They were much better than the Whitley which was a slow old thing, flew along with its nose down. You felt very exposed because you were going so slowly. You could see the flak following you up and think that's bound to catch you – you see it start behind and keep bursting nearer and nearer. That's going to get me soon!

'We were usually told to bomb from about sixteen thousand feet so there'd be a lot of aircraft in a small space over there! We were told which target to hit – the navigator had all the details. He used to get it in the bomb sights, give the details of the run-up and let the bombs go.

'It was very easy to get lost. After one raid we got back to England next morning about six o'clock. It was getting light, but we hadn't the faintest idea where we were! We flew around for a while, getting short of petrol, we even considered ditching in a field with the undercarriage up.

'We were turning all these things over, discussing what we should do, when a Spitfire flew up alongside us. He saw we were an English plane so we followed him in. The first thing we did when we got down was to open our bomb doors and we found a thousand pounder hung up! It had been triggered, so if we had crash-landed there would have been quite an explosion.

'I wouldn't say that the navigator was all that good. Once we nearly bombed Sweden. We were meant for Berlin and the navigator said, "Oh, there are lights over there, shall we go and bomb those?" That was Sweden! Lucky we didn't! We generally decided if there were lights on there must be some catch somewhere. They used to have these dummy targets. They'd set a few things on fire hoping that you'd go and drop your bombs there and some probably did.

'If you had a fighter on your tail you'd be inclined to jettison your bombs there and then and get the hell out, or get into cloud if there was some about. The thing was, the nights chosen for bombing raids usually had a moon and not much cloud. You could even have a few days' leave, go home and you'd get a telegram saying come back straight away because there's a moon period, with good visibility. They wanted as many crews as possible. So to hell with your leave, back you went to take advantage of the moon period.

'Berlin was one of the longest trips, and Turin, over the Alps. But Italian flak was about five thousand feet below us so we weren't bothered. In fact we laughed at it, took the mickey off the Italians. We just cruised around at our leisure and dropped our bombs where we hoped was the right place.

'We weren't trained to use a parachute. People were always pinching them – you put it down for a minute and somebody would pinch it so you'd go and pinch somebody else's. They didn't even bother with parachutes when you were doing circuits and bumps! It wasn't worth it because you wouldn't have time to put them on. With the Spitfires and Hurricanes you didn't get into the aircraft without a parachute, you sat on it. On bombers they were much more casual – get inside the aircraft and chuck the parachute behind the corner. I think there would have been one mad scramble – who's got my parachute? Who's got mine!

'We didn't complain. There were too many other things on

your mind. You'd say, "Oh I see so-and-so's gone," his face is missing when you go to the mess. You've had a raid, how many did we lose last night? Oh, a couple didn't come back so you wait in the mess to see who it was.

'There was quite a bit of feeling among the regular staff, ground staff, against us. We came in and got our stripes quickly. They'd been in the service for twelve years, twenty years, before they got theirs. One bloke on the maintenance, in the sergeants' mess, was always pointing it out to us, how unsafe the planes were, our chances of crashing or not coming back, generally trying to put the wind up us. Those were the sort of people, when there *was* a crash and your gear was taken to the stores, who'd go and pick it over, take the best stuff and send the rest to your family.

'When you'd done six trips on Halifaxes as a second pilot you went back to Whitleys as a captain. We did one trip on the Channel ports. The next night we went out just as it was getting dusk to do our night-flying test, two or three circuits and bumps. I did the first couple of circuits without any incident and then the pilot officer took over. On his first take-off he swung right off the runway – which could happen with twin-engined aircraft. The torque is trying to push you one way and if you don't keep your rudder on the back stick you will swing off. That's what he did. We tailed through the rough. Whether he did the props in I don't know but we staggered off the ground and got to about five hundred feet.

'He said, "The undercarriage is not coming up!"

' "We'd better do a quick circuit and go in again if we can!"

'As soon as we said that the port engine started banging and cut right out. We tried to make a circuit as quickly as we could but with the one engine it was a bit difficult – we got into a sort of a flat spin. As I say, it was dark, we lost our bearings!

'We thought we saw the lights of the flare path but judging by where we ended up it must have been a railway siding. We were still trying to straighten it up but we hit the ground. Immediately the starboard engine where I was sitting burst into flames. Then it was all fire, just like that, as quick as that!

'We were scrambling to get out. I was sitting next to the pilot. I didn't see him but apparently we both did the same thing which was to try and get out by the pilot's escape hatch over the pilot's seat. I couldn't find it and I thought I'll go back down the fuselage – I wasn't too keen – you thought very quickly – all these thoughts run through your mind. To get down the fuselage you had to crawl under the fuselage petrol tank – I'm not too keen but I could only see that way out!

'The starboard side of the aircraft had broken open as we hit the ground – there was a river and we caught the undercarriage in the bank which took most of the shock off for us. I stumbled out and found myself on the engine that was on fire – got up quickly! It seemed the other pilot came out almost immediately, and the wireless op.

'The rear gunner was down the other end away from the flames – he turned his turret and got out the back. He came up out of the darkness and we were wandering around for a minute or two like idiots until the ammunition and the flares started going up. Then we moved a bit further away. We found our clothes were on fire – we walked up to the river and splashed it over each other. Some locals came up to us and said are you English or German? (*Laughs*.)

'We soon told 'em, but they were very good actually. They took us down to this little village near there and the doctors gave us a drop of whisky and an injection for the pain.

'The RAF ambulance turned up and took us to hospital, which was quite near. Part of it was a mental hospital. They took us into the wards there and dressed our burns. They were wondering how to treat us and they were saying, well, the last burns they had, they'd put on treacle and flour! Luckily they didn't use it on us – they thought about it – they didn't realize how serious it was. They said in three weeks it'll be healed up, you'll just have pink skin there.

'Well, it was all quite a painful operation! They decided to put our hands in bunion bags which were a new thing then, sort of like plastic bags. They used to flush it through with a solution of milk and inflate it with oxygen. It's supposed to keep the plastic off your hands and enable you to move them at the same time. I must say we didn't think much of them. The bags didn't stay up, they came down on your hands which were extremely painful.

'They put gentian violet on our faces – my wife came to see me and she didn't know who was who. She saw three people sitting there with gentian violet all over their faces! But the nurses were very nice, they wanted to do their best for us. They had to feed us and they were very gentle and understanding, how to feed us and do the usual functions for us. They couldn't do enough, could they?'

*Mrs Cookson:* 'They were marvellous. Norman's mum came with me and the head porter put us up for the time we were there. It was difficult because there were two extra and we hadn't got ration cards. They were very good to us.'

*'Had you been married long then?'*

*Mr Cookson:* 'About six months. The people from the village came up. They'd been saving up their chocolate bars and biscuits for Christmas and they brought them up for us. After a while an RAF MO came to see us and he got us transferred to an RAF hospital. We were put in the newly opened burns ward there which was actually in the officers' wards. Some of the other patients were a bit "off" because we weren't officers, only NCOs.

'They had just got these newly introduced saline baths which were a great thing. They put us in and took our old dressings off. The relief was marvellous!

'We were there a few weeks until Sir Archibald MacIndoe came along to see us. He said he'd take us down to East Grinstead for plastic surgery. I was there for the next two and a half years.'

Norman had been severely burned, especially his face, ears and hands. Even after the long time he had spent in hospital the extent of the scarring was distressing to see, particularly on his hands and ears.

'East Grinstead was a place on its own. You think, two and a half years in hospital! But it was a different hospital. Sir Archibald, apart from being a surgeon, appreciated how we felt. Military hospitals in those days liked to keep up the discipline. First of all we had to wear overall blues, which dated back to the First World War, and they'd only got two sizes, too big and too small! Trousers held up with a bit of tape, white shirt, red tie, and a blue jacket. We were supposed to wear these when we went down the town. We didn't think much of it.

'We were allowed out in the afternoons, from about two till four, and given free passes to the local cinema. Sir Archibald soon changed this. He got the blues abolished and allowed us to wear our own uniforms. We could go out in the evenings as well for a drink. He made things generally easier because he knew – which we didn't realize at the time – that we were long-term patients. If we didn't have a few freedoms we could get so sick and tired of each other we'd be arguing and carrying on all the time. It's not a good frame of mind to be in when you're going to have surgery every couple of months.

'Sometimes the hospital had an outbreak of infection and they were losing grafts, so they closed down for a while. I had to go into a general ward. They used to have a daily issue of beer. We had a barrel down the bottom of the ward in the evening for those who were still in bed, and we'd go and get a few jars and have a bit of a "do". They used to get a film occasionally. But if you'd been down for an operation that day you'd come back, wake up, it'd be dark and somebody'd be sitting on your bed dropping ash all over you when you felt like nothing on earth! Later on they opened recovery wards.'

*'How old were you then?'*

'At the beginning of the war I was nineteen. We crashed in October 1941 so I was twenty-one. There's another thing about the crash. When one engine cuts, you've got the second which is pushing you round the other way. You trim it against that engine. When we tried to do that nothing happened, it didn't work. The trimming wheel didn't do its job. I don't know whether the wires had been cut but that was a possibility – it was mentioned afterwards, wasn't it?'

*Mrs Cookson:* 'Norman was a bit delirious from time to time, and he mentioned this particular friend of his – '

*Mr Cookson:* '*Johnny* – '

*Mrs Cookson:* 'The padre came to the hospital and he said was there anything we wanted to know? I said we were wondering how Johnny was and if he could get to see Norman. The padre came back the next day and said Johnny'd also been in a crash, he'd been killed, and they suspected that there had been sabotage.'

*Mr Cookson:* 'The planes were dispersed all round the airfield and it was quite easy for people from the neighbouring villages and towns to get across to them. It was the time when they were expecting an invasion. We used to stand outside at night with broomsticks because they'd got no guns. We were going to get the parachutists with our broomsticks! A couple of you together walking up and down the perimeter fence jawing about things in general, you couldn't see much, it was dark! Anybody who wants to get to an aircraft has bags of opportunity.'

*Mrs Cookson:* 'Once the padre told me they'd been sabotaged I got a bit scared. He immediately swore me to secrecy. But he was most upset. I don't think he expected to see them so badly burned. I didn't, quite honestly. But we were almost grateful for it. It was on my mind that something might happen. Only the day before I'd said to Mum what would you do if there was a telegram? Would you bring it to me straight away, and she promised. I thought if Norman was killed Mum would not want me to know until the last minute. And I wanted to know. But I knew, I always felt, that he wouldn't get through it. So I could really say that it was a relief. Although it was a shock and they said he might be blind, it's a dreadful blow, but at the back of my mind was the thought, well, this is the best.'

The first of the wartime bombers – the Stirling – came into service with the RAF in November 1941. Its defects – it couldn't climb very high and it was slow and clumsy – soon became apparent. Sir Arthur Harris said, 'It's murder, plain murder to send my young men out to die in an aircraft like that!' But some men who flew the Stirling to bomb Germany and Italy speak highly of it now: after all, it brought them home again. *Ron Dixon* completed two tours of operations on bombers as a flight engineer, the first of them on the Stirling.

'We had no end of trips in the Stirling and came back with only three engines because one had failed. I flew T-Tommy and there's a picture of it in that book – she always got us back! We had one bad crash but fortunately we got away with it. Everybody expected to be killed and that's all there was to it. I've often thought if television had been invented in those days, they would have had a birthday! The news would never have finished, would they? They make so much now of any little thing that happens! But probably it was a good thing, because half the public never knew what was going on.

'My uncle was an ex-Flying Corps man and he used to tell me a lot about aeroplanes. Growing up in those days when aircraft were only just coming into being, I got very interested. I used to spend a lot of my Saturdays and Sundays cycling up to de Havilland's at Stag Lane to watch them fly. But I only went to an ordinary school and left when I was fourteen, same as loads of other boys. My dad said to me one night, "What do you want to do, what do you fancy doing?"

'I said, "I'd like to fly aeroplanes but I don't suppose I ever shall. I haven't got the education or the money."

'My father, an electrician, was one of the subcontractors when they built the new de Havilland place at Hatfield. He got to know one of the directors, Mr Hearle, quite well. De Havilland's ran an aeronautical students' school, which was like a college but you learnt aircraft. The only problem was, the parents of most of the people that went there had to pay for them and you didn't get any wages. My old man took me over there and we had an interview with this gentleman. He said, "I'm willing to take you in but we shan't be able to pay you."

'Coming home my dad said, "I can't afford to pay for you so that's that." The only other thing was to join the air force, which I did as a flight mechanic.

'When the war started in September, panic! We had to camouflage all our aircraft because they were silver then. We had to camouflage them in green and brown paint. We had six Hawker Harts lined up out on the tarmac every morning. Six pilots used to come out, mostly instructors, and fly these aircraft all round Wales and the Midlands looking for German paratroops.

'It was a right cock-up because nobody knew what they were doing. Our flight commander used to say, "Go and get yourself a parachute, Dixon, you can come up with me for two hours." I wasn't officially a flyer but I used to go up as a passenger. I got to like it and did quite a lot of hours flying with this bloke. One day when we came in I asked him if he thought I could put in for a pilot's course. But it was all toffee-nosed in the RAF in those days. If you were only an ordinary working-class bloke you didn't get on much.

'From there I was posted down to Stradishall, as a fitter, and I used to work in the hangars on engine changes, or overhauls. We had these Wellingtons flying on missions. I used to think it must be smashing to go so I went to see the adjutant to ask if I could try for a pilot's course.

"Well, yes, there's no reason why you can't apply for it," he said, "but I don't suppose you'll ever bloody well get it!" Anyway I filled in the forms, sent them in, and carried on working there.

'In 1941 an Air Ministry order came out that the new bombers needed an extra crew member called a flight engineer. Any ranks in the technical trades like fitters or electricians could apply, so Joe Bloggins put in for it. Within three weeks they sent for me, I had been accepted. We were given four weeks' training but all it did was confuse us!

'The particular crew I went with was Sergeant Bland's. He was an American in our air force. He was the type of bloke, if he wanted to do something he would do it. He was the skipper!

'Going out on one op an engine failed. I feathered it because we were losing oil. By the time we reached the German coast we were down to five thousand feet. He said, "I'll have to have that engine back!"

'I said, "I've feathered it for loss of oil! If we've got no oil it's gonna seize up!"

'"Oh I can't help that! We'll have to have it back!" He unfeathered the engine and started it up. It had only been running for a couple of seconds when there's a hell of a vibration. I was looking out the cockpit and saw a big mass fly off! The rear gunner called up, "There's a big hole in the fuselage down here!"

'I chased down the back. Half the reduction gear had come through the top of the fuselage! Of course with that the vibration stopped. We'd dropped to about three thousand feet. In the Stirling with a bomb-load on but only three engines you just couldn't keep height. We had to turn round and go back.

'When we got out to dispersal the old sergeant-fitter said to me, "What's the matter, Ron?"

'"I think we lost a bloody engine!"

'He shone the torch up and there was only the wires and pipes there! No engine left at all! We had to go in front of the CO for that. The skipper got a rollicking because he'd unfeathered it against my orders. So that was that little trip!

'The Luftwaffe was pretty good in the first years of the war. They used to shoot us down like sitting ducks. The first tour of ops we did we used to fly over there, no radar equipment or anything. Half of us never hit the targets, especially if it was a cloudy night, pitch dark – you couldn't always find the things!

'The German fighters used to come up underneath and you couldn't do a damned thing about it. They used to fly in pairs, the JU88 and the Focke-Wulf 190. The JU88 used to come in on the rear of you and take the two gunners' attention, and the Focke-Wulf would come in and rake you all down the side! (*Laughs.*)

'In a Stirling the engineer's position is just back from the cockpit, nearly adjacent to the wireless op. There used to be armour plating behind the instrument panel. I used to squat down like this – the instrument panel was up there. The night we got shot up he raked us all down the side. The shell went straight through just above my instrument panel. If I'd been standing up the shell would have gone right through my head! (*Laughs.*)

'Unknown to us, they'd also shot both the tyres away so as soon as we landed we couldn't control the thing. And we'd got no flaps hardly. I'd been able to wind them out a bit but they weren't sufficient to pull us up. We tore across the aerodrome at about 160–170 miles an hour, crossed a road – there was a little ditch at the end of it. The undercarriage dropped into that, what was left of it, and so did the engines! The fuselage just tore out of the wings across the road and we finished up in the gardens of married quarters (*laughs*). Fortunately a bloke had dug his garden, the nose stuck into it and tilled it up so that stopped us going through the houses. We all got out all right.

'If you crashed our squadron always gave you a week's crash leave. When we got back we were posted! I said to the skipper, "That's because you crashed the bloody aircraft!"

' "No," he said, "this is going to become a Pathfinder squadron. The only people they want are experienced crews with experienced navigators." We'd only done a few trips and they didn't think a lot of our navigator. We were posted on to a main-force squadron.

'When we got there I felt this pain coming up in my forehead and I had to go sick. I told the skipper and he said, "That's hard luck. We're on tonight, a minelaying trip." We used to call them a piece of cake – there was very seldom liability of being shot down or anything. When I woke up in the morning in our billet there was nobody there!

'I went up the flights and said, "What's happened to Eddie Bland's crew?" They said they got shot down into the sea. Apparently what happened was they flew over a little German flak ship and it started shooting at them. My skipper being what he was decided to go down and shoot it up and he got shot down!

'That left me floating around on my own, without a crew. But I found one with a Canadian called Mike Wilson. I carried on with them till they finished – I did three more than my thirty to finish with him. Our last trip was to Turin. With the Stirling you were lucky if you could get twelve thousand feet maximum with a bomb-load on. Crossing the Alps, to be safe, you'd to get up to about fourteen thousand feet. We didn't, we got to twelve, and going over there one of the engines packed up through over-heating.

'We carried on over the target – we were going for the Fiat factory at Turin. We did a couple of runs and it was always pretty quiet – as soon as we arrived the ack-ack used to pack up. But on our first run one keen bloke was still firing and he happened to hit the starboard outer and the port inner and put them out of action. That left us two engines and we'd got to get back across the Alps! Never! But the navigator said he thought he could navigate through the Brenner Pass. We came through there at about eight thousand feet, couldn't see anything, it was as black as pitch.

'All the way back from France there's me and the skipper trying to hold it up – in the Stirling you had two control columns, you had two seats – trying to hold it up like that to keep the wing up! Half-way across France the exactor control on the port outer engine started leaking. I kept topping it up but I used the lot – we were down at low altitude. I went round and got the thermos flasks and what coffee we'd got left and poured that in to act as a liquid. In the end I had to go round and ask the blokes to have a pee into this flask so I could top it up. Anyway, we made it back to England.

'When we got out of the aircraft into the bus we were waiting for the skipper. What's the matter with him? I went back in and said, "What's the matter, Mike?"'

'He said, "I can't get my bloody leg off the control column!" He'd put his leg over it and wedged his foot under a little shelf to try and take some of the strain off his arms. What had happened, he'd ruptured himself! We had to cut the spoke out of the control column to get his leg out. They took him straight off to hospital.

'I finished that tour in December 1942. I'd met my wife the August before. We were talking about getting married and she said, "I'm not going to marry you until you've finished your flying!"'

'When I finished she said, "Do you think you'll go back on ops?"'

'"No, I think it's pretty safe now."'

'We decided to get married in April 1943. It came round to 1944 and D-Day and the adjutant sent for me one day. "Ah, Dixon, you've been posted back on operations!" They crewed me up and as we came down the tarmac the skipper said to me, "That don't carry much weight with me!"'

'He meant the DFM (*the Distinguished Flying Medal*) – I'd got it for that last trip to Turin. "Well," I said, "it doesn't worry me, they just gave it me, I didn't bloody ask 'em for it!"'

'I started flying with him and I got on very well with the rest of the crew. He was a bit snooty because he was a flight lieutenant and three of the other blokes in the crew were officers. By this time they'd brought the Lancaster out, one of the best aircraft that's ever been built – it was even better than some of the things they're building today. I did twenty trips in them and we never had any trouble. The old Stirling would take a hell of a lot of punishment but the engines were no good. It was a real old bus of an aircraft but I used to love it.

'When we started flying the Lancaster, someone else in the crew had to be able to fly. The natural thing was to train the engineer up because he sat at the side of the pilot. So what we used to do, the skipper flew it out with the bomb-load on and I flew it home. They were so easy to handle! Even if you got in the slip-stream of the one in front of you, you'd jerk about a bit but she'd soon come back on an even keel. They were really light to fly.'

*'Did your parents know you were on bombers?'*

*Ron:* 'Oh yes.'

*Mrs Dixon (from the kitchen):* 'Not half!'

*Ron:* 'When I got my posting to aircrew my dad never spoke to me for six months, did he?'

*Mrs Dixon:* 'No! No!'

*Ron:* 'He never spoke to me for six months. If I used to come home on leave he'd never say anything, he'd never offer to go out for a drink – '

*Mrs Dixon:* 'If we were up there when the siren went he always used to leave home and go down the pub, never stopped with us. But he changed after Sam Western's son went out the first night and never came back!'

*Ron:* 'Yes. One of his drinking friends in the village, his son was the same as me, a flight engineer. He got killed on his first trip and then *his* dad would never speak to me when he saw me. I don't know why they did it. Especially Stanmore, it was a little village and everybody knew everybody else, but I can't understand why they did it.'

*'Did you realize what the losses were like?'*

*Ron:* 'Oh yeah. We had a dispersal truck which took us round to our aircraft. If you were the first one out, as you got out, the bloke would say, "Don't forget, I'll have your ration tomorrow night! Because *you* won't bloody well be coming back!" They used to say those things to you! But you never used to worry about it, I don't know why. I think you only worried if you really got in trouble, like the night we lost that engine. I thought, well, we ain't gonna get back tonight. We always used to get an orange in our ration and a bar of chocolate. I usually saved my chocolate to take it home but this night I ate them both, we ain't gonna get back. But we did!

'I think one of the nicest sounds I ever heard was when we used to land in a Lanc. I used to pull the throttles back and you could hear all the exhausts popping back. That used to be a lovely sound.'

*'What was the routine when you were going on an operation?'*

'In the morning maybe, a buzz'd go round, there's ops on tonight. Petrol bowzers going around, you'd see the bomb trolleys going to the bomb dumps and all that. You'd go back to your flights and say what is it? Is there a battle order tonight? And they'd say yes, briefing's at six o'clock. You just used to idle your time away in the afternoon, that's when it used to play on your nerves a lot, because you didn't know where you were going, you had to wait all this time. You used to smoke cigarettes by the dozen.

'Then you'd have your flying meal, go to briefing – the pilots and navigators always used to have a pre-briefing – and then the main briefing for all the crews was say six o'clock, or eight o'clock, or ten o'clock at night. You'd all go in, sit down and the CO'd come in, the flight commanders, the weather blokes, the technical officer.

'The CO'd say, "Well gentlemen, your target for tonight" – and he'd pull the blinds back from the big wall-map. You'd see these red lines going up like that. (*Laughs.*) If it was Hamburg or Italy – Christ! We've got to go all that way! – or Nuremberg, Schweinfurt – anywhere about four and a half hours' flight across enemy territory, blokes used to groan, but if it was an easy target, like round the coast, they used to cheer!

'From there you used to come into the crew-room, get your gear, get in the bus, go out to your aircraft and wait there. If you got a couple of red Verey lights sent up from the control tower, that meant the operation was cancelled. All the blokes used to moan like hell because they'd been mucking about for hours, probably half the evening, so they couldn't go out. They weren't very often cancelled.

'The anxiety before you went was the worst. I often used to say to blokes afterwards, the war we fought was totally different to anybody else's because one day we'd be at war, fighting for our lives, then you'd probably have two days more or less holiday. I used to go to Cambridge to be with my wife. Well, the next day I might be back at war for two or three days. We were non-combatant one minute, and combatant the next. I think that's what used to get to you in the end.

'When I came out of the air force we'd got a son then. We bought ourselves a little house in Cambridge but I'd to get a job – that was the whole worst twelve months of my life. How my wife stood me I don't know. In fact modern girls today wouldn't, the marriage would have packed up. I think a lot of marriages went on the rocks in that twelve months.

'It was the change, you see. You'd been used to doing what you wanted – OK, you had to obey orders that they told you to do, but your free time you could do what you wanted. I used to have this urge to go out every night on the beer, I used to go to the cinema, and the money I earned was only four pound eighteen a week! But after about twelve months I began to think, this is no good, I can't carry on like this and then I started to get better. I went on to shift work and did thirty-two years.

'I'd rather have been doing what I did than stuck in the army in trenches or in the navy down in the bowels of a ship. Being up in an aircraft never worried me. I was over Hamburg on the night of my twenty-first birthday. But *now* I can't bear to fly, I can't even bear to be in a lift! I'm very sorry about it because it means I can't go abroad on holidays, can't go to Spain – I can't bear the thought of going into an aircraft. All those other people there and the aircraft being confined, all confined together in a narrow space, very difficult to get out. I can't travel on the London underground for the same reason. I'd be all right if I could go into the cockpit, it's being a passenger upsets me. Never felt like this during the war when I was actually flying. It's something that has developed over the years since.'

# 3

# ALLIES

THE RAF WAS AN INTERNATIONAL SERVICE. CANADA, AUSTRALIA, New Zealand and South Africa declared war on Germany in 1939 and sent young men to Britain to fight. Their contribution was invaluable: forty-six per cent of the pilots came from the Dominions. Some bomber crews contained people from five or six different countries. Other personnel came from the Continent, particularly after the fall of France. Poles, Czechs, Belgians and Free Frenchmen fought with the RAF. *Josef Frankel* had served in the Czechoslovak air force before the war.

'In the Czech air force we were lovely boys and pampered. We had a small but I would say quite pleasant air force, efficient for its day – don't forget it was 1925 up to 1938. We started with old French aeroplanes, the Spad, and I flew an aeroplane which was built in 1914, a hundred horsepower, called AI. We inherited about three of them from the Austrian Empire. In those days flying was so different. In the Czech air force when you said Joe you knew who it was, like a big family. The British air force for us was the ideal for a real flyer. That's why the regulars came with so much enthusiasm to England. Unfortunately many were lost because they were in the first line.

'We were mad flyers, everybody was flying, and loved it. We did up to fifteen, twenty thousand feet photography. Photographed the Germans already in Austria on the frontier, their fortifications, and also ammunition dumps, but we had open aircraft! Can you imagine at fifteen thousand feet, an open aeroplane, with a camera overboard. Cold and came back with frozen noses!

'We were flying also before the war with the Little Entente, Czechoslovakia, Romania and Yugoslavia. Some bloody fine allies we had! But it was nice because we managed, the selected boys, to fly there for meetings. That way we got the wings. The old crocks in the officers' mess had all their medals from the First World War and we had nothing, not a badge, so in Romania it was a recipe for getting the wings. You landed, you are welcomed by two officers usually, little moustaches, painted cheeks, and wearing corsets, like a woman! But you were kissed on all four cheeks, taken to the officers' mess and tonight there'll be a party in your honour, and you paid for it. There were gypsies and prostitutes and wine. It was a terrific party and cost you five hundred crowns – which was for an army officer a bit of money, but we are getting flying pay so we could afford it. If you were very generous, to seal the friendship you get another hundred crowns which one of the high-ranking officers pocketed, and the next day we are called to the regiment and get the honorary wings! Romanian ones. CC – two sort of entwined Cs – King Carol's regiment.

'We were on night duty when the Sudeten affair happened. My squadron was billeted in a monastery, flying to the frontier. We saw from zero height, ten metres, the Germans chasing Jews in pyjamas from the Sudeten early in the morning across the new border. Couldn't do anything. After that it was waiting for the Germans when they come in. Nobody believes that nothing will happen. It's the end when they lost the Sudeten. It was now so small a country, when you played a squeezebox you had to have a passport!

'The boys, those who started in 1925, '30, were very good, but all those old boys from the First World War couldn't take it in. They went through the First World War and were made big heroes, which was natural – the liberators – and they sat on their laurels and nothing happened. It wouldn't have helped against the Germans. But it was sad because the young generation didn't have a chance.'

*'Do you think Czechoslovakia should have fought in 1938?'*

'Only if they would have even more heroes – dead heroes. Like in Poland, the Westerplatte, there was some sort of heroic stand, it didn't lead anywhere. It was a very sad thing. We were deserted even by the English. Everybody washed his hand. The French didn't want to know, Mr Chamberlain said why should we fight for a country which we don't know even where it lies, things like that.

'It was getting more and more difficult. I had to get out. My brother perished. The Germans got him. Hitler was already in Czechoslovakia. I had a cousin, I told him, you must leave. He said, "They can't do anything! I was an officer in the First World War! I have gallantry medal, this medal, that medal – they can't do anything to me!" A week later his wife got already a note that he died in Mauthausen.

'I had to escape. I had to sleep every night in a different hotel because Bratislava was a babel, and ninety per cent were enemies. But there I was very lucky again because I met a girl from a night club in Prague. We got talking and she told me, "I have boy-friend, public notary." Good God, a public notary is issuing passports so we broke into his offices with her help, and got passports, the books, photographs of all the air-force boys, stamps we made, everything, and the boys got away. I got to Belgrade and that was all right. Plain sailing more or less.

'When I came to Syria, then still a French colony, there was an old colonel with a white moustache at the border. Fell round our neck, each separately, and kissed us and said, "Bienvenu en France, mon ami!" Shook our hands and kissing us. I told him discreetly, "Look, we didn't eat for two days", so there came a huge Negro legionnaire and brought us a big bag full of sardines, oranges and bread. Tins of sardines without openers, my boys had to open it with some sort of pocket-knife, and cut themselves.

So we were in the French Foreign Legion in Beirut. It wasn't long, I don't complain. The boys had a bad time because they were not used to this sort of life.

'We went on this ship, to Marseilles, and within twelve hours they told us, "Oh, we have you for the French air force!" We said fine, we didn't like the Foreign Legion at all. Bed bugs everywhere. Horrible. We are sitting in officers' mess, and suddenly bombs are coming down. Through the window we saw the port and the marvellous ship *Le Havre*, the flagship of the *messageries maritimes*, in flames and burning! Not one machine-gun fired, not one anti-aircraft gun fired!

'In the evening we are already on the train to Arques which was the biggest camp I have seen in my life. The toilets were placed in the middle of the camp, huge toilets for twenty thousand men, so wherever you were they stank. Then came tailors: we got French uniforms. We found accommodation for ourselves because we got money, and I rented a house with three or four other officers and went every day swimming waiting what will happen, and nothing was happening at all. We were still there when Pétain received from the Germans the points of Armistice. And amongst them which gave us a strong impetus was, you must hand over all Polish and Czech soldiers fighting on your side. We knew it was high time to disappear.

'My boys raided the armoury and armed themselves with rifles, ammunition and hand-grenades, and they were called to the commandant of the camp and he raised hell. The boys must give the weapons all back!

'Next morning the boys, all two hundred ten of them, all beautifully armed, even a trumpet they stole somewhere, said no. Off we went. The general was screaming! He wanted to shoot all of us. I told the boys – they rattled with the locks and everything was fine. We were heading for Spain till we got to Collioure and ran out of petrol. The mayor of the town came to us with the tricolour, "OUT!"

'I said, "Don't be silly!"

'"I've no accommodation for you here!"

' "Don't worry. There are holidays, the school is empty, my boys will sleep in the school!"

'He said, "Oh."

'We went to the school and my boys with their rifles looked very impressive. Collioure was very nice, the citizens were very nice, they helped us, and then I heard of a destroyer at Port-Vendres. I ran like mad there, saw the magnificent destroyer, and after long negotiations I was allowed in, spoke to the captain, and I told him I'm bringing a bomber squadron to England! It was a cheek, but the intention was there. He said, "I can't take you, but I call a ship."

'They found a ship, mainly carrying fruit in the good old days, and the captain told me the minute the ship appears there will be twenty thousand people here, I warn you, so you must be here. I ran back again, got all the people together. We leave the lorries on the hills, march the little streets down hill to the port, the ship appeared at some sort of rocky harbour, and there were about ten, fifteen thousand people, you cannot imagine. Polish Jews, British old soldiers, Belgian soldiers, Foreign Legion, masses of Poles, a Polish general in a wheelchair, it was incredible. There was fist-fighting and people hid their faces. It was very very hard. The ship was for three hundred and eighty passengers and there were over two thousand on it!

'We arrived in Liverpool and glad to get over! We were immediately separated, the Czechoslovakians, and we marched to the railway station. We had a trumpeter, fixed bayonets and rifles, to impress, and people were doing this (*giving the Czechs the thumbs-up sign*). No Czech knew what this means, thumbs up! English are funny! Look, they are putting their thumbs up!

'We came to Cholmondeley Park, a big estate with a manor-house somewhere in the background which we hardly saw, and thousands of tents. There were more of those places, but Cholmondeley Park was notorious. There were still remnants from Dieppe, the Poles, some Czechoslovakian Telegraph Regiment – I don't know how they got there. All sorts of peculiar people. Nothing to eat, lice everywhere, it was terrible. I slept unshaven, straw all over my beautiful blue uniform, and they said there are some officers who want to speak to someone who speaks English. I looked at a lot of general-staff people, all with red, you know, army, so I went "Ah!" It was a young brigadier. He said, "Josef! What are you doing here?" He came to Prague in 1938 as a newspaperman to write articles about democracy in arms. I was called to headquarters, and I took him to the Škoda works and everywhere. We had three wonderful weeks. And this man was the first Englishman I met in England! Coincidence! He said, "You were so nice to me in Prague, what can I do for you?"

' "We want to fly. Can you do something about it?"

' "Will be done!"

'Within six hours came masses of lorries with food, something to eat. I would say he simply asked somebody – probably Air Ministry – "We have two hundred men who want to make a Czech squadron, what should I do with them?" I think in England they had so many worries, 1940, June, July (*laughs*), you can imagine!

'Then we went to Wilmslow. We had a breakfast there and I remember a Czech boy, he gets for breakfast porridge, sausages, bacon, bread, jam, marmalade – so we are well set, aren't we? From there it was smooth sailing. Soon we got the name 311 Squadron, Czechoslovakian Bomber Squadron, the first commanding officer spoke Russian. It didn't help much because Russian and Czech is still a hell of a difference – at least like German and English, I would say.

'We went *en bloc* to Honington, a pre-war station, in East Anglia, where still a batman had striped waistcoats in the officers' mess and everything was fine. It was bombed once or twice, nothing serious, and from there the boys started being air force, getting the whole spirit of air force. As we had pilots from the Czechoslovak airlines, they didn't need long training to fly a Wellington, it was like a DC1 or DC2, they could fly them after short training. Within forty days of landing in England we did the first raid! That was I think a very good effort.

'Then we move to East Wretham, a big estate with a huge house which belongs to an old lady who had to be taken out of her bed. She made a contract with the air force, everything was fine, and then when we came in she stayed! East Wretham had grass, no runways, but there everything was happening. We were screaming for pilots, the boys came back from training and we had the odd English boy.

'We had a lot of difficulties, with names, with the language, and so on. I spoke English well enough. There were some who were quickly learning, but the young people started learning because the Czech young generation, they were Anglophiles. The air force officers, their dream was the British air force. So they tried to read the *Flight* magazine and some navigation books which I translated for them, little booklets which we got, but nobody speak well enough to be able to translate maintenance manuals for the mechanics.'

*'Communication in the air?'*

'This they learned quickly. There were difficulties because we had two brothers, one was second pilot, one was air gunner. The name started with *five* consonants – we got, "Josef, what's that?"

'I said, "Cross it off! Smith One, Smith Two, finished." When they were starting the initial training, we formed the crews, we are putting them together by characters. It wasn't like in the big British air force where you had six, ten thousand men. Everybody knew everybody, you see, so you had to know who likes him and who knows him to build up the crews. In flight training there was the blackboard, so there was Sergeant Slavik and crew, Sergeant Blank and crew, etc. and there was a boy standing in front of it, and he says in Czech, "That Crew is a fine fellow, he flies with every pilot!"

'We were a bomber rather than a fighter squadron because all the people there were bomber pilots and mechanics. We also had Czech airline pilots. By his mentality, by his training, by his frame of mind, he's rather a bomber pilot than a fighter. I feel always that the bomber pilot has a more difficult job because he goes there, drops the bombs and comes back. It wasn't fun, so the bomber pilots were very brave. Not that I am taking their part, but it was a different job than the fighter. We had boys on Mosquitoes, and some of the best we lost them. Went over Berlin, the first Mosquitoes with one four-thousand-pounder. I tell you, the air force, when we saw the horrible beginning, the poor Wellington! But the boys went out and back and they sang on the plane and they did a good job.

'I loved my job in wartime. One has to live it to know the life of the squadron. They were taking off in three minutes, five minutes, ten minutes intervals according to the possibility. They had a late supper which was at three in the morning, could have been called an early breakfast. Five o'clock, six o'clock. One wasn't back. The boys were sitting and waiting, didn't go to bed, till they said, "Ten minutes, he can't have more petrol." Everybody knew – they lived with the boys, we were very close. We had a crew which went down in a dinghy in the North Sea, was very tragic, where we had contact with them till the last minute. Two froze to death – two were saved by the Germans. One lost both feet, they were amputated. Both were prisoners, they survived. After the war they came back.

'The spirit of the squadron was very good because the boys stuck together. Even the non-flying people, you know. That's just so important. We had Hanka, a red-haired Jewish girl of twenty-three, the squadron could never exist without her. On paper she was a clerk in the technical section somewhere but her job was to go round and collect socks and shirts and repair the boys' underwear and sewing on buttons, and she was so wonderful – Hanka this, Hanka that! She is married in Canada now and the boys are going to visit her. She is of course seventy – '

*'How did she come to be in England?'*

'Well, how the Jews came, you know. Suddenly they were here, they escaped. Often children, and they were brought up by the Catholic Church. The way people got to England, it was incredible. They came via Poland and Russia – they didn't want

78

to get into Spanish prisons or internment. We were lucky that we found this destroyer. It wasn't there for us. But we had New Zealanders with us, the odd Canadian, Aussie, and they fitted beautifully in.

'I was in the Committee of Adjustment – usually it was two officers in a squadron – when somebody was missing or dead you took all his property and got it safely. Usually put in a parcel and sent to Air Ministry – they had places where they put it. Went through the correspondence. Tried to trace family, or relatives. Our padre was one of the mainstays of the squadron, great fellow. There was Mr Glass, the man was about sixty, white hair, golden spectacles, a well-spoken gentleman. He had a big box and there he had all his paraphernalia, he was a musical clown, known in Italy before the war. He said, "You see, sir, these boys, they will die before I finish the war! I try to make them happy." He went to buy for the boys shoelaces in the village, he did everything for them. When he did his performance in tails and white tie he was a man of the world, and he was a batman to officers. That was to me a hero.

'From my experience, some didn't get to the target, but dropped their bombs and came home. That happened in all squadrons, Czech and others. I had cases, the plane came back and the second pilot came out of the aircraft and broke his arm, ran into the propeller! Stopped the propeller because he was so scared. He came out of the aircraft, he shit himself. A New Zealand flight lieutenant had to be taken from flying altogether. There are people who couldn't take it. It's understandable. These few flights I had, I had here (*in the thigh*) a bit of shrapnel, nothing serious but it wasn't fun! Hamburg was a nasty target, when you went, it was like Christmas trees coming at you.

'The losses were very heavy. Many of them are buried in East Wretham. I was there a year ago with my wife in the cemetery, about ten or twelve of the boys are buried there, killed in training or landing, on their return badly damaged. The losses were considerable. That's actually the main reason why we were transferred Coastal Command, to preserve a few Czechs. Our losses were not bigger than the rest of the Royal Air Force. We were in friendly contact with all the squadrons. When you took off in East Wretham you could see eight airfields. Marham and Feltwell and Newmarket – airfield next to airfield so all had big losses but there were few of us only so it was more evident, and the replacements were not so quick. They couldn't supply so many so quickly. We got Canadian Czechs, American Czechs, and two South American Czechs. They were not flying but engineering and both of them remained in the RAF after the war, very intelligent nice boys.

'I went to a submarine, twenty-nine days, and that was not fun. I learnt I could instruct the boys when we came later to Coastal Command, what happens on a submarine when we drop the depth charges. The operations room briefing took root, debriefing took root, you had these huge areas where we operated, but we had very good control. Girls mainly doing it, huge maps, thirty yards by twenty yards, the whole Atlantic, movement of every aeroplane, every U-boat, every British unit, every convoy all the time traced.

'As they wanted me to know about everything I was sent to a Coastal Command squadron, to know something about operations there. The next morning there was a raid. They had short-nosed Blenheims, horrible things, with a single machine-gun. I introduced myself to the commanding officer and he said, "Do you want to go on a raid?"

' "Very much so, sir, that's the reason why I'm here. As navigator."

'He said, "I don't send you as pilot, you know! As navigator and air gunner."

' "You do it often these raids?"

' "Not very – we do the odd raid on the Norwegian coast."

' "Oh fine."

' "Briefing is in the evening, take-off about five or six in the morning. Early to bed, and you will be called, all right."

'I wake up, it was eight in the morning. They didn't call me. Obviously they didn't want me to go – I understand it. Ten aircraft went out, and none came back. Actually one came back and it crash-landed and all five were killed.

'This Coastal was hopeless, you know. The sea was so big, you can't imagine how big it was! It's endless – and the square search for a navigator, and the zigzag searches – it was hard. We had losses. The losses are very nasty because the poor Wellington had no defence against the JU88. It was not a pleasant service, the boys were not happy. It was not eventful, nothing happened for ages, and they came back dead tired. Eleven hours' flights in the Wellington, staring at the sea all the time. That's why navigation was important because they had to cover an area for their own safety. We traced them, we had to know where they are. We had even homing pigeons. We used to take them and release them so that they are in training, but we never used them.

'We had sometimes fighter escort, when we were passing the Channel Isles where the Germans were. They were there stooging about for half an hour, three-quarters of an hour, till we passed and got safe away again. These were horrible Beaufighters, they disappeared – it was incredible. Just sank into the sea, like a brick. But never a signal, nothing. I remember once a French boy, pilot, just vanished, and the leader of the fighter aircraft said, "He was there and I turned around he wasn't there!" Never heard of him again. Up to date we don't know what happened. They were blaming the plane, the kite was wrong. Apparently when it came to a critical speed it dropped like a brick and everything stopped, you couldn't use radio or anything. It was the end.

'The first Coastal Command station was Torbenny. It wasn't finished when we arrived, I was the first aircraft to land there. I flew out as navigator and we had to fly twice, up and down to chase the lorries away, because the Irish workmen hadn't finished yet. It was a very happy station, nice there. The boys liked it because it was ten minutes to the sea and we had a beautiful summer, plenty of swimming and bathing, and the losses were not too bad. Scotland was bad. I was with them there. It got worse. Torbenny was the best still as far as losses were concerned.

'We were patrolling the Bay, generally speaking. The Bay of Biscay. We were Western Approaches, what the navy called 15 Group, the headquarters is in Portsmouth. The boys used to go, in Czech, "Biscay is a dog! Bad! Nasty!" The weather was very often very bad, and when you wanted to see something you had to fly low. To fly low is always dangerous because if you had some engine trouble there is no room to operate. If you are high you don't see anything. The boys were keen enough to do something, to find something. If they sighted a submarine, then they were allowed to call the navy, fast boats, and they polished them off. And the blockade runners. Once we had a crew landed in Gibraltar and the tail gunner was killed. A JU88 attacked us. They flew also from France, the Germans. They landed in Gibraltar and the tail gunner was dead.

'The spirit during the war was unique. The sense of humour. I remember notices in messes everywhere, don't waste food! Somebody wrote, leave it to the cooks! I had a little experience in France, but it was horrible there, everybody cursing everybody, oh, they were very unhappy. But in England, they always had for the RAF boys in the pub, the uniformed men, "Hello soldier! What do you want?" He was a general, or infantryman, or airman. "Soldier! What do you want?" In wartime one did appreciate it. We had a very nice pub. The owner was an Australian, and he was a father to the air force. The civilians who came in, they loved us, it was always very nice, almost like a club. When we would get a day off when there was no operations, he knew that we liked to have a drink, stay longer, so he locked everything and said, "Come into my living room and the pub is closed."'

82

# 4

# MASS PRODUCTION

O NCE THE WAR HAD STARTED, AIRCRAFT PRODUCTION HAD
to be stepped up dramatically. After the defeat of the British
armies in France, the only way to strike back at the Germans was
through air power. Sir Arthur Harris, Commander-in-Chief of
Bomber Command from 1942, argued that Germany could be
defeated by air power alone. This meant building up a huge fleet
of thousands of bombers. At the same time production of other
kinds of aircraft had to be kept up, especially fighters and aircraft
for Army Co-operation and Coastal Command.

In the first stage of the war, up to the time of the Battle of
Britain and even beyond, improvisation was the essence. With
aircraft factories under attack, and Fighter Command in the
Battle of Britain hanging on by the skin of its teeth, every chance
had to be taken.

*Rob Thirsk* had joined de Havilland's at Hatfield just before the
war. He came from the north of England where for a time he had
worked in his father's business. But it was taken over and he had
to move elsewhere. He decided to go south and try to find work
in the aircraft industry. 'So there you are! I'm a young man!
Wishing to earn his living, with no particular skills, some administrative ability, and the yen to get back into business if I could.

'By the time of the phoney war, I'd been elevated to the status of charge-hand. We had an intake of people and stupidly an outflow. Although we were recruiting people they were still being called up! We decided we were not going to be put in the bloody infantry, we would join up and go in what we chose. So I canvassed all the recruiting offices I could and was run out of all of them as soon as I mentioned my occupation.

'However, for some reason I had to go to the south of London and coming back I found a recruiting office in the side of Admiralty Arch. There I enlisted, in the Fleet Air Arm. I got home and told the boss, a fellow called Jock Allardice – he went up in the air. "You stupid B, what's the good of the bloody navy having to teach you to be a sailor and me having to teach some farmhand to be a fitter?!" Which was logical.

'"Anyway," I said, "you've done nothing up to now and I'm not going where somebody decides to put me. Apart from anything else the earnings are better!" I joined as a petty officer. That was hit on the head within a fortnight. I got pay-books stamped, "On loan, civilian rates of pay", and was told to report to de Havilland's. Something like that. They were on the ball. I think by that time I'd been thrown out of every recruiting office in the district.

'The war in Hatfield didn't seem to have started. Work went on as usual, on *civilian* aircraft! Air-raid warnings went and we spent our afternoons down trenches at the edge of the aerodrome. Jerry seemed to come more often than not at lunchtimes so we were all streaming out of the canteens with our lunches and coffees in our hands, and he was up there going somewhere else. In the end we'd grown largely to ignore the warnings.

'On the day he hit us he shot up Hatfield first. The klaxon went and everybody seemed to think that this time it was serious whereas previously it had been a laugh. I went to my shelter and as I turned to have a last look round I noticed the air-raid warden crossing the junction at the bottom of the corridor. They had white hats. He threw himself down against the wall, and showers of glass were coming sideways. I decided it was time I was in the shelter. I won't forget the feeling.

84

'To get in this shelter you put your head in, your feet in, and your backside was the last thing that went in! I thought, I'm going to get one in my bum! However, the plane went over, showering glass, machine-gunning as it went, very low, with a roar. We were used to that because our own pilots used to shoot us up often enough, if they were in a good humour. Geoffrey de Havilland particularly. He'd shoot the chimney pots! I don't know whether it was good spirits or bottle spirits! Anyway this thing went over. And there was dead silence.

'We sat in the shelter wondering what was to happen next. We heard four dull thuds, not impressive at all, just dull thuds. The shelter rocked, it *seemed* as if it was about to fall over, filled with dust, and we lost our breath. We all sat still waiting. There was a loudspeaker announcement: would volunteers take stretchers to the 94 shop.

'Stretchers were hung along the walls of the factory. Two of us lifted one off to go to the 94 shop which was in fair ruins. The bombs had been very cleverly laid – it was the only way he could have bombed it. They'd hit flat, skidded – you could see the skid marks – rose again and lobbed straight into the hangar.

'Twenty-eight were killed and eighty-odd injured. There were bits of people that were hardly recognizable. One fellow I picked up was covered in brass pins – he looked just like a porcupine. He lost a lung, an eye, and the use of an arm but he survived! He'd been married a week. About one o'clock they announced that the factory would shut down for the rest of the day and we went home. But that shop was in production the next day.

'I got a call one day to clear out the Tiger Moths and so forth and leave a space for Hurricanes. My first question was, well, what's a Hurricane like? How big is it? That's up to you! So I went to Heston. There was a Hurricane on duty there. I went down and measured it and came back with what information I thought necessary. I needn't have bothered! By that time they were at the door! So we shoved them in where we could get them.'

'*You couldn't get information from Hawker's?*'

85

'In time we did but at first no, they'd nothing to give us. We had four planes just standing there for some time. We knew nothing about fuel flows and hydraulic pressures or how to arm them. And this was at the time of the Battle of Britain!'

*'When every plane was needed?'*

'Right! They were damaged. One had taken its path between two trees. Wings were shot out, fuselages bent, undercarriages wrecked. A friend of mine had moved to Witney and was in charge of salvage there. He was very proud of the stacks of ingots he produced from boiling up crashed aeroplanes – German and English – and invited me down to see it. I was walking round his scrap-yard and all the components I wanted were just lying there poised to go into a boiler! I nearly wept. I said, "I want all these!"

' "Oh no!" he said, "look what we're doing with them!" They had stacks and stacks. Anyway we made an arrangement where I would go down periodically, tie labels on the bits I wanted and he'd send them. We established a department with mostly women employed to take the bits to pieces. We had to have some men because it could have been dangerous. They could have released sprung items and killed themselves. But the fellows were qualified to sort out what was safe and show the girls how to undo the nuts, so we were getting some of our spares.

'But then we were involved with rows over inspection. As you know, that's crucial on aircraft. Safety! The spares should have been inspected! Practically every one of these second-hand parts was below limits. Inspection was turning them down as rapidly as we were gaining them. Then suddenly all these objections were scotched by the air force. They said to our directors, "Look here, if the thing'll fly for twenty minutes, it's good enough for us! Twenty minutes will deter an enemy! If it can *take off* it will deter! And it might get one. Or go on for longer than twenty minutes!" That's what we worked then. If a plane breaks up in the air, nobody's going to notice. It was just a question of repairing them and to hell with protocol! Get them in the air.

'One time I went to this place at Witney and tripped over a

wire. At the end was a constant-speed unit! I had it dug out and there was another! There were seventeen all wired together. Constant-speed units feathered the props so you could climb to a greater altitude! We had only seventy machines fitted with those and here were seventeen lying in the dump! And we hadn't *any* for the Hurries we had. So we salvaged those and they went back into service. There was a tremendous row about that!'

'*Why?*'

'There was no record! Either somebody had stolen something or was using constant-speed units that had come from some odd source!'

'*Who made the row? The Air Ministry?*'

'Oh yes. The Ministry clerks and the accountability people.'

'*So they were watching things pretty closely?*'

'Aye, a long time after. I suppose if you thought ahead – well, I'll get my arse kicked for doing this. But nobody was thinking further than the next few days. It was quite enjoyable on occasion.

'About that time we got the go-ahead for the production line. People were seconded to us – a gentleman called Grinham from Standard Motors, a mass-production expert. He organized the line, the pits, and so on. But we were a long way from proper co-ordination. When we got an apparently complete Mosquito at the end of the line and tried to make it work, we discovered all kinds of snags. We couldn't get the undercarriage doors to shut, bulkheads weren't glued in, and tailplanes – they would have fallen off!'

'*Why weren't they glued in?*'

'An oversight – one *presumes*! Each componenta history card so you look down. Glueing a bulkhead was an operation that should have been signed up. It wasn't. Your first reaction is to say the silly bugger's forgotten to sign it. But the careful bod says, I wonder. Well, everybody said, "Of course it's glued!"

'"I don't care, I want it out! I want proof!"

'The bulkhead was taken out and it wasn't glued! All the others were now suspect. We tracked back the history of these things and it all came to one place – there's something wrong with their engineering. We created a section of about seventy men to sort out these snags.

'We took the plane in whatever condition it arrived and put right whatever we discovered wrong, till we were satisfied. If we found a thing wrong on one, the first thing was to go and see if it's wrong on number two, three and four. One way and another we were going down the line looking for trouble. And finding it and warning people and gradually you raised the standard.

'Westbrook* had arrived by now, with instructions to get production going. I went along to see the great man and was attached to him as one of his PAs. He'd sort out jobs for me – they give you some idea of the working pressures of the time.

'We were manufacturing Mosquitoes with submarine-detection devices. Much of the stuff that was coming from America was being sunk off the Irish coast. Marshall at Cambridge got the contract but he didn't want to change over from the very profitable contracts he'd got repairing Wellingtons and other bomber types. His labour force was used to it, whipping them out, very nice for Marshall. He didn't want to start something new. But he'd accepted the contract – I suppose he didn't have any choice.

'I went down to see his manager who fed me, wined me, and did everything possible to slide me away from the main point. This went on for several days until I realized I wasn't getting anywhere. Now Hatfield had sent down some people to train Marshall's staff. I went down and asked them what was going on. They said, "We'll never get it done! He won't put the labour on!"

'Armed with that information, I told the manager we'd just

*T. C. L. Westbrook, CBE, was de Havilland production controller from 1942 to 1945.

have to have the labour from their other production. Our job was more urgent! He said I'd have to see Marshall.

'He was a character. He was about my height but he was the same size in all directions, and he used to go round with his pockets all crammed with masses of notebooks – he took a note on everything. He'd got a remarkable memory as well. A forceful personality! He used to get things done. But he wasn't God. He had to build those Mosquitoes and that was that.

'Well, he refused. I'd been there a week when I was summoned to Westbrook's office one Sunday afternoon: "Well, how are you getting on?"

' "It's hopeless! He won't put the labour on!"

' "All right," Westbrook said, "I'll see to that. You go and sort out the men. If necessary take them from here. As far as Marshall's concerned, tell him, unless you get his co-operation, you'll put your own men into management."

'Whatever Westbrook did on Sunday night I don't know, but when I got there on Monday morning, oh boy! There was a red haze over Cambridge. "Ever since ten o'clock this morning Mosquitoes have been arriving here! What are we going to do?"

'Westbrook had got on to various squadrons and told them to send the machines. They all arrived at Cambridge. The moment I showed up I don't know whether I was run, or carried, or escorted or what, but I arrived in Marshall's office. I saw this beetle-faced fellow foaming at the mouth, stamping his desk and telling me I was going to be hanged, drawn and quartered. To get out of the office, x-y-z, and so forth.

'I explained the situation, told him how urgent the job was – we had to stop the enemy sinking the gear before it got here – what was required, how I summed it up, and where he could get the labour from – from his other projects.

' "Get out! Get out! OUT! Take him out!"

'I said, at the door, "Well, of course, you realize I'm only going to get my own management and put them in! Ring up the Ministry if you've any doubts!" I was leaving the place then, I thought I was probably safer. Before I reached the gate the

Tannoy went to ask me to come back. The manager met me. He said, "He doesn't want to see you. In fact he doesn't want to see you ever again! But I've been told to co-operate with you!" And so we got the project going.

'That was Westbrook's attitude, you see. Just chuck 'em in! I suppose he thought, if they drown I'll get another. If you've got a lot of money backing you, you can do that. He was only a turner, I think, in Weybridge, and he was a union man too. He got noticed through solving union troubles. Beaverbrook picked him up. He lived in the factory – he had a bunk next to his office. I was there myself one night at twelve o'clock, pushing something through the design office door. I walked past his office, saw a light on, opened the door – I was surprised at the light. And there he was! At his desk!

'None of the old crowd at Hatfield – the established de Havilland men – liked Westbrook and shifted him out as soon as they could at the end of the war. There was a de Havilland personnel factor, a prejudice. Pre-war people were in senior positions, almost regardless of their attributes. Wartime was exceptional – I don't suppose I'd have gone very far except for the war. It took you away from home – the hours were seven days a week. I had a lot of fun on occasions. But it was quite a firm. After the war, in one year they had a new Heron, the Comet, the Vampire, and the Venom, all prototypes, in the Farnborough Show! All in the one year! That was de Havilland!'

Several of Britain's most important aircraft factories were in the London area. They had to keep up production while coping with the disruption of bombing and bomb damage. Their workers were expected to help with the rescue services, as well as continuing to build planes. *Harry Laurel* remembers the strains of trying to do two, if not three, jobs at once.

He is now a fresh-faced, vigorous, elderly man (in his eighties), smart and militarily erect in his bearing. Before the war he built coaches for London Transport. This work stopped when war was declared and the factory was moth-balled. He and a pal found fresh jobs at Fairey Aviation, which at that time was building planes like the Albacore for the Fleet Air Arm.

'Now you know aircraft is very very fussy indeed. We weren't allowed to touch one for about six weeks. I'd done nothing but walk round with other men and watch them work. I started on the pilot's screen – they're very heavy because they were double glass about half an inch thick, bullet-proof. I wasn't allowed to drill a hole, except under the tuition of another workman.

'Anyway, I got the hang of it after about two or three months and began to get quite proficient. If your work doesn't match up you're in trouble! (*Laughs.*) They want to know why! Shift this and shift that, take these out and rebuild it! I grew to be a very exacting engineer because I damn well had to be. It done me good! Because that kind of – what shall I say – *fineness* wasn't necessary on buses but it is necessary on aircraft. It made an engineer out of me which I wasn't.

'I suppose I was about two, maybe three, years on Albacores until we finished the batch, about six hundred I think. But it was a terrible job. You're laying on your stomach, you haven't got the end of a room to move, and when they start riveting outside, the noise is deafening! Today they give you earphones, but we had nothing like that. When you come out of it your head was ringing with the vibrations. I think it done my ear in.

'When the bombing of London started, we weren't allowed to work. As soon as the bloody warning went, out went the lights and you were in pitch-black darkness. We had to make our way out on to the sports field where they'd already dug our trenches. They were equipped with stools and steps and God knows what not, but of course what they didn't do was allow for drainage. When it rained, the water used to run down the steps. Only earth floors, so you got that much water in the bottom. No light down there. We used to feel our way round, find the form and lay down on it. You know what, you never fell off! If you did you'd land in about three inches of water. Whether the old subconscious kept you on there, God knows!

'At the same time, I was on the civil defence – they scooped me in, after I came off night work. We had to do something. If you wasn't on the wardens you'd to be on the fire service, or something else. You weren't allowed any spare time whatsoever. I had to join something so I joined the wardens.

'We were on patrol every night, and I got several incidents that I had to go on. He dropped a thousand-pounder – it was a pile of bricks. They said, "Look, we've got the mother and father but we believe that somewhere in there is the baby. See if you can get him!"

'There was me and about four more and we started shifting the bricks one by one. All of a sudden one bloke – "I think I've got him!" That was the bed he was in. Now this is as true as I stand here, we got to that cot and it was full of blood but the body had gone, there was nothing there. I can remember getting hold of the mattress, holding it up like that, and it just dripped blood. But the kiddie had gone, completely. Whether he'd been right in line with the bomb when it went off I don't know – blast is a queer thing.

'Then there was the night I went to Blythe Road. Oh, it was terrible, that was! The carnage was awful. Killed about fifty-odd people. And there was another incident near Baron's Court station. He dropped a five-hundred-pounder and it hit a couple of houses, way up the top. On the third floor up there was a grand piano, right on the edge – the front of the house was gone. There was myself, two soldiers and a policeman. Down in this cellar under the house we could hear the cries of a couple down there. A bloke came up, "I'm their next-door neighbour. It's a Mr and Mrs de Jong."

'We had to get 'em out because they were pinned down. The copper said to me, "Have you got a wife and children?"

'"Yeah, but not in London, I'm just an ordinary warden."

'"Would you go down there?"

'I said, "Well, somebody's got to go down."

'"We'll put a rope on you. We got the old lady out but we can't get Mr de Jong out because he's been pinned down by a

92

big baulk of timber, one of the joists underneath. He's pinned down by that."

'I don't know why the hell *he* didn't go! Why he picked on me, I was a young bloke. They lowered me down on a rope and I explored round as much as I could, and I got to Mr de Jong's head. He was pinned down to about there and his head was out. I said, "You got any pain, guv'nor?"

' "Yes, there's something sticking in my leg."

'Every time they put a rope round him and tried to pull him he screamed. Do you know what it was? A big piece of glass was stuck in his leg – every time we pulled it drove it in deeper.

'I said, "Right! Pull me up!" I told 'em what was wrong and the copper said, "Look mate, he's gotta come out, he can't stop there because he'll bleed to death! I suggest we put the rope round him and give one bloody good tug and let him scream the house down!"

'That's what we did. We put a rope round his shoulders and there was about five of us all told. We gave one great heave and he did scream an' all! But we pulled him out.

'The ambulance was standing by. The copper said, "Would you go with him to the hospital?" It was West London Hospital – they'd turned the basement into a casualty centre. I went with them and gave the doctor the details. Thanks very much. He said, "Where are you going?" Back on the job. "So" – this is the doctor – "can you give *me* a hand?"

'We went down to the basement. They'd got these trestles and they were surrounded with dead bodies. The doctor said, "Look, all these are presumed dead, but I have got to certify them because you can't bury persons without a doctor's certification that they are dead. I'll put the stethoscope on their chest but I must turn them over and put it on their back and I can't turn them over on my own. Are you willing to help me?"

'I finished the rest of the blooming night down there. I went into that hospital round about one o'clock in the morning and I didn't come out of it till six. I would say roughly there were about forty dead down there and they were in a terrible state, covered in brick dust and dirt and shit, some of them had smashed heads where the masonry had fallen on them. Awful state. Actually, it shook me up, I couldn't deal with it, it was something I wasn't used to, but I'd a good stomach, fortunately.

'I spent the rest of the night with that doctor turning these dead bodies over and helping strip the clothes off so he could get the stethoscope on their back and certify them dead. They *were* dead. We never found one alive. But it was a lousy job. I don't think I could do it now. I'm *sure* I couldn't.

'At that time we'd been working seven days a week. We had no day off whatever, and we were so bloody tired. I was up on a trestle one day and I went to sleep standing up! Fell off the damn trestle! Didn't do me a lot of good either! Two other blokes had similar accidents, they were so dead tired they just went to sleep standing up. I think they saw the red light then and said, "It's no good, we'll have to do something." Every third week they used to give us the weekend off – it gave us a chance to recuperate our sleep.

'When they stopped weekend work altogether – from Saturday afternoon – I'd got nothing to do. But they were advertising in the paper for volunteer drivers – London Wholesale Dairies, Shepherd's Bush. I started taking out milk. I used to go straight over from Fairey's and report to the canteen up at LWD. I could get a meal up there which was a godsend, because we were on rations, and you couldn't live on 'em. I was living on porridge. I couldn't cook for the life of me. Where did two ounces of margarine go? And two ounces of sugar? Two ounces of meat! Well! You could have eaten the whole damn lot in a day. So it really paid me to stop in there and I did.

'I was well browned off. My wife and children were down in Devon, and I had nothing to go home to, nothing! Fact, when the bomb dropped out the back and brought all the damn ceilings down, I thought that's it, I shut the bloody door and I never went back for a long long time. I slept up the post, I made the post my home. Was rough, but there you are. A lot of people had it more rough. I never lost anything fortunately.

'When my wife came back from Devon we'd got all the ceilings down and there was no glass in a lot of the windows. Oh blimey, it was a shambles! It took about six months to get the place right. You couldn't get any repairs done – there was millions in the same boat.

'One morning I went in to Fairey's, I'd been up all night, on warden, on an incident. I went to sleep standing up, and it was only the fact that I was holding the vice stopped me falling down. They sent me over to first aid and they put me to bed! I slept the whole day. They woke me up at five o'clock to go home! You see, you got very very low! You weren't having the compensatory food to keep your strength up, you were using everything you'd got. In every direction. I went fifty hours without sleep, two nights and two days, non-stop. Never got a chance to sleep.'

At Supermarine's pressure was on to produce Spitfires. A shadow factory was built at Castle Bromwich to expand output. But both there and at Southampton, great teething troubles were experienced, as *Eric Lovell-Cooper* recalls. These had to be got right because the Spitfire, unlike the Hurricane and other early fighters, remained a front-line aircraft throughout the war. It had remarkable potential for development, and the later Marks were in use in all major theatres of the war until the end.

'Beaverbrook dismissed Pratt, the boss of Supermarine's, when the bombing took place – he blamed him for the poor output of Spitfires. Of course it was nothing to do with Pratt, he was just the manager of the outfit, but he got the blame. He took the dismissal rather to heart and went home and shot himself.

'There were no ifs or buts where Beaverbrook was concerned. You either did it or you'd get the chop. The cannon on the Spitfire for instance. It was a brilliant idea but we hadn't made it work. Some of the COs of various stations which had Spitfires were so upset they refused to arm any of their squadrons with cannon machines. They preferred the .303. The trouble with the cannon was everything on paper looked perfect. When you fired the gun on the ground it was perfect. As soon as you got it in the air and started chucking the aeroplane about nothing happened!

'Beaverbrook put me in with a chap from the Enfield works and a professor from Farnborough. We had to get it right. It became serious because the enemy were armouring their machines against .303 ammunition and we were unable to shoot them down with the ease that we did in the early part of the war. Something of heavier calibre had to be used. The half-inch machine-gun was too large to go in as a replacement for the .303 and the cannon really was the only available thing.

'We soon came to the conclusion that the gyroscopic effect of turning and twisting the aeroplane threw the mechanism that fed the cartridges into the gun out of action. The effect of Gs on the spring was more than it could take. Consequently you could fire one or perhaps two shots and then the thing would stop.

'As soon as we realized what was wrong we were able to get down and do something about it. We developed very quickly an auxiliary spring which was about four times as strong as the original spring, then it was my job to see it would go in the aeroplane! It was all right making the gun work but it wouldn't be much use if it wouldn't work in the aeroplane!

'In a couple of days we had an alteration to the wing that would accommodate the new requirement and from then on everything in the garden was lovely and everybody got an extra stripe!

'After the bombing of Southampton we were dispersed. Beaverbrook got a gang of chaps together, they were all good business-men, go-getters, and we had four of them down at our place. They had a fine old time. We fed 'em and wined 'em – there was no shortage or anything like that. They lived in the lap of luxury, they could go where they liked and do what they liked and that was all they cared about. They were helping the war effort. Their job was to go round the countryside and demand the use of various premises to build planes in. They collared any premises that they thought would be useful and various bits of the Spitfire production were put there. Various foremen and what-not were in charge and went with them. We had garages and laundries, tramway sheds, bus sheds, you never saw such a collection, all sorts of things. You name it, we'd got it.'

*He shows me an orange-bound photograph album. On the inside cover is a cartoon of the leading characters at Supermarine during the war with himself as the conductor of an out-of-tune orchestra.*

'Do you know at one time I was controlling nearly every blooming aircraft on fighter work in the country? I had Westland's under my control, Cunliffe Owen's, Folland's, oh, there were two or three others. My men were out there doing their best to keep them in order. And of course there was Castle Bromwich. That was a scream! It was a mass-production factory and if you went inside it you'd have thought my God, how marvellous, but if you knew how we were trying to mass produce in the early stages you'd have laughed your head off.

'The machines produced by Castle Bromwich were really Supermarine machines taken up there to finish off. Castle Bromwich was making an awful hash of things. The trouble was that Morris (*Lord Nuffield*) had the job to do. He was the motor king, marvellous chap who'd produced thousands of cars! He was the man who was going to mass produce the Spitfire. Well, Morris's *works* could have done it but Morris was quite incapable by himself. Fortunately he had a very good second-in-command – Oliver Boden (*Vice-chairman, Morris Motors*).

'He organized the building of the works at Castle Bromwich and got it going. I was amazed how quickly they got to work. There was a desert waste you might almost call it – looked like a rubbish dump when I first saw it. Within a matter of weeks a factory was standing there, all ready to drive into. Pavements and tarmac in front, and a big airfield behind it. Unfortunately the chauffeur was driving him to work one day and he opened the door and there was Oliver Boden dead inside. He'd died in harness, as it were. Of course that put the whole thing in a flummox and Morris came to the rescue. It would have been better if he'd stayed out of it. From then onwards the thing became an awful shambles.

'They made a big mistake – I suppose they hadn't much option really – they thought that any draughtsman could draw aeroplanes. If they could draw motor-car parts they could draw plane parts. They thought that putting the Spitfire in production meant building it like a motor car. I suppose if you had enough time you could do it but they'd got a comparatively short time and they made a hopeless hash of it. The motor-car people used to draw everything out about four or five times full size, all the details, and they put every hole in accurately dimensioned, you know, to within a thousandth of an inch to where it should be. The tools are made accordingly, they stamped the parts out and the parts were all perfect.

'Well, it might be all right for mass-producing motor cars but mass-producing aircraft is a very different situation. Ninety per cent of the holes in an aeroplane have to be matched up with other holes and if you drill them separately they never will match! Their first attempts were absolutely hopeless. We used to take bits and pieces of the Spitfire up there to try and make it look as if they were producing aeroplanes. Meanwhile everyone was shouting, when were they coming off the line? We had bets on when the first production would come off the line at Castle Bromwich and we won a bottle of whisky about once a month! I should think that went on for about a year before they actually produced an aeroplane.

'They had to take Morris's people off the job and Sir Alex Dunbar from Vickers took over. He licked the place into shape. When I went up to see him at Castle Bromwich he'd got a bed in his office! I thought this is how managing directors live, is it? The sooner I become a managing director, the better I shall like it. Being able to lie down on the bed whenever you feel in the mood. Apparently he suffered with his heart rather badly and had to rest frequently.

'Once they got going they were perfect. I used to go up there quite a lot. They were streets ahead of us, especially on the machine side. They had all the modern machinery – I believe it was nearly all German! I remember Westbrook before the war importing shaping, drilling and automatics from Germany for the Supermarine works simply because our people hadn't got the sense to make them. They were still dodging along with the old-fashioned manhandled turret lathes and what not, whereas everybody else was using automatics. I think our actual workmanship on the machines was just as good as the Germans' but the ideas were completely out of date!

'One of the snags on the Spitfire was icing up of the muzzle on the cannon. The cannons poked out a long way in front of the wings and they used to ice up. These guns were gas-operated and didn't work unless the gas went back along the barrel – you could fire off one shot and that was all. They wanted some method of stopping water or ice forming on the barrels. With the small machine-guns, they doped a strip of fabric over the opening in the wing where the guns fired through. When you fired the guns you blew the piece of fabric off and everything was all right. But the cannons froze up and nothing happened.

'Well, somebody thought of the bright idea of putting a rubber cap over the end, but where do you get them? Oh, says someone else, there's a place opposite Castle Bromwich! Let's pay them a visit and see what we can get. The place was very convenient – we marched in and said we'd like to see the manager! They showed us into the manager's office and sitting behind the desk was a woman, middle-aged, quite nice-looking. We said, "Oh, we'd very much like to have a talk with the manager, can you arrange for us to see him?"

' "I'm the manager!" she said. That put us in a bit of a flap, but we said, "We're having rather a problem with our cannons – they want some kind of a rubber protection to go over the end. We think that you people here would be able to supply us."

' "Oh yes, I think so. What size do you want?" She brought out a thing like a test-tube stand in a laboratory, and it had these rubbers on, various sizes, from the minute to the immense. She handled them with the greatest aplomb. "This is the largest one we make. Do you think that would be big enough?"

'We said, "No, we want an elephant-sized one!"

' "I think we could manage it. I suppose you'll want it in fairly thick rubber?"

' "Oh yes, we don't want any flimsy stuff."

' "How many would you want?"

' "Can you let us have about ten thousand straight away?"

'I think she was expecting to supply about half a dozen. I don't know whether they got the whole contract from the Ministry but millions of them must have been used during the war. From then onwards every time the aeroplanes went out on a sortie they had one of these caps over the muzzle of the cannon.

'As time went on Castle Bromwich really produced the goods. The snag was that once they got started they didn't want to stop. We were constantly having to put new things on to the Spitfire right from the very beginning. Castle Bromwich moaned and groaned every time anything new came out, even simple things like jettison hoods. You had to slide back the early hoods to get out. But pilots found that was rather critical. Sometimes they jammed and they could neither get in nor out. So they wanted a quick device to do it. This was our first contact with Jimmie Martin (*Sir James Martin, managing director and chief designer of Martin-Baker Ltd*). He thought of things that other people never thought about.

'I was with Joe Smith in his office one day and in comes Jimmie Martin with a Spitfire hood under his arm. "I'm Jimmie Martin! How do you do, Smith!" That didn't go down too well with Joe, I can tell you. However, he hadn't got time to say anything.

'Jimmie said, "About your bloody Spitfire hoods. I've got a job here, I think you'll appreciate its worth when I show it to you." He'd got a Spitfire canopy, just the sliding part, with a little red rubber knob hanging down there. He said, "You pull this and the thing flies off. There you are, what's wrong with that?" That's Jimmie – a very practical bloke. Joe got on his hind legs then. He said, "When I want your advice I'll come and ask for it!" That didn't suit Jimmie at all. Anyway they got to a state where I think old Jimmie said, "All right Smith, you can stick your bloody Spitfire up your arse, for all I care!" and stalked out of the office.

'Joe turned to me, "We can't let him get away with that! You'd better go and fetch him back!" I ran after him – fortunately he'd left his car a little way away from the entrance so I was able to catch him up before he got in it. I said, "Look here, don't take any offence. Joe's in a bit of a state. He's got a bit of a short fuse. He doesn't know what the hell he's doing half his time. You'd better come back. I think you've got a very good idea there. We're going to make him see it!"

'He came back and they parted the best of pals. Having a drink and shaking each other by the hand. Glad to have met you and all that sort of thing. From that day onwards I was Jimmie Martin's friend at court and anything he thought was worth while I was the first to know about it. It was a very useful adjunct as far as I was concerned.'

*'Did you use the hood?'*

'Oh yes, it was so simple! A kid could have fitted it. That was the beauty of Jimmie's things, he went right to the heart, as it were, and produced something that could be used. Other people were designing and redesigning the hood in order to make it work, he took the existing hood and put a red rubber ball on it, two bits of tubing and a wire and the whole thing worked. The wind took it, the wind did the rest. Previously the pilots had to strike it back like that. If it jammed they were stuck there, they couldn't get out. Simple as that.

'I suppose I was one of the earliest civilians, other than Jimmie Martin's own staff, to test his ejector seat. He had to persuade pilots to burst through the hood to get a safe ejection. The snag with the hood arrangement was that you were supposed to fire it off in case of emergency before you ejected. When the hood had gone the cockpit became such a cave of winds it was almost impossible for the pilot to climb out.

'Jimmie suggested it would be much better for them if they

crashed through it with the ejection seat, so they put a spike on the top of the seat to break the Perspex dome. He offered a gold watch to the first pilot who would eject under those conditions. He said it wasn't very long before one of the pilots turned up and demanded his gold watch. From then onwards that was the standard method of ejection from the cabin.

'Jimmie had a contraption in his backyard which was rather like an enormous fire escape. You sat in the pilot's seat at the bottom with all the paraphernalia that you normally have in the cockpit, hood and stirrups to put your feet in, and so on. When you wanted to eject you pulled the hood over your head and that fired the cartridge in the thing at the back. You shot up this fire-escape ladder arrangement at an alarming rate of knots until you were about eighty feet above the ground.

'By that time the effect of the propulsion had more or less died out and you stayed up by means of a ratchet which engaged with the rungs on the fire escape. Then you could be lowered by a crane arrangement which was worked from a drum down below, but it's a funny sensation when you pull this hood down. You get to feel for all the world as if you're pulling yourself through the bottom of the seat. Actually it's the seat pushing up against your bottom but you don't realize that. One thing I did find out was that my feet came out of the stirrups twice in the course of the journey up the ladder and I was able to pull them back in, which struck me as rather amazing. The whole thing only lasted a few seconds. When you take the hood off your face you find yourself about eighty feet above the ground waving about in the air! You hope to God that the lowering mechanism is going to work all right!

'Another job we did with the Spitfire – Farnborough developed an aircraft camera which was capable of taking photographs at about thirty thousand feet. You could then blow them up and actually see what they were. We mounted one of these in a Spitfire behind the pilot, pointing downwards. It had a roll of film inside which was electrically operated, so it could take a series of pictures as you went along.

'We had to double the quantity of fuel to get the range to go to the further parts of Germany. The only thing we could think of was to take the guns out and make the leading edges of the wings one long tank. It would have paid us to have rebuilt the leading edge as a tank, instead of which we took an ordinary Spitfire wing and tried to make it petrol tight which wasn't very easy. We had to bung up all the leaks with various compounds. From then on the Photographic Reconnaissance Unit was built up and they must have had, oh, a dozen Spitfires going at one time, flying over Germany.

'One difficulty we had to deal with, chaps used to come back half-frozen because there were no heating arrangements in the machine. They had to rely entirely on the warmth of the engine flying back into the cockpit to keep them warm. They used to come back nearly frost-bitten! I don't think they lost many. Or very few. The Luftwaffe couldn't get up quickly enough. The Spitfires flew at thirty thousand feet taking pictures and were away again before the Germans could intercept them.'

*'What did you think of German fighters?'*

'I sat in the first Messerschmitt we had over here and I thought, my God! if we'd designed our machine like this it would have been an absolute winner. The only snag with it was there was no room for adjustment. I'm a big man and I could never have flown the Messerschmitt machine. You sat with your legs out straight in front, rather than slightly bent, and there was no room at the top for a big man – you had to be just the right size. But the controls were absolutely marvellous. Ours was like a wheelbarrow compared with that. You could touch the thing and you would feel it moving while you sat there and watched it. Our machines were really inferior – well, the Spitfire was better than anything that they'd got but it was only the fact that we were fighting over this country that enabled us to beat the Germans off. We didn't do so well when we had to fight them over Germany.

'As regards the later planes they had – I did see those at Farnborough when the war finished. They brought several of them over and they appeared to be far in advance of anything we'd got on the stocks. Whether they would have been effective as fighting machines was another story altogether. At that time we had nothing comparable with them. They had got much further advanced with the design of turbo-jet aircraft and if they had got them to work satisfactorily they'd have outgunned us quite easily.

'They also had this Messerschmitt swept-wing rocket-type aeroplane which used to put the wind up our photo-reconnaissance pilots. They'd suddenly find one of these things hurtling down at them when they were flying at around thirty thousand feet, and it would be gone in a flash, zooming in to climb above them again. Their endurance was short – only about twenty minutes' flying, I think. By the time they got into position for a second attack they had to think about getting back home, and by that time the PRU machine had got too far away for them to catch up.

'After the war we developed the Swift. Our air force was practically without any fighters. The Americans were all out for this Korean war and told us to get some planes in hand at once! "You haven't got an air force capable of modern warfare. You'd better order a thousand straight away." That's how the Swift and the Hunter started.

'Well, the Korean war was almost over by the time the machines came into service. So who was going to pay for them? The Americans didn't want them now. It became a question of finding fault and the result was the cancellation of the contract. But do you know, our finance people told me afterwards, we made more money out of cancelling the contract than we would have by completing it! They had to pay so much indemnity for the work we'd done.

'Our chief finance chap wasn't really an aircraft man at heart anyway. He began to feel there was no money in it. I remember him saying once, we only get twelve per cent profit building aircraft, but we can get twenty per cent if we build something else! He was all for diversifying. I suppose he was right to a certain extent but to an aircraft person like myself it was absolute heresy.'

To cope with the expansion of production, other firms needed to be brought in. In London these included several companies which had built or serviced coach bodies in peacetime, such as the London Passenger Transport Board and Duples. *Harry Powell* was one of the workers who came into the aircraft industry for the first time during the war, helping to build the Halifax.

'I've brought you my one and only credential. That was the very last Halifax we did and we made seven hundred and ten altogether. (*He shows me a group photograph of aircraft workers, women and men, in front of a Halifax. The women wear turbans and overalls. He's in the far corner, aged about twenty, grinning at the camera.*)

'I was grade three. In 1938 I'd fallen off a roof. The people I worked for sent me up to repair a window, a fanlight, and I fell off. It wasn't a very long drop but I broke my back and fortunately that made me grade three. I'm quite sure I would have been one of the first to have got killed if I'd been a soldier.

'I was in the shoe trade then but of course they wouldn't allow me to continue in that, not that I wanted to. I wanted to do something for the war. They sent me to a training centre. I was there for three months, ostensibly to learn precision engineering. It was some mad ambition. I knew that toolmakers were very highly paid and it sounded glamorous, but it wasn't for me. It all came to nowt because I just couldn't file, as it were, a two-inch cube into a one-inch cube. The sides just weren't at right angles, one to the other, and in the end I finished up with a half-inch cube. So they sent me to Duples in the Edgware Road. They'd just cleared their factory of all they'd made before – coaches and trucks. They'd been given a contract by the government to produce Halifaxes under the aegis of Handley Page, who were not very far away in Cricklewood.

'When I got into the factory there were cleared floors, a few benches, the tiniest handful of people, and a lot of material. We were given drawings and from week to week there were modifications on those drawings as we learnt, *felt*, our way. Of course we had enormous difficulties for the first year or two. We were supposed to turn out one plane a day, and it took us about a year and a half to turn out the first five!'

*'Why did it take so long?'*

'Well, there were a lot of reasons. The management knew nothing about making aircraft to start with. They'd been used to turning out coaches and trucks on a large scale, but they were totally unused to the techniques of aircraft. We couldn't get material, we couldn't get a lot of advice from Handley Page – they were jealous of losing their ... – they were the ones who had designed the plane to start with. They were well away with their production and they just didn't want to pass their knowledge on if they could possibly avoid it. This was very early in the war, about 1940, 1941. And the idea of the workpeople themselves being a consultative body that could help in production was totally unknown in those days. We did finish up with a works production committee.

'In the end we ironed out all the administrative problems, but there were times in the early days when people were hanging around. We had women who had *nothing* to do – nothing whatsoever! They could spend the whole day knitting (*laughs*) if you can imagine it. Men played football out in the fields – by that time we'd moved out to Aldenham. So we were outside in the countryside playing football and literally doing sweet bugger all.

'When we did get started, the nose section which we worked on was *crammed* with gadgetry as you can imagine. We were all working one on top of the other under the most dreadful conditions which couldn't be helped. There was no way of improving them. Certain things had to go in first and that was it, but if anything had to be taken out for modification or because the AID didn't like it – and they were very very fussy, we used to *fear* AID – everything had to come out before you could get to those little bits and pieces that went in first.

'Eventually we ironed out all those things – once we'd got up
to about number two hundred things began to roll very efficiently
but (*laughs*) the confinement and the post-natal period was really
awful.'

'*The Ministry didn't create a fuss about the delays?*'

'Well, I think they understood the difficulties. It was a learning
period, still early in the war, and the really big bombing raids
came in the latter part of the war.'

'*What sort of hours did you work?*'

'Nominally nine to five, but we were working all the hours – I
once did a seventy-two-hour shift. Average hours were somewhere
round about twelve, thirteen, fourteen a day. The seventy-two
hours shift was interesting because I came out totally exhausted.
I was living in Hendon then and I came home early on the third
day, as it were, went to bed, and woke up ostensibly feeling
refreshed. I had my breakfast, went down to Hendon Central
Station to go to work again, and found I'd only been asleep for
about an hour! I was totally disorientated. When I got down to
the station I suddenly realized that I was in a sort of time warp.
I've never experienced it since, or before for that matter. We
worked *enormously* long hours and with such willingness – a
phenomenon which of course has totally disappeared today,
unless you work for yourself.'

'*And the pay?*'

'It took the larger part of two years, two and a half years,
before the wages really went high. It was a high wage compared
to what they were working at in most factories. I think the main
reason was bad rate-fixing. There came a moment when I actually
got my name in *Reynolds News* as a sort of Stakhanovite – I did a
hundred-hour job in ten hours and got ninety hours' bonus for it
on top of my pay. But between you and me it wasn't really a
hundred-hour job at all. It should have been priced much lower
than that. The rate hadn't been adjusted as we became more

tuned to the production of the Halifax. But I rested on my laurels. I had a lovely big headline in *Reynolds News*.

'My main job was doing the cabin-heating ducts, the radio mast, and one or two other things. It suited me very well. Oddly enough I worked on asbestos right through the war – the ducts were covered in asbestos. When I heard about the asbestos problem over the last few years I thought how lucky I've been. I worked entirely on my own and on occasion I'd go down to the airfield at Leavesden to adjust the portions that were in this section. On two occasions I managed to get a flight.'

*'If Handley Page were unco-operative, how did you know you were doing the job right?'*

'There was liaison with them but it was not of a very high quality. We went down once or twice to see their factory in the very early days – we were sent in little groups ostensibly to pick up hints but there wasn't very much we could learn and they were rather reluctant to show us. There was no contact after. Once the work began to roll the contact with Handley Page died almost totally.

'It was a lovely plane, but you know there hasn't been a single survivor. Not one Halifax survived the war.* I feel very upset about that. I think there are three Lancasters floating around somewhere. We've got pictures of it but no survivors. In a sense I always feel a little guilty about it, who knows, you might have left rivets undone or faulty inspection. When the Lancasters came along all this was ended. The Labour office came to us. We were all interviewed at the factory and told where we would have to go. I was sent to Feltham, to Fairey Aviation. Terrible!'

*'You'd no choice?'*

'I was directed there. I had no choice. I didn't really know what I wanted to do. To me the world had come to an end. I'd

---

*There is now a Halifax in the RAF Bomber Command Museum at Hendon.

been so happy for the four years that I was working on Halifaxes, to find that it had run away for me was a terrible thing. I reckon we all had traumas when the production came to an end, as I suppose happens in normal industry anyway – if you're happy.'

*'Did you find out what happened to the other people who worked there?'*

'No, there was no keeping in touch. It all withered away – they were wartime relationships really and they were all doomed to disappear. When I went to Fairey's down at Feltham my wage dropped from about £15 a week, which was a lot of money during the war, to £4 10s. That was the end of the aircraft industry as far as I was concerned.'

*'What did you do there?'*

'Oh, I don't know, I've washed it out, a bad dream. I know I was working on a wing spar, and fitting bits and pieces on that. By that time it was getting on towards the end of the war and the people at Fairey's were all beginning to look after their jobs after the war. They didn't want dilutees as we were and there was animosity all round, you could feel it in the air. I was very unhappy and depressed. In the end I drilled an enormous hole quite deliberately – I got sacked – I just couldn't stand any more of it. They couldn't prove it was me but they suspected me and slung me out.'

*'What did you do after that? You went into something completely different?'*

'I sold elastic and combs on the black market! You couldn't get elastic and you couldn't get combs (*laughs*) and you couldn't get nail varnish. But you could get something called stocking stop, which was nail varnish – it was just another way of getting around the law. I found someone who could supply me and I used to go out on the street with a dirty old suitcase rather like those characters outside Selfridges who sell perfumes. I made a fortune in eight weeks but I was in and out of police stations. Oddly enough I was never charged.

'I used to get great crowds of people around me but the guilt and the discomfort I had in doing something I knew I shouldn't be doing stopped me from carrying on. I mean, in a matter of half an hour I could sell out everything I had and go home with a fortune because I was grossly overcharging. I only had to take a reel of elastic out and go like this and I was surrounded by people. I did that for eight weeks and after that I went back into the shoe trade for a very short period, and then I went on to the knowledge of London and became a taxi driver.

'When I was a small boy I lived in Norbury in South London. Every Saturday afternoon I and a number of friends would walk all the way to Croydon aerodrome and watch these enormous four-engine biplanes going off to India and wherever, taking weeks it seemed. They were Handley Page air liners of Imperial Airways, Hansas and Hannibals, everything began with H. I never ever dreamt I would be making a Handley Page Halifax. But they were the best years of my life, the ones I had in the aircraft industry, because it was the only time in my life that I ever worked with a large group of people, and we all wanted to work. It was a wonderful feeling which I don't think this country's had since, of patriotism and getting something done. It was a very nice experience.'

Aircraft firms had to change over to mass production, and then maximize output, but they had also to keep up with the latest technical innovations, two very different roles. Sometimes, their staff found themselves engaged on both aspects of work in the aircraft industry, like *Stan Atkins*.

'I finished my education and went straight into the drawing office at Fairey's. I did some right jobs on the Firefly and the Swordfish. One of them was fitting a thirty-six-inch searchlight under one wing, a pukka searchlight such as they stood on the ground and shone up into the air. I designed a box shaped like a torpedo for the batteries, and there was a very crude radar. The idea was you would pick up a submarine on the surface at night, guide the

Swordfish on to the target and switch the light on. There he was bathed in light! Another Swordfish would dive down and bomb it.

'We fixed all this up – oh, I had a right lark with that! We blacked the hangar out, shut the doors and switched the light on. It shone this searchlight – a terrific beam! It stayed about a minute and then went oh-oh-oh and died away. Batteries exhausted. Everybody was very pleased because that was all it had to do – last half a minute or so otherwise the submarine would knock it down with its gun.

'But they never tried it out because a Catalina (*flying boat*) fitted with a similar lamp was practising in the Irish Sea. It picked up the submarine it thought it was liaising with, dived down and switched the lamp on. But it was a German submarine waiting for it and he shot him down. So all interest in that was lost.

'Special jobs. We devised a new method of blowing up the Jungman dinghy. On the Swordfish there was a big dinghy stored in the top centre section. The idea was when you crashed, a remote control blew it out and with air bags in the tail it floated. I gather when you got in it you were seasick in about five seconds flat.

'On one occasion, in a hell of a storm, the thing blew up in flight. That, I think, was the only Swordfish that crashed inadvertently. Anyway, they decided that they would change the chemically operated head to an electrically operated one. So we put it to the test. It was all set to go on the catapult, the engine tipping over, great rope round the tail-end, and they fired it. It just went off the end of the catapult into the water! This thing which was supposed to operate and blow the dinghy up failed and it sank complete. Gone! Just hanging on the end of the rope.

'They pulled it up and there it was dripping, propeller blades all bent. So, you know a navy chief? Nothing'd stop them! They'd do anything! "We'll have another go after lunch!" You could hear them hammering the blades with sledge-hammers, to straighten them about a bit.

'After lunch they put this very sorry-looking thing on the catapult. The fellow who invented the electric switch had been

111

trying it in a bucket of sea water. It worked every time! So they threw the plane off, catapulted it over the side, nothing happened! It sank again! This poor fellow was out of his mind! One more try. Have some tea first. Off we went for tea.

'When we came back they'd got it back up on the catapult. It was in a shocking state by then but believe it or not they fired it and it worked! We were all proud! The naval commander came along. "I do NOT consider one go out of three very promising!" We were absolutely *crushed*! But we changed over to the electric switch and I don't know of another crashed Swordfish. That was the first time I went anywhere for the firm.

'Then we had another one, rocket take-off. I got to design the framework – it had two barrel-like contraptions on each side with rocket projectiles, for take-off. I had this fairly well designed when they came up and said, "We want it to carry torpedoes with air-rudders like a tail-plane!" I had to splay these things out, then they said, "Ah, now, wait a minute, each bit you design has to be carried by no more than four men on a heaving deck. Keep each piece under two hundred pounds!"

'We had another look over it and eventually it's all right. It was dispatched to a trial ship. I had to go and see a demonstration of the rocket take-off. It was at an aerodrome somewhere up near Oxford.

'They had a grandstand built of scaffolding, and all the big wigs from the Admiralty, the Army, the Air Force were there on a jolly. They had this gadget like I've done but on a Stirling bomber. The Stirling taxied up the aerodrome and when it got about level with us it just blew up! Disintegrated! Bits were flying towards the stand – people were ducking, running. When the smoke cleared away it was, ah well, back to the drawing board. There was no "Oh, poor bugger" or anything like that! Nobody thought of the pilot, not a thought. You're just a cipher in the services! They can do anything to you. I was most depressed.

'Another time I went up to see a bloke from Coastal Command and he wanted to know if it'd be safe to tie bicycles on the ends of planes' struts. I said, "I've seen a Swordfish changing station with the wardroom armchairs strapped on the bomb-racks so I reckon you can tie bicycles on! What do you want it for?"

' "We fly agents from Malta into North Africa. Vichy French. We lost one because we couldn't get away quick enough. So what we want to do if we land is set fire to the plane and get the hell out of there. We want to jump on a bike and go!" These bikes had long step-nuts on the back axles, so one guy could stand on the step-nut and the other fellow pedal like hell.

'Years afterwards I met one of these blokes and I said, "Did you ever use the bikes?"

'He said, "Oh yes! The next flight we landed in a bog and it tipped up on the nose! We couldn't get off, so we took the bicycles off, located a road, and rode into town, Tangiers or wherever. We knew where to go once we got there."

'In the middle of the war I got a job with the British Air Commission in the States. Everybody thought I was mad to go. They more or less said goodbye. My boss went the week before and they were transferring German prisoners to Canada on the same boat. There was a screaming and fighting when they tried to get these Germans on board – "You wish to murder us! You know as well as we do this ship will never get to the other side of the Atlantic!"

'One chap jumped overboard and started swimming across the Clyde – it was a hell of a set-out! They never saw the Germans during the voyage. When they woke up in New York one morning, these Germans came out on the deck and burst into tears, almost without exception. They realized the propaganda about no ship crossing the Atlantic was all lies.

'We were stationed on Long Island, Roosevelt Field. We had a lot of Wrens on the station. People used to say, "What uniform is that, my dear?"

'The Wrens used to say, "I'm a Wren!"

' "What's that?" When they heard they'd say, "Oh! You must come to dinner! Do bring a friend!" And as often as not they'd bring me!

'The funniest things happened over there. You learn such a lot about Americans and their mass production. I'd designed a shelf for a radio receiver on the Grumman Avenger. We would then put the drawing out to tender to get parts made. They'd come in and people on the line would fit 'em in. A bloke came in the office one day, an American: "Ah! Your bloody English inches again! This is nowhere near right!"

' "I measured it myself!"

'We went down and I looked at this plane. He was right – it wouldn't go in by about two inches. So I walked along the line. The next one was TBM – that meant torpedo bomber – M stood for General Motors. The one after was TBF – that was built by Grumman and the shelf went in easy. I said, "Get the General Motors rep!" He worked for Buick before the war. He comes in: "What's up, Stan?"

'I said, "We're not building these aeroplanes right!" We measured it. I'd had five hundred of these sets made. Because the frame was out of position it actually altered the line. It was a thin frame where the fuselage ought to have been a bit fatter – you could actually *see* it if you looked along the line. "Well," he said, "it's not going to make any difference to the performance, is it?"

'When we checked up, number five jig in Jersey City was wrong. They never put it right. They all came in with the frame in the wrong position and no one turned a hair, never turned a hair. So much for mass production. They used to tell me things about the car production lines – if they were bolting on a front assembly section and they were pressed for time they put three bolts in instead of four. It would go out like that – they'd sell the car like that. They'd say, "Never heard of accidents happening through that!" That was their attitude. Oh, they were a rotten lot! But they were all right, they were nice to work with.

'Oh yes, America was the place to be during the war. Life was just out of this world but I didn't kid myself. These people wouldn't spit at you normally, it was the uniform. I was a civilian incidentally. I didn't have a uniform but I used to go out with the Wrens and they used to think I was a uniformed lad in mufti!

'We came back about eighteen months later and the ship was

loaded with troops. I remember one day one of these soldiers said, "Excuse me, sir! Where are we heading?"

'I said, "Europe, I suppose."

' "That's what I figured. Why can't we *see* it?"

' "Well, it's probably a thousand miles away yet!"

' "But there's nothing in between, is there? We're on water, why can't we see Europe?"

'I thought he was pulling my leg at first. I said, "It's the curvature of the earth!"

' "Buddy," he said, "this ain't the earth, this is water! Where I come from, Omaha, Nebraska, Lake Something-or-other, is flat. Water's flat. You can't have water curved, it would run all up to one side!"

'So I had to draw the globe. "That's the Pacific and that's the Atlantic!"

' "Do you mean to say they're *curved*? Jesus!" He was absolutely mystified. But this crowd, they were high-school people: most of them had been to Omaha High. They were really taken aback about British money. "Can't use greenbacks? Can't use the green stuff?"

' "No, you'll have to change it."

' "What do you mean, *change* it?"

'I said, "Four dollars will give you one pound!" Oh, the idea of giving four dollars for one of something else was terrible!

'Things were much the same in England when I got back except for the bombing. They'd extended the drawing office so much! I was in there one day, drawing, and something made me drop flat on the drawing board. I was looking down the office and the sides went in and out, about a foot. The windows were big, not one broke, but the hut went whoo! bang! Bloody great crash.

'I rushed to the phone to be first to the chap on the roof. He said, "Come out and look straight up in the air!" There was a perfect blue sky with one little cloud slowly expanding. He said, "That's it. It exploded up there, on entry into the atmosphere." Scattered bits all over the area, little bits of metal were floating

115

down twenty minutes after the bang. The V-bombs! They were bastard things!

'The other thing I noticed when I got back was the influx of women into the factory. *Girl* draughtsmen! There wasn't one when I went and I had a team of four when I came back. Two were bank clerks from Newbury, one was an artist from Maidenhead and the other was straight from school, in Slough. Before the war even the typists were men. We had some very clever women then, way above me in mathematics.

'You know, I remember just after the war all the design team at Fairey's were invited to go to Farnborough and look at the captured German aircraft. Some of them were phenomenal! They were far ahead of us on jets, but they fiddled about on production – lucky for us! After the war a pal of mine, a squadron leader, grabbed a set of Luftwaffe maps and it was most interesting because the Fairey Flugwerke was plainly marked as were the AEC Wagenwerke and EMI – they were all outlined in red. They knew where we were, no argument about that. The RAF headquarters in Uxbridge – they'd got the lot! It made you realize that there was absolutely nothing you could hide, not in daylight at any rate.'

# 5

# BOMBER COMMAND

$D$URING 1942 AND 1943, THE WEIGHT OF RAF EFFORT went into Bomber Command. The pattern of recruitment, training, and service became established. *Len Port* was typical of many thousands of young men, attracted by the glamour of the Brylcreem Boys. He tried to join up at the age of seventeen in 1941. The recruiting centre told him to come back on his eighteenth birthday because then he wouldn't need his parents' consent.

*'Did your parents know?'*

'They didn't at the time, no, they knew when I'd done it! My mother said, "I don't know what your father's gonna say!" But he didn't say anything. In those days people were getting called up anyway.'

Len was sent to the training centre in St John's Wood, like thousands of others. 'We marched in whistling the RAF march. Just a little way down on the right-hand side there's a block of flats, and that was where we were billeted. They were all empty and full of RAF recruits. We ate in the underground garage. I was in London seven weeks.

'To phase out the training we went to Ludlow, in a field for about four and a half weeks and then down to Initial Training Wing at Torquay. That was ten weeks, or thereabouts. We did all the ground subjects, navigation – I was on a pilot's course to start with, most of us were – meteorology, airmanship, hygiene, can't remember the rest – quite a number of different subjects.'

*'Was it a good course?'*

'Pretty intensive. The instructors were all ex-teachers, middle-aged chaps. Ten weeks there and then examinations. I passed everything first time so I was yanked out and posted to Theale near Reading to grading school. We flew three weeks on Tiger Moths and at the end of that time were sent to Heaton Park, Manchester. There were *thousands* of RAF guys waiting for the next stage. I was graded bomb aimer so we all had to reshuffle, change flights, and then on to the troopship at Liverpool. From there down to South Africa.

'There was a lot of animosity towards us. Chaps were getting beaten up, couple of stabbings while I was there. The South African police were reputed not to like us, and the Tank Corps for some reason or other, but we didn't have any problems. Leaves we went on holiday, and I stayed on a farm, Afrikaans family, had a lovely time.'

*'How did they train you as a bomb aimer?'*

'Waste of time I subsequently discovered. It was fifteen weeks' bombing and gunnery, and we spent a lot of time doing theory of bombing which was not necessary at all. Actual bombing was quite fun.

'Eventually, in about February 1944, I arrived at Advanced Flying Unit which was up at Bovington near Wolverhampton. By then you began to feel that all that training was just a way of phasing out aircrew from the inception at St John's Wood to bomber squadrons, replacing those that were lost. After AFU there was OTU and other transit camps in between, they were still trotting us off to different places.

'At OTU the different crews get together, bomb aimers, navigators, pilots, wireless operators and gunners. You more or less sort yourselves out into crews. My pilot was a lovely chap, shiny white teeth and very well brought up, about six foot one, thirteen and a half stone. We had a flying officer-navigator, Sam, from Canada, very nice chap, and two Canadian gunners. I was quite surprised at the attitude of the Canadians. They were all officer rank but quite casual about it. Up to that time we were saluting everybody. I introduced the rear gunner to my sister and they got married after we finished flying. We had quite a good mob.

'First phase of OTU was circuits and bumps with the pilot, learning to fly Wimpeys (*the Wellington bomber*). The wireless operator confided in me, "I've seen his log-book and he's a below average pilot!" (*Laughs.*) But he was terrific! I can only think the reason was he was very cautious. Instead of flying through clouds he'd try and fly round them, he'd avoid flak and things like that. But his landings were lovely, he always used to kiss the ground, coming in just over the hedgerows.'

*'Any views about this system of crewing you up?'*

'I haven't experienced the other (*American*) way, but in theory you're supposed to look at each other and think oh, I like the look of that fellow, you know. I'd no regrets. We got on famously. Our average age was twenty-one.

'While we were there we had to do a leaflet raid over France. On the way back, pow! the old engine dropped. The skipper said, "We'll have to go straight in!" Right ahead of us I could see an airfield, an American aerodrome. There were all these Americans chewing and watching in some amazement at this antiquated aircraft going round the track.

'After we landed, somebody called, "Say, do they still use those?"

' "Ooh yes, we still use 'em!" They took us to the officers' mess – no sergeants' mess in the American air force. Had a lovely meal there, smoked salmon, coffee with cream, and ice cream.

'Next, we went to a conversion unit on Stirlings. Same rigmarole. Circuits and bumps first of all. There were pranged Stirlings all over the place because they used to swing quite badly – very high undercarriage. Story was that when they made the Stirling

119

they had to reduce the wing spread because it wouldn't fit in the hangars! So they had to increase the angle of attack for take-off and made a longer undercarriage. This long spidery under-carriage. Slightest cross-wind and it swung – and if it swung the undercarriage used to collapse. But our skipper never pranged one – he liked the Stirling. Very manoeuvrable and lots and lots of space. He used to throw it about all over the place.

'Our next posting was Lanc finishing school. We weren't there very long and then we got posted on to squadron. Chop squad-ron – one of the original Bomber Command squadrons.'

*'It had lost a lot of crews?'*

'I think it probably had. You didn't know all the crews on a squadron – people come and go. When you've been on it a short while, when new crews came in, you'd say to yourself quite callously, "I reckon they'll get it, they'll get the chop!" Used to get quite callous. You didn't have all that much feeling about people dying or getting killed. But you didn't know all the crews so when one went missing you didn't notice it unless they happened to be friends of yours.

'As our gunners were Canadian they had lots of Canadian pals. There were two in particular that I have a pilgrimage for now and again – I go up to the RAF memorial at Runnymede. We were in the same hut. I remember the wireless operator, a chap named Sam Roberts, quite old to us, about thirty-five, sitting at the small table we had writing a letter to his wife. He'd got a picture of her and his child, and he was writing this letter and crying. They were lost over Duisburg – somebody said their wings fell off. They used to lose the odd Lancaster for no reason at all, metal fatigue or something like that. They used to fall apart. Lost over the target and nothing was found of them.

'When we got to the squadron they had these lovely new Lancasters lined up! They said, "Try 'em out!" so we sat in them. Only one had a benign atmosphere – we were unanimous about it – E for easy, but another crew already had it and they were senior to us. I think they had three trips to do so we said we'd wait. We took it over and we never had any trouble. E for easy. Not a thing went wrong. We had problems with other ones, on three engines, icing up and all that kind of thing.

'Anywhere we went we all went together, like a lot of silly kids. Flying was a pleasure – going for an air test for example, that was fun, I liked stooging around on our own, no discipline, nothing to do.

'We had to go to Woodbridge where all the pranged aeroplanes were, to pick up a Lancaster. It had M-Michael on the nose and Q-Queenie on the rest of the fuselage! An amalgam. We flew this thing back, and we could either have it Q-Queenie or M-Mike, so being silly buggers we said we'd have it M-Mike, thirteenth letter of the alphabet.

'We flew to Cologne on that and it was a beast, one engine kept giving us trouble all the way. We were icing. We just got to the top of the cloud at about seventeen thousand feet, and that's as high as we could get with it. Not very nice with the others three thousand feet above, likely to drop their bombs on you! The skipper said, "We're not flying that again," and we didn't.'

By this stage of the war, the bombing onslaught on Germany was thoroughly organized. Planes had the latest technical devices like H2s and Window to deceive enemy radar; Pathfinder Force to find and mark the target; the raids were almost routine. But German defences had been greatly improved and British bombers faced a fearsome task getting to the target and home safely again.

'The day before a raid there'd be a battle order, pinned up in the sergeants' mess. All the crews would come in and look at it – we're on! Mostly I did daylights so the drill was you went to bed early and in the early hours of the morning an SP would come and wake you up. I was always the first out because there was a pre-briefing which involved the pilot, the navigator and the bomb-aimer. That took an hour, say, and then the main briefing took place. Doors opened and it was like a cinema coming out.

'The squadron commander would tell you the target – there

were big maps on the wall and a red ribbon with pins used to show the route of the raid. All the heavily defended areas were like little balloons outlined in red with stripes across. The meteorologist used to give you the weather and so on. Then you put your clobber on, got your parachute and escape gear, chocolate and sweets – we used to keep the chewing gum and give the sweets to the girl who drove the crew truck. Get to your plane at the due time, start motors, take your place round the perimeter track and off you go!

'Our policy was always get up the front! No matter where we were supposed to be, get up there! In fact we were so far at the front one day – we were bombing Trier, on the Moselle – we bombed before the Pathfinders! That was the only time I saw my bombs hit. We were a little bit unorthodox really.

'We'd wobble about. We got told off for wobbling too. As we were approaching the target we saw two Lancs blow up, and we couldn't see any flak. Everybody got the wind up, the whole bloody bomber stream was weaving. Our wing commander was a regular, very stern, and he used to fly as well. He said, "I've noticed crews weaving over the target area – use your guts and fly straight and level!" '

*'Didn't he want his crews to survive?'*

'I don't think it did any good really, but it was good for your morale.

'Ground crew always used to wave us off, and civilians, especially on a Sunday. There'd be quite a few of the locals over the other side of the wire. They'd wave and we'd wave at them. I started ops in September 1944, and finished on the thirty-first of December, doing twenty-eight in that time. It was fairly intensive.

'The hairiest part was going into the last turning point. We weren't terribly worried because we didn't think we'd get the chop, but I suppose we were a bit apprehensive. If you weren't right up at the front you'd see the others had got to it, and they're all wheeling round, going into their bombing run. You'd see the flak coming up. When you turned on to the bombing run, you began to feel a bit edgy. You got into it fairly slowly, it seemed to take a long time, then suddenly you were in it! You were tense and your mouth was a bit dry.

'I was the only one talking at this point, and the navigator said after one of the raids, "You sound as if you're on a practice bombing run!" I didn't particularly feel that way. For the rest of the crew it was a bad time. I didn't open the bomb doors till we were practically there. As soon as I did, a draught got going – not for me but for the rest of them! The navigator was holding on to his maps – that was the testing time! You felt exposed, all these bombs down there! It was a relief when the things dropped off, and I said "Bomb doors closed!" Peace reigned again, there were no draughts and they felt a bit better.

'The actual raid looked like a cauldron, all different colours, boiling and bubbling. The photo flashes are blinding, and the flak is quite blinding too, on a night raid. Over Cologne you could smell the cordite, it was so thick.'

*'Were you attacked by enemy aircraft?'*

'I'm not sure. On one occasion we were going to Stuttgart. We were flying above cloud, in bright moonlight, and you could see other Lancs – you could see miles in the moonlight. I was in the nose looking round and I could see an aircraft out to starboard. I assumed it was a Lancaster, but at that point the mid-upper gunner said, "Starboard ghost, skipper!" so we went straight down into the cloud. He said it was a Focke-Wulf 190. We stooged along in the cloud for a bit, came up for a look-see, went back down – you were beautifully silhouetted on the cloud. You could see all these black spots like bees all over the place! Any self-respecting fighter pilot would have had a field day! We didn't like firing the guns anyway because you had to clean them afterwards. If you fired at some bloke he might take offence and have a go at you.

'We didn't suffer much damage but others did. One pal of ours, his wireless operator was killed. In fact his head was blown off. He fell out of his seat into the gangway. Our pal had to put his navigation bag over the top because the head was lying there looking at him. Another time we were tucking into our flying meal and the crew of a Halifax that had been shot up came in. There was just three of them, looking very shaken and the pilot was carrying a flying boot which apparently was his flying officer's leg.

'Another pal of ours was flying in front of us, I knew what plane he got in, and it just disintegrated. My only concern was that we flew right through it! I was waiting for us to hit a bit of a wheel or something but there was nothing. It exploded and the rear gunner thought *we'd* been hit because the flames went straight by us. It was a big whirling oily smoke but there just wasn't anything there!

'When we went to Merseburg I saw two planes go down, but they were well in front of us. All we said – when we reported it – oh, chop dead ahead, or chop to starboard. The navigator logged it. They both appeared to catch fire and turn over on their backs. I said to the skipper, "Watch that chop in case it comes to us!" The main concern was to get out of the way! I didn't think at the time of the horror that was going on inside that aeroplane – these blokes upside-down and the plane engulfed in flame, that kind of thing. I don't think we were very imaginative. We knew it was happening but we couldn't get a mental picture of it. It didn't worry us too much. We were very young at the time. We were full of self-preservation really.

'There must have been a lot of collisions at night, especially when the visibility wasn't good, when you were flying in cloud. When the aircraft started buffeting you knew there was another just in front and you were in its prop wash. I don't remember being all that frightened. The training wasn't all that much use, except being acclimatized to aircraft. But for that we might have been frightened.'

'*Did you get superstitious?*'

'Don't remember anything, no. I can't recall any. No talismans or anything like that, scarfs or stockings. We were too young, young idiots, you know. We were full of beans and round the pub at night. There's something about bad luck! You never said good luck to anybody because it would always bring bad luck.

'Airfields could be creepy places. Security on ours was so poor, oh! it was non-existent! There was a spate of Lancs blowing up on take-off. Once I had to go back to the plane, dead of night. I climbed up in there and it's very eerie you know. I'm sure there was noises especially when you get to the cockpit. You've got all these fluorescent gauges, I'm sure there was noise in it, you *feel* it, like an entity, you could feel the hair curling on the back of your neck.

'Some people had bad feelings about their next trip. I was in the parachute room and a chap was saying goodbye to one of the girls, he wouldn't be back, and as I recall he didn't come back. That girl was called chop Annie – her reputation was whoever she went out with got the chop! We had a flight engineer, very debonair, from Shepherd's Bush, bit of a wide boy, curly sleeked-back hair, a ladies' man, and one night he had a date with this girl. He'd a couple of false teeth at the front there, covering a big gap, and while he was getting himself spruced up, we hid his teeth and wouldn't give them back so he couldn't go out with chop Annie!'

*'What was the discipline like on the squadrons?'*

'None. No. It was very free and easy really. We were just a group of individuals – we used to amble about – we used to wear our sweaters, battledress jacket, I don't think we dressed to kill. There wasn't a great deal of discipline – it wasn't necessary. You knew what you were there for. We didn't question going on ops because this is what it was all about. It didn't occur to us to question it. One chap did one night. The aiming point wasn't where he thought it ought to be – a factory or something – it was in the built-up area. He was questioning it and the intelligence officer said, "We've bombed that, they filled the holes up so we bomb them again." But he wouldn't go, he refused. They took his stripes away, called it Lack of Moral Fibre – in his case it might have been true principles. We weren't that principled. The thought of being LMF and having everything taken away – we'd rather take our chances. The more intelligent you are, I suppose, the more you would feel it, but I don't think we could have been all that intelligent.

'After I finished ops there was nothing to do. And by that time I began to think flying was dangerous, you know. I thought if I stay in the air force I'm going to be flying again and perhaps that's not such a good idea. So I decided to take the demob papers.'

The most professional group in Bomber Command was Pathfinder Force. This was formed under the leadership of Group Captain Donald Bennett to find and mark the enemy target. Skilled crews were recruited on a voluntary basis. The force might also include a Master Bomber or Master of Ceremonies, who would control the raid from above the target, flying round during the forty minutes or so it took for the attack to be completed, an extremely dangerous task. *John Hudson* performed this role on several occasions during the war. He was a regular who joined the RAF in peacetime, in a very different world.

'It was a great privilege to be asked to fly. Everyone wanted to fly and this was the only way most people could hope to do it. Many young men went into the RAF to learn, taking four-year short-service commissions. They hoped to leave with their £400 and use that to set themselves up in civilian careers. But the expenses in the RAF were such that unless you had a private income it was difficult to make ends meet, and many of them mortgaged their £400. If they were exceptional they might be picked for a medium-service commission and stay on. A lot of them did very well indeed. Several finished up as air chief marshals. If you were lucky you were all right.

'The life in the RAF pre-war was terrific. Every day you could look up in the sky and think where shall we fly to, today? You'd set off and go and visit your pals at the other stations, have a few drinks and lunch with them, and then back home again. At weekends you were free and could set off in your plane wherever you wished to go, maybe up to Yorkshire to visit your mother, parking the plane in a nearby field. No trouble in using an RAF plane for such a purpose. It was a lot of fun. You could land the planes anywhere if you got lost.

'Instruments in the 1930s were extremely primitive and unreliable – they only had the altimeter and the speedometer and both were inaccurate. Engines often stalled. What did you do? Looked around for the nearest bit of space where you could land it and went straight in there. You'd be dropping like a stone anyway.

'In the thirties, the front-line mobile squadrons of the RAF literally had old stringbag aircraft. The only time they came in touch with any signals equipment was in the one aircraft out of a squadron of twenty-two which carried an old GP set. This had a range of about fifty miles if you had the aerial let out, and most times the aerial used to fly off when you let it out!

'We heard that we would be the first squadron to get Wellesleys (*the predecessor of the Wellington*). By the end of the first day the new planes arrived, every pilot in the squadron had been converted. All we did was sit in the cockpit for two minutes while the instructor explained the controls, and then off we went. We had a lousy airfield. It was shaped like an inverted V, very short runs, and we had to land uphill. We'd been brought up well on Fairey Gordons which had no brakes so we got used to it.

'Of course things did happen. We had a young pilot officer who was a bit of a card, drove a little black MG. The last time I saw him he'd gone through a plate-glass window drunk as a coot in the middle of Winchester. He came in one day with a bit of a hangover, went over the top of the hill and they'd lined up all the aircraft in two rows, in front of the hangar. He went straight down and wrote a complete line of them off! It was all good fun!'

'*He remained in the air force, I presume?*'

'Oh yes, yes. He did very well, actually. Finished off an air vice-marshal. It was all a jolly holiday really and this is what people joined the air force for.

'We lost a number of pilots with the Wellesley because of its faults. I had the misfortune to hit one of them. We were doing practice bombing in the winter. I came in to land in a blinding snowstorm and finished up with one side of the undercarriage collapsing completely. She cart-wheeled right round, the petrol tank ruptured and about a hundred and fifty gallons of high-octane fuel gave me a lovely shower bath. And then at that precise moment, the bombs that we'd been trying to drop decided to start smoking. The fire-tender crew which came dashing up to see what had happened mistook it for a fire. They doused me with fifty gallons of foam. When they'd finished I was in an igloo of foam, completely cocooned. And couldn't breathe! (*Laughs.*) You'd get funny things like that happen!'

This happy existence started to change in the late 1930s when a war seemed increasingly probable. The RAF began to introduce new types of aircraft.

'We had the Whitley which was out of date before it even started. It was the slowest thing that you could meet anywhere. When you were flying it you felt like getting out and walking. It was as bad as that. And they were going into action! They did all the early leaflet raids, and we were still using them as late as '43.'

*'How was it they were kept on?'*

'Shortage of aircraft. Pure and simple. They were trying to bomb Berlin with those things! The early Halifax was just as bad. As soon as he'd bombed the average pilot being harassed by flak all over the place used to put 'em straight over into a steep diving turn, one way or the other, which was the quickest way out of the target area. On the Halifax if you banked over like that, it got steeper and steeper till the thing went over on its back and

128

spun in. They couldn't understand why they were having such heavy losses.

'One day a bod got into one of these spins when practising corkscrew evasion and couldn't get out of it. The plane went over and all sorts of queer things started happening. Fortunately he had a bit of height and by juggling the engines, switching some off, trying to boost it up with another – he didn't know what he was doing – he managed to get out of it. Came back alive and told the tale. So they recalled all the Halifaxes, and if you look at the Mark II or Mark III you find that they've got huge square rudders. But they lost a hell of a lot of aircraft before they found out!'

*'How much did you know about the German planes and German tactics before the war?'*

'Not a lot. It wasn't until late '38 that people started taking an interest in German matters. We started getting a bit of intelligence, and a few leaflets and booklets on the German air force, which you had to pick up, but all the main things that you really wanted were never touched on! For instance, we used to operate as day bombers on dead-reckoning, navigation and map-reading. Well, if you can imagine anyone flying dead-reckoning and map-reading over Germany at night in battle – I've yet to know how they did it! You couldn't even navigate in this country on that basis.'

In February 1942 Arthur Harris was appointed Air Officer Commanding Bomber Command. A decisive self-confident personality, he introduced a fresh determination and purpose into the air war against Germany. Known to his friends as Bert, to the general public as Bomber, Harris was nicknamed Butch by aircrews, short for Butcher.

'Butch Harris decided the targets. Everyone thought the world of Butch. It was a good thing to be controlled by a man who made decisions, right or wrong or what. Believe me he did. All

129

the people they had up to the time of Butch taking over in '42 wouldn't drop a leaflet on the Germans in case one of them landed on someone's head. That's no way to fight a war.

'The targets were all fish and the favourite was whitebait – Berlin. Saundby, Butch's chief of staff, was a great fishing expert and he was able to name every target. We had the lot, whitebait, herring, trout, plaice, you name it.

'Butch would have his morning conference. They used to brief the operational staff at Bomber Command on the weather all over Germany, take the operational state of the aircraft and decide how many they'd put on a particular target. If one hadn't been attacked for any length of time and was in the right area Met-wise they'd lay it on. Having got to that stage the wires started buzzing, the old teleprinters, and the groups were informed of an operational order.

'Each group commander was usually connected on a circuit and they would sit at their group headquarters. The only thing they didn't have was television. Thank God! I shudder to think what it would have been like if they had! Can you imagine all that lot trying to make themselves look image conscious! Most of the discussions as to various things were done at group level – minor modifications – you had to conform to the overall plan.

'It used to be terrible in the war because a lot of the group commanders were more concerned with dropping a heavier weight of bombs than they were with the safety of their crews! Butch Harris had a thing about heavy bombardment and tonnage. The normal all-up weight for Lancasters was sixty-five thousand pounds, with everything on board. They experimented with bigger bomb-loads, bigger fuel-load, getting it up to sixty-seven or sixty-eight thousand – I can't remember offhand what the limits were. Once they started doing that, the problems started arising!

'To stand any chance of staying alive, you had to get up to about fifteen thousand feet by the Dutch coast. Most of the Bomber Group met up on a rendezvous and merged into one stream, crossing the Dutch coast at a certain point for safety, on the principle that if you all go through in the one narrow gap, the people either side can't get you and you've got more chance of getting away with it. This was the principle that we adopted all the way through on tactics. The fighters were scared to attack you. There were so many bombers in the stream their chance of collision was pretty high, so all in all you got the better of the bargain.

'You were very vulnerable to flak below fifteen thousand when you were crossing the coast. There were guns everywhere you looked. Your only safety was in height. In a fairly new Lancaster with a normal bomb-load on, some people used to get up as high as twenty-two thousand feet, or even more. But if you had a duff aircraft, an aged one, or you had the extra bomb-load to carry, which they did have, a lot of the people found that they weren't even getting up to fifteen thousand by the time they got to the coast. They only did it once. The second time they went the whole of the North Sea was lit up! They didn't release the whole bomb-load or anything like that, but they'd had a real scare on this business and I should think a lot of the crews formed a pact amongst themselves and said we're not going to carry the bloody things there. A very high tonnage of four-thousand-pounders went down in the North Sea.'

*'Did anything happen about that?'*

'Well, you report all these things, but they're brought on by the people who organized it. You're faced with two things, aren't you? You want your aircrew back – it used to take eighteen months to train a pilot to the stage of efficiency where he can take a Lancaster and a crew over to Germany. Right. Now the difference say between dropping six thousand pounds of bombs or seven thousand on a target is negligible as far as I'm concerned, or as far as anyone's concerned. Makes no damn difference whatsoever. It's far better to get an aircraft over there with a crew as safe as you can, and drop six thousand pounds of bombs in the right place than have a crew shot down crossing the coast with its bombs on and lose the crew, the aircraft, and not bomb the target. The answer's simple, isn't it? By being too keen, you were operating outside the capabilities of the aircraft and anyone who tried to do that was a fool.'

*'Why did they do it?'*

'It was all competition between the different bomber groups! It was a very nasty period, I can tell you! I'm under no illusions about it! I operated in Two Group, Five Group, Three Group, with Coastal, you name them. The only group which had any idea what it was doing and planned things properly was Eight Group, and that was entirely due to Bennett, and the fact that Bennett himself was a highly sophisticated navigator, pilot, anything. The most efficient airman I've ever met or likely to. He was young, he'd been shot down himself over Norway, escaped and came back to become AOC Pathfinders which was about the biggest job of the lot in the war. When he started the Pathfinder Force he had to fight to get any special recognition whatsoever for his people. We were at the sticky end of it, catching it in the neck all the time.'

*'Why was this?'*

'Operating! Simply operating. We were the ones who were carrying our lives in our hands going over there night after night. There was seldom a night when you didn't get shot at, or risk something, or get caught out with the weather and come in on very sticky dos.

'The German night fighters were just as clever, if not cleverer than ours. They had the aircraft to do it in and they were very good, the way they used to come in, particularly the various types of approaches. Even now you can get nightmares reading about some of the raids where they operated the Wild Sows and the offset guns and all the rest of it. You don't stand much chance in the Lancaster with pea-shooters which couldn't knock anything down. We were using those things from the Western Front in the First World War, the .303s. They've got a range of next to nothing.

132

'With the German night fighters, they'd come in – some used to operate down below, some to one side – and position themselves with the upward-firing guns. They were a menace because they'd get on the blind side underneath the aircraft where no one could see them. They'd wait for their moment, pull the throttles back, pull the nose up slightly, and take a Lancaster from the nose right down to the tail with the cannon. Some of them didn't even do that. They'd go for the wings and get the tanks first. Once you'd got a twenty-mill cannon shell in the tanks, that was it. Oh, it was a very dicey business! It was a good thing half the people didn't know what was happening. I'm sure they wouldn't have gone if they had!

'Of course I was relatively old. By the time I was flight commander, I was an old man, twenty-six or twenty-seven! They used to look on me as a father figure. You went into the mess and someone stood up to offer you a seat! Still, there you are, we survived.

'Flying to Berlin some pilots took the view they should get in and out of the target as quickly as possible. Be the first one home, that way there'd be less chance of getting hit. They'd charge into the target, getting all they could out of the engines and to hell with whoever used the aircraft after them. They also knew that with lots of planes being damaged and others running out of petrol there'd be hardly any airfields to land on. We always knew who they were because they'd get home about an hour before anyone else.

'Sensible and reasonable pilots, and I regarded myself as one, would be careful how they used the engines and would take indirect routes, so they arrived back later. I always tried to fly so that there would be about two hours of petrol left when I got back to England. I flew around for twenty minutes and then came in. An experienced pilot would bide his time: he was safe while he was up there.

'When we got to the Battle of Berlin in '43, the second night we hit Berlin the temperatures were round about minus forty. There was a bit of heating in the cockpit but the poor old gunners at the rear end had nothing. No heated clothing, no anything.

'On our squadron, ninety per cent of the rear gunners were out of action after the second night – they'd all got frost-bite where the oxygen mask fitted, and the fingers and toes. To replace them we had to go to the OTUs and grab all people there – some had just started training – some had never been airborne. We made up the battle order with them. Some had never fired a gun. It didn't make much difference. They were only a pair of eyes. They couldn't do very much with .303s. But it was the principle of the thing that was so bad.

'It was Berlin every night from then on – even though we didn't go we were briefed every night, stood by, and it was only the weather that stopped us. Harris was determined that we were going to hit Berlin. He'd got a phobia against the place. He'd a biggish force and he wanted to really hit them. The weather turned nasty in October, November – it was *terrible* weather! Fog every night. There's no means of getting them down. If you send seven hundred or eight hundred bombers off to Berlin you didn't stand an earthly of getting them back again unless they got in fairly quickly. They'd only got so much juice – you'd got very little in the way of landing aids.

'Europe's a very funny place to operate over. The weather usually comes over from the west and hits us first in this country and then it carries on and either swings up a bit towards Norway or swings down a bit towards the Mediterranean. We had a fairly big cyclone centred over Europe with cold weather which created a fog every evening as soon as dusk fell. By six or seven o'clock in the evening you'd got fairly thick fog. You were in for it.

'Well, when the whole of England is covered with that and you've got say thirty aircraft a station to land – if you've sent thirty aircraft off, you want them back. But to get them down was practically impossible. Butch had to draw his horns in. We were losing anything up to forty or fifty aircraft a night on those dos. You can't afford to lose them more than once or twice at the outside. You didn't have the rest to spare. On the Pathfinders, we had bigger crews than the others because we carried a set operator on H2s – if you lose four crews, that's thirty-two personnel gone for a burton overnight.'

*'Shattering for morale –'*

'I'm surprised that we maintained morale as long as we did. I know I was pretty depressed at times.'

*'How do you think morale was maintained? Because it was maintained, by and large.'*

'It was maintained, by and large. A lot of the people were more afraid of being seen as Lack of Moral Fibre than they were of going on the raid. There's always the old business of the First World War – if a rifle bullet's got your number on it, that's it, you can't do much about it. You get a bit of a fatalistic attitude. You say, well I'm all right at the moment, and with a bit of luck I'll be all right, so what! And that's the way it goes.

'It's a very difficult thing, Lack of Moral Fibre. I ran into it more on Mosquitoes at the end of the war. That was unusual, because the Mosquito was the easiest number ever. Look at it this way, nearly all the training for new pilots and navigators was done over in Canada. They'd go through the training course and at the end of it there's a requirement for *x* number of them to be kept on as instructors.

'The result was a tremendous lot of instructional staff were left out there who were having a marvellous war. Many of them married Canadian girls and they got to be well known by all the Canadian families, fêted right, left and centre. They'd never fired a shot in anger and I think most of them were determined not to! They had a pretty good life.

'Towards the end of 1944, we were advancing towards Germany, and it began to be apparent that things were going well and they'd have to close that lot down over there. They said, what's the best way to use them up? The answer was Mosquitoes. Well, they were most disgruntled. It was obvious if they could stick it out for a few more weeks or months they weren't going to get anything.

135

'The first inkling I had of this, we had a wave of these crews come in and I put the first of them on the battle order. He was away about an hour, came back and said something was wrong with the engine. We didn't take much notice of it because these things do happen, but when he did it a second time and a third, that was it. Rolls-Royce engines don't behave like that. Right! Let's go out to the aircraft and see what it is. Off we went, no trouble at all. I had to read the riot act to this chap. There's only one answer, the next time it happens, there'll be a full inquiry and I shall put you forward for LMF and you'll really get something then. We didn't have any more trouble that way.

'The Mosquito was the cat's whiskers. We would have been well away at the beginning of the war with a few Mosquito squadrons. We could have hit Berlin for a dozen in the first few weeks – you could afford to fly one of those things in daylight.

'In winter we could take off at about four o'clock in the afternoon, in the dusk. By the time we got over the Dutch coast heading towards the target, which was invariably Berlin (*laughs*), you were up at about thirty thousand, pretty safe, away from everything. You could steam into Berlin, in the knowledge on many occasions that you had fog on the Continent. We'd send about a hundred aircraft, converge on Berlin, having done a bit of dog-legging around the place to alert the fighters and make them try to get up, and fox them a bit.

'We'd collect over the target, drop a load of four-thousand cookies, the air-raid sirens would be cracking and so on, down they'd go fairly accurately, and back everybody would steam. Used to take about three and three-quarter hours, roughly, and you'd be back in the mess by half past eight, having a normal dinner. You'd have tea before you went, dinner when you got back. What a way to fight a war!'

'*When you became a Master Bomber, did they give any training for this?*'

'It's just experience. You see, it's very difficult to control anything up to a thousand heavy bombers! We used to go out, from the various groups, all stretching down the east coast of England.

136

Each group probably had anything up to two hundred aircraft and by 1943 they were mostly Halifaxes, Lancasters, a few Stirlings which went out shortly after that. They were nearly all four-engine jobs, all roughly about the same speeds, same height, same bomb load or getting on that way. You had to get those four groups all converging into one solid stream of aircraft which was about ten thousand feet thick, about five miles wide, and about fifty miles long, all going along the same way.

'We used to attack Berlin from some most peculiar angles to see if we could fox them. We used to go past Berlin, suddenly turn round and attack it from the rear. They'd all be floating around Leipzig and Stettin and places like that expecting us to come in there, and we'd just turned in our tracks.

'I hadn't flown a Mosquito by night. Quite a sensation taking off with a four-thousand cookie – it made the aircraft pendulous. The first time we were about half an hour from the target and my navigator said, "Oh, I do feel ill, I don't know what's wrong!" I did all the usual things, got him to check his oxygen supply and so on. He said, "I think it's just the fact that I've never been this high before." I let him sleep till we reached the target, when he felt a bit better.

'After we'd bombed I headed north for Hamburg, the quickest way, dropped down to two or three thousand feet intending to come back fairly stately. We were screaming down when the Germans picked me up with one of their master searchlights. They must have thought here's a sucker, a God-damned Mosquito coming down to ten thousand feet, all alone. The first thing I knew was this damn great blue searchlight got me, with about twenty others. My natural reaction like we used to do in the dear old Lancaster was an absolutely steep diving turn, and get the hell out of it. On the Mozzie which is fingertip control, we actually rolled! God knows what the ack-ack crews must have thought down below. There we were beamed, doing a barrel roll, the shells following, and the cockpit was full of paper and maps and the navigator standing on his head. Anyway we came out of it and I was a bit more careful from then on!

'I left the RAF in 1959 when the Minister, Duncan Sandys, decided that in future air battles would be decided by pressing buttons. You didn't need men to fly them. There were all these wing commanders, colonels and captains – two hundred of them in each service – and they could be got rid of. So they went and I was one of them. We all got a letter from Queenie and an invitation to a royal garden party, and that's about all I got out of it. After thirty years, apart from a small pension. We arrived back in this country, straight from Germany, in September 1959 and we'd got no home, no furniture, no money, no anything. We had to start all over again.'

1. Men and fuselages crowded into the main assembly shop of a Fairey factory in 1938. The aircraft is the Fairey Battle, which suffered disastrous losses in France in 1940.

2. RAF pilot training: link trainers and operating tables. Pilot training was intensive and could last up to eight months.

3. Airmen working by floodlight servicing aircraft in December 1940. In that year a stint of three or four days' work without sleep was not unusual (see pp. 180–81).

4. Thirteen people work on the wing of a Halifax heavy bomber early in the war. Shadow factories in particular often had difficulty getting work organized efficiently (see pp. 105–108).

5. Working conditions at a factory producing the pilot's cabin of the Halifax still look somewhat primitive after nearly six years of war.

6. Women workers inside the famous geodetic structure of the Wellington bomber (see pp. 141–46).

7. Mass production of the de Havilland Mosquito, May 1943. Goering said, 'it makes me furious when I see a Mosquito. I turn green and yellow with envy!'

8. The light capstan section of a machine shop working on the Lancaster bomber, 1942. The women in white overalls are inspectors, checking the quality of production.

9. The Supermarine factory at Woolston after the bombing in 1940 (see p. 6).

10. Night fighter pilots of a Fighter Command station waiting for briefing.

11. Pilots of the Hurricane I of 87 squadron in northern France scramble for their aircraft in November 1939. The airfield is grass, heavily frozen.

12. The Duke of Gloucester inspects a huge Avro Lancaster of 467 squadron. Its slogan refers to the notorious request of Goering to call him Meyer if enemy aircraft flew over Germany.

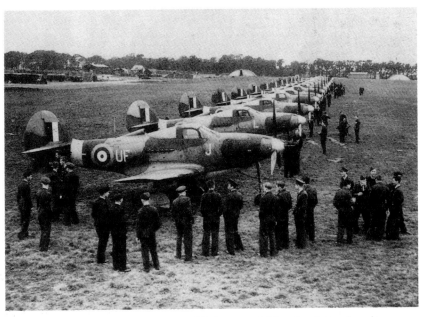

13. A line-up of the Airacobra, one of the less successful American fighters brought into RAF service early in the war (see pp. 29–30).

14. Bombing up a Stirling in October 1941. This massive aircraft was underpowered, slow and vulnerable. It suffered heavy losses during the war (see pp. 61–66).

15. A mass training flight of the Vickers Wellington takes the bomber over Paris. (For the memories of a WAAF stationed in the French capital shortly after liberation, see pp. 248–51.)

16. Devastation of the Krupps works at Essen in April 1945. (Aircrew who visited Germany at the end of the war were shocked by the devastation bombing had caused, see pp. 304–305.)

17. The crew of a Warwick and their dog on the way to the aircraft in December 1944. Pets, airmen and WAAF occasionally and illegally went on operations (see pp. 192–93).

18. Cramped flying conditions inside the Whitley bomber, 1942. This obsolete aircraft was called 'the flying coffin' by aircrew (see pp. 47–58).

19. Shipping strike by Beaufighters off Norway, 1944. Attacking shipping was one of the tasks of Coastal Command (see pp. 174–79).

20. WAAF at work at Bomber Command headquarters at High Wycombe (see pp. 251–57).

21. Wellington bombers in flight. At night aircraft so close together faced a serious risk of collision.

22. One of the hazards Allied aircrews feared most over Germany: flak in 1941. German flak became even more powerful and dangerous later in the war.

23. Whitley bomber ditching in 1942, the crew already in the dinghy. (For one pilot's experience of coming down in the sea, see p. 49.)

24. The wreck of an RAF bomber shot down near Berlin in 1943. Aircrew sometimes managed to survive the most damaging crashes (see p. 64).

25. The Lysander over the Egyptian desert, practising collecting a message from the lorry below. Used for army cooperation, this aircraft was already out of date at the start of the war (see pp. 16–20).

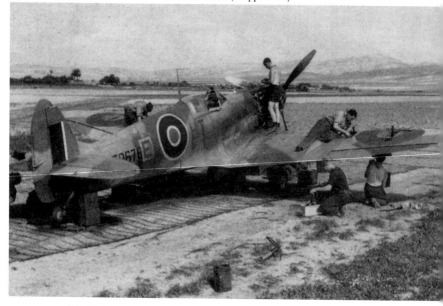

26. RAF fighter repair and maintenance men working in North Africa in 1943 (see pp. 200–203).

A Hurricane of 73 squadron crashed on its nose on its way to Cairo in December 1940. Many aircrew survived several crashes.

28. An electrical storm at Cairo lights up Handley Page Halifax IIIs in 1946. Weather could be as dangerous to aircraft as flak and enemy fighters (see pp. 48–49).

29. Looking tired and worried, the crew of a Stirling are debriefed after returning from a raid on Berlin in 1943. Berlin was one of the most feared enemy targets (see p. 134).

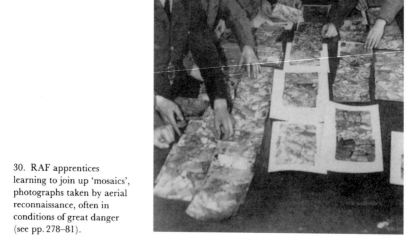

30. RAF apprentices learning to join up 'mosaics', photographs taken by aerial reconnaissance, often in conditions of great danger (see pp. 278–81).

# 6

# WOMEN WORKERS

As PRODUCTION EXPANDED ADDITIONAL WORKERS WERE needed to staff the factories. As men were called up they had to be replaced and supplemented by women. Some had already begun to enter aircraft factories before the war started. They came from all parts of the country and from many different backgrounds. *Mrs Tyrone* left her home in the north of England to look for work in the south. She found that a job at Vickers factory at Weybridge was a different world to the Lancashire textile industry in which she began her working life.

'I was a doffer in the mill. I left school when I was fourteen. The first day I went there I took my ball with me, thinking we'd have a playtime! We had a playtime all right! I got the sack from there. I says to the bloke, "You're not telling me what to do!"

'He said, "I'm your overlooker!"

'"I don't care where you overlook, but you're not telling me what to do, talking to me like that! I'm not here just for you to shout at, you know! I'm going home!" I put me coat on and went home. When I got there my mother said, "What are you doing home?"

'"I've walked out."

'"Well," she said, "you can just walk back again. If you don't, I'll drag you there by your hair!" So I had to go back!'

139

*'Did you get your job back?'*

'You can guess what I went through afterwards! But I didn't go through it silently, believe me. Then I went in the weaving shed. Place called Vantona, they used to make blankets and towels. Funnily enough, the woman on the looms in front of me used to go to the pictures and she'd tell me the whole story the next day! It was all lip-reading – I couldn't hear a word she was saying, especially with the looms going.

'I couldn't afford the pictures – I never had my father. I never knew where he was, so of course my mother didn't get widow's pension. She had four kids, I was the youngest, and she depended on our wages. Mind you, you daren't open your wage packet before you got home or you'd have got a bloody good hiding.

'I liked it up the weaving shed but it did get on your chest – it killed my eldest sister. She was thirteen years older than me. You walked in the place – bare feet, you never had shoes on because it was so hot. It was so oily the floor looked polished as though you'd just put a load of varnish on it. The cotton was like little worms – you didn't connect it then, I don't think anybody connected it. No extraction fans or anything like that. Wherever you looked – the lights were on – there were these little worms in the air!

'My mother had TB too. She got pneumonia so many times it was unbelievable. On her way to work she used to go down a back street, cough her heart out, bring blood up and then go on to work. She had it before I was born so they kept their eye on me. When my eldest sister was ill they took her in the hospital and the doctor said to her husband, "How many cigarettes does she smoke?"

' "She's never smoked a cigarette in her life!"

'The doctor said, "Her chest is absolutely riddled!" – as though she'd smoked about sixty fags a day.

' "Oh no," he said, "that'll be the cotton mill." She worked in the mill and he worked down the pit. Her lungs just gave out.

'When I started with this cough they thought I had contracted

TB. I wasn't getting enough to eat really, that was the base of it. I used to get tuppence for my dinner. We couldn't pay our rent. We did a moonlight. Well, that's what my mother had to do. We used to look for a house that was quarterly rent. You moved in and they didn't want no rent until the three months was up. About three days before we'd do a moonlight! We lived at Rochdale, Leeds, Bradford, Wigan, Todmorden, oh, we moved everywhere – I don't think we ever paid any rent. In Bolton I got one pound nine and thruppence a week, for me and me mother – she never got any other money but that.

'Once I got in hospital I never coughed once! The doctor used to come and look at me chart at the bottom of the bed and say to the nurse, "How many times did she cough in the night?"'

'She'd say, "Not at all, doctor!" I'd get underneath my bed-clothes, I felt such a fraud taking the food off 'em. I had three good meals a day there and a warm bed and that was what I wanted really.

'There used to be three of us on my money. Then we had the means-test man in and he said we were allowed eleven shillings each a week so he'd make my money up to thirty-three shillings. I said, "You won't because I'm off." My mother kept me up all night telling me not to talk to strange men because it was dreadful me going to London on my own. I don't blame her for being wary because I'd have been more than wary if I'd realized what was happening. We used to walk up and down Bradshawgate (*a main street in Bolton*) backwards and forwards, I don't know why – pick up blokes, I suppose! And yet there was nothing in it, you never did anything wrong in them days. My mother always said, "If you lose your virginity I can tell the minute you come in that door!" I used to look in the mirror and think, "Now I wonder how she can tell?" You believed every word they said, didn't you?

'I started at Vickers, must have been 1936. I came south to Aldershot first. I was sixteen. I went on the Naafi and had to tell a lie and say I was eighteen otherwise I couldn't have gone. I was a big girl for my age, you see. We were Naafi girls and being ignorant and Northern and green they thought we were there for

141

just one reason! We soon clamped down on that! When we got fed up of reporting them we packed it in. There were five of us and this girl Ethel on her half-day went down to Vickers and she got jobs for us all!

'When I got to Vickers I was on the wings of the Wellington bombers. I used to crawl inside and do the landing lights. You had the blue and the blue and the red and the red. We did that night and day. You had to be slim to get inside. We used to do about forty a day. It was quite interesting. Once you got in there you had the canvas over you – it was something like a Meccano set, the geodetics.

'The thing that annoyed me, that I did kick up a fuss about at the meetings, was that if they drilled a hole and it shouldn't have been drilled, they'd fill it with chewing gum. Oh yes, that was nothing. I used to say to 'em, "Boys' lives depend on that bloody hole that you've done there and bunged up with chewing gum!" But that was done the whole time I was there. I complained and complained and nothing was ever done about it. So it must have been, you know, standard procedure, I dunno.

'You'd walk through the factory and you'd know exactly which department everybody came from. If somebody was a bit of a leaner and he'd think, "Oh, I'll have a walk round the factory," he'd only to go past another door and they'd say, "What are you doing here? You don't belong here! Get back to your own department!", which was really very good. And then every Thursday morning, for them that didn't live in their own houses, they could have a bath! You didn't bring any towels or soap – everything was provided. No charge for the bath but you were only allowed half an hour. And six minutes in the toilet! They were knocking on your door – you used to give them your clocking-on number – mine was 295 – "Come on, 295!"

'I'd say, "Oh! What's the matter with you?"

'I lived in a bed-sitting-room – very very meagre. The old woman who run it, she was going on for ninety then, and she'd buried three husbands. When I complained I was cold in bed she said, "Well I don't know, those blankets were smashing fifty years ago!"

'I got sacked there twice, you know. I'm too outspoken, that's my trouble, I get in a lot of trouble with it. I started back the next day in another department –'

*'You just went in, without any difficulty?'*

'No, none. Not during the war. No problems at all. They were crying out for people. They must have had about twenty thousand working there during the war. The foreman was a woman, she was called Mrs Wood. She got the MBE after the war for her services to Vickers. I got very friendly with her later – I used to buy her a pint of beer in the working-men's club. She was one of these women that every word she said was 'f'. Even with the directors and everybody else. I was coming out that day and I started crying and the managing director stopped me to see if I'd had bad news. I said, "Not really, I've just got the sack."

'He said, "Oh, have you? What did you do?"

' "I hit Mrs Wood."

' "I've wanted to do that for the last ten years!"

' "Well, she's not saying 'f' to me! But I think I've cut off my nose to spite my face. I'm only in rooms and I've got my rent to pay!"

' "Oh," he said, "you start in the morning. You start in the tinsmiths." So of course I did do. I surrendered me green overalls for me blue ones.

'My sisters came down to work at Vickers. I came down and they all followed me, both my sisters and my brother-in-law. He used to push the cotton waste in these big vats in Bolton and he got dermatitis through his fingers. It went nearly all over his body. His toes and everything. He got three hundred pounds' compensation so with that he came down. He found a flat and a job.

'My sister is five years older than me, very North-country, very thick. She said to me one day in the factory, "That woman over there's getting a penny an hour more than me!"

'I said, "Perhaps she's doing a more important job than you and me. What's a penny an hour?"'

'She says, "I'm not having it!" She went up to the foreman – he was talking to some high-up people because they had good suits on and attaché cases. They were in a little circle, about four of them, and the foreman with the white coat on. She said, "Excuse me, but that woman over there is getting a penny an hour more than me!"'

'He said, "Don't worry, my dear! We'll give you tuppence an hour!" Things like that she used to do. You'd think to yourself, oh, I'll see him in a minute but not when he's talking like that. Oh no, she pushed right in the middle of them and spoke to him. What she didn't know was I was getting fourpence an hour more than her! She still doesn't know!

'I met my husband there. He came down from Bolton to find a job. There were seven of them, hadn't been working for ages! I didn't know him in Bolton, I'd no idea. When we went up the pub on the Sunday night the landlord said to me, "Do they want anybody at Vickers?" This was before the war. He said, "Them blokes have got an interview tomorrow" – they all got a job! My husband went in the rolling mill. The metal was in a black roll and he'd put it through what they called a mill and shape it. It was a very tiring job, like turning a mangle for two hours.

'Funnily enough about six weeks before the bombs dropped they'd put a notice up in the surgery. Anybody who wanted to join the first aid could have two hours, from nine to eleven every Thursday, and come down for instructions. I thought to myself, two hours off work and get paid for it! So I joined and I can't stand the sight of blood.

'My mother was living with me then. We used to hear the German bombers coming over and she'd say to me, "Can you hear that noise?" You could tell the difference between our bombers and theirs. An' I said, "Yes, it's searchlights going round. What they're doing, the searchlights are on a kind of a handcart and they're driving round the streets. If they hear a noise they put it in the sky" – she believed anything like that. I mean, she

144

never knew. I thought if anything did happen and the bombs did drop she wouldn't know what was happening. It was dreadful to have to lay in bed and listen to 'em, knowing there were German bombers coming over.

'It was either the first or the third of September, a beautiful day. They had soldiers and an anti-aircraft gun, but this particular day they got very lackadaisical and the old shift went off and the new shift hadn't come on. There wasn't anybody on the guns. The Germans just came, dropped their bombs and went. We had no warning, nothing. There were three blokes on the toilet! By the time they got 'em out *rigor mortis* had set in so you can guess what a sight they were. People you'd worked with from seven o'clock in the morning till half past twelve were killed. It all depended which part of the factory you were in. Had it been another twenty minutes we'd all have been in and it would have been a lot worse.

'At first they wouldn't let anybody in. But it came over the Tannoy would all the first aiders come in. Oh, there was a hell of a queue of minor things – even where I worked it was a glass ceiling and you got the blast. They said you take that queue and you take that queue – they were all more or less minor scratches. You just put a bandage on – I'd passed my exam by then – we used iodine in them days. Then this boy come and he was holding his ear like that and the blood was just coming down his fingers – he was about sixteen. I said, "What have you done?" He took his hand away and he'd a big hole in his head. I could see all inside his head, in that instant. That was my lot! I dropped on the floor and they just rolled me under the table! When I came round I was no use. I was as white as a sheet, I was shaking.

'Later on they were running from place to place to find their dead and injured. They didn't know where they were taken to. Even Woking came into it because they had mortuaries there and people kept saying have you tried Woking, and have you tried such a place.

'After that you were scattered all over the place. They'd confiscate garages and put machinery in. You'd have your own little clock to clock in and out and they'd come and pick up what you'd done and bring you more raw materials. It was very well organized, I'll give 'em that. We took over Walton Studios and I worked there.

'They opened a nursery, ninepence a day. My eldest was the first one there: I was waiting for it to open. She had about five nurses looking after her for quite a while, and then it got really packed. You'd no excuse if you'd only one child and it wasn't school age – you could go to the nursery. One thing they didn't have at Vickers was part-timers. So you couldn't go while your kids were at school, like nine to four. No, you had to work your seven days a week and twelve hours a day. It was either from seven to seven or eight to eight. You could do either but that machine was never stopped. The minute you'd finished at seven or eight somebody came and did the night shift, and you had to do a month about. A month on days and a month on nights. We used to do it alternately. If my husband was on days I'd be on nights because of the kids and the sirens.

'I've been back to the factory since although I live in Tooting now. They found a Wellington bomber in a loch and I got invited to go over to Weybridge to see it. I called in and saw one or two people that I used to know there. It was in the experimental shop. They'd cleared it all out. The place is beautiful now – we never worked in them conditions. You never washed your hands till it was time to go home, you had germs and all. *Now* there was even fitted carpets in the toilets! It's beautiful now. Everything was altogether different.'

*Maureen Day* began work as a wages clerk at Hawker's factory in Kingston in 1940. She still lives in the same house as she did then, though now the neighbourhood has become 'yuppified'. 'It used to be so friendly round here, but now nobody speaks. You wouldn't believe how it's changed!'

'I was seventeen. We used to analyse the wage sheets for the factories – there were quite a few. I think the average pay would be about £8 a week which was quite good money in those days. We had to go to the bank, get the money and check the right amount was there. We had huge great bags, big as cricket bags, to carry it.'

'*You walked?*'

'No, we had a limousine. And that was lovely because we were chauffeur-driven. You can imagine the likes of wartime with a chauffeur and four young girls in a car. We used to get booed and hooted and God knows what, really!'

'*They thought you were idle aristocrats?*'

'Yes, right! And we didn't let on. There were five of us in a small office and we used to share all the cards that came from the wages office. Bonus cards and wage sheets and things like that, and pay out the men as well. They were horrid cards, a sixteenth of a penny, an eighth of a penny. We were not allowed to give them a fiver – the old big white fivers – unless they had eight pounds. Seven pounds and less, they had to have pound notes. In those days it wasn't easy to change a five-pound note.

'We used to work through the air raids. We were given a medal for that. A big round blue one with a ribbon on, worn with pride! We didn't know then that the men used to dive into the shelter! Quite often they'd be in the shelter the whole time the air raid was on, and we'd be working away like mad.'

'*Why did you carry on working?*'

'Well, somebody had to get the wages out. They wouldn't work without. If they were a halfpenny out they'd know and come and knock on the door. Bear in mind we worked every day. Only Christmas Day off. I think at one time when we did night work, we had one day off a week, either Saturday or Sunday. We had to work nights to get the men's money out. It was absolutely essential that the money was ready. Don't forget that they were paid weekly. And by Jove there were a lot of them. It was just a continuation. As you finished paying out on Friday, you started all over again, on Monday. Another job we had, stamping the insurance cards! Oh! I hated that. We used to spend hours on Sunday afternoon – bump, bump, bump! Cancelling all the cards, hundreds of them.'

*'I didn't know wages clerks worked nights!'*

'Oh yes. It was very lonely because there were only two of us in the whole office! Very lonely! You didn't ever come in contact with the factory, you had to go through quite a long way to get to them. We could hear them, we knew they were there. In the office we had the AID (*an inspector*). Honestly, I think if a German had said "Boo!" he'd have died of fright, but he was going to protect us girls! He had a gun, yes oh yes. He was the one that guarded the money.

'We were all there under sufferance when you think about it. We couldn't leave. I wanted to join the Wrens, I wanted to join the Land Army. They wouldn't entertain the idea at all. Even though I went and got my papers for both. No! We just had to work there. What we did, we used to wash our hair sometimes because hot water wasn't easy to get during the war. You were only allowed so many inches of bath water. We used to wash our hair and rinse it and put the fires on the desks and dry our hair while we were working. Our boss used to phone us up to see how we were getting on. We'd gee up and bash away at the machines and make noises as if we were phoning somebody, but we did work, believe you me.

'And we were so badly paid! The union representative came round and said, "Do you realize you don't get very much money?"

'We said, "Well, there's a war on!"

'They said, "You don't have to get as little as that! If you join the Transport and General –" so we did and we did get a rise! I'd started at nineteen shillings. I gave my mother twelve and I had to pay fares and lunches and clothe myself out of what was left.

'I was thinking back to when the first bombs dropped. The air-raid warning went. We finished at half past five and the all-clear

148

hadn't gone at six o'clock. We were getting worried: it was very late. I got to Kingston station and there were no trains because of the bombs. I said, "What bombs?" We hadn't had any. We'd heard this funny noise whilst we were in the shelter, but it was brick-built, very heavy doors, and every time there was a crump we said, "Oh, someone's banging on the door!" It never entered our head it was bombing.

'I had to come home by bus that night, and when I *did* get home, my brother said, "Did you see the craters?" I remember thinking, what's a crater? Whatever would it be like? It was pretty frightening. But you never thought of not going to work. I wonder what people would do today.

'We lived here then, in Battersea. The siren used to go before I left the office. Trains were in complete darkness. My father was doing warden duty at the time. We often used to cross each other. As I came from the Junction he was going to his post. I remember him saying, "If you do hear a bomb, for heaven's sake don't run towards it! Stay *still*!" I was under the arch at Clapham Junction and heard these bombs whizzing down! I thought to myself, "What the devil did he tell me to do?" I couldn't for the life of me remember.

'We were machine-gunned one lunchtime! Along Elm Road there was a sweet-shop, and sweets were very scarce. My friend Kathleen and I went to get some and as we stood at the shop we heard this plane coming along. It was so low it was unbelievable. We stood in this shop doorway and I said, "Gosh! It's coming along the road! Do you think it's coming down?"

'The young fellow that was serving said, "It's not one of ours!"

' "You're joking!"

'But he'd disappeared, he was under the counter. Kathleen and I stood there and I said to her – it was so low that we saw the pilot – "God! It *isn't* one of ours!" Then it started machine-gunning us so we dived into the shop. He went around machine-gunning quite a few places in Kingston. When I got back to the office old Potty – all nicknames you see – Miss Potter came in and she was furious. She said, "I was walking across the road and this silly man threw me into the gutter! Look at my suit!"

'I said, "Yes, but you were being machine-gunned!"

'She said, "I don't know about that! I might have missed that! Look at the state of my suit!" Clothes were so scarce in those days!

'As soon as I left Clapham Junction I used to run because in those days they wouldn't open the subways and let you come in. I used to fall in the front door and go oh! oh! dive under the table and have something to eat. I used to get my head under the table as soon as I arrived home. Then I used to go to bed, I was so tired. Towards the end of the war I had to do fire-watching, which meant that once I got home I had to go to the post, if there was a warning. If there was a purple alert. There were so many fires it was unbelievable. They used to drop an incendiary before they dropped the bomb. The whole sky used to be alight sometimes.

'What used to worry me was my mother. She used to say, "Oh, I'm not coming, I'm too tired, I'm going to stay in bed!" and you'd hear the bombs falling. The doodle-bugs were ghastly. Living here we were a right target. A rocket actually dropped on the church over there. That's when most of my wedding presents went for a burton. We had a young serviceman and his wife staying here. Their baby was buried in his cot.'

*'Was he killed?'*

'No, he came out almost laughing! This house absolutely shook like mad, it *moved*, it's never been the same since. I've spent thousands on this place. Downstairs we had a beautiful bay window. The doodle-bugs and the bombs shifted it. Every time there was a bomb at the back, the whole lot would shift out, the whole structure. We'd push it back and do all sorts of things. We didn't have windows for years, not proper ones, because they were blasted out. As soon as we had them in they were blown out again. It was incredible that the houses stood up round here. They're pretty strong. They're just over a hundred years old.

'The war was horrific but we had lots of fun. I suppose you

have to. We used to go skating and dancing. We did a lot of dancing. It was lovely music, soft and sentimental. Sometimes there wasn't a man there under sixty or over fourteen. We'd go to the Grosvenor, to the tea dances there. They were half a crown and you got a cup of tea, a biscuit and a scone. Lovely dancing! And *there* you'd quite often get servicemen. Don't forget I had a young man in the forces so you *daren't* look at another man! You really didn't.

'If we missed the last train the soldiers gave us a lift all the way home, and they really were gentlemen as far as we were concerned. When I look back we were so naïve in those days, it's unbelievable. I'd get in the train at Kingston, and the train would be in complete darkness. An old gentleman one day shone his torch at me and said, "You're not very old, are you?"

'I said, "No."

'He said, "You'll be *shattered* by the time you're thirty! Your nerves will be in absolute shreds! You can't take this as a young girl!" The siren had gone, you see. He looked at me and stared, and I thought, I don't think so! (*Laughs*.)

'I left Hawker's when I married – they wouldn't employ married women. Unless they kept it secret. You just took it all in your stride. When my daughter was eighteen, twenty, I used to say, "You're not going there!" and I'd think, well what did I do at seventeen? We went all over the place during the war, and no lights, and it was all right. You'd never think, I can't go. But *now* I don't go outside the door after six o'clock, unless I have a taxi. I used to go to evening class, but I won't even do that now! It's all wrong, isn't it? It's all wrong.'

*Mrs Connor* began working in the aircraft industry when her family left the East End during the Blitz and went to stay with relatives in Slough. Like Maureen Day she found she was in a reserved occupation and couldn't leave.

'What I remember about the war is you couldn't sit out and get fresh air. The roof was camouflaged, the windows were darkened, so were the fanlights. When you worked long hours it was claustrophobic – horrible. It was a very grey period, wasn't it? We weren't allowed out. You couldn't leave the premises. You weren't allowed to sit down. You often tried but you had to stand up all the time. Some of them did suffer with varicose veins, but I was lucky, I was one of the younger ones.

'I went to work at P. D. Cowl's on the Slough Trading Estate. I first went there when our house was bombed and we left the East End. We made dinghies for aircraft so I learned rigging. I was taught by an ex-naval rating, wonderful old man. P. D. Cowl's originally made Lilos, that's probably how they got the contract.

'We also did the tanks for various planes like Spitfires, Halifaxes, Lancasters and Mosquitoes. They came in to us just metal and we coated them with a cotton fabric. It had several coats of latex over plus canvas, and these were then doped. As it was a reserved occupation we had to stay.

'When we changed over to injection moulding it was very hot. There were presses and it meant standing in that heat. We didn't wear uniform, we just wore our own overalls and we had to use Rosalex – it's a barrier cream. Our clothes were dreadful and our food because everything smelt of rubber. When we started getting the American tanks from planes that had been damaged to be recovered, we were struck how superior they were to ours.

'Later on we started doing the long-range tanks for the bombers, and we also had to make special tanks for jettisoning. Small tanks. We worked in twos, with another girl. A few men worked there. The latex rubber was done by a man, and the lifting and moving. They got paid quite a bit more than us, it could even have been double. We never objected because they had families to keep.

'When we did the long-range tanks they were twenty-two feet long. It was semi-skilled work. The patterns were cut out, like a tailor would cut them out, and I covered the tanks. You had the pattern and shaped it round, overlapped it, so the different coats were different sizes, and then as I say they were covered with canvas and dope. It was mostly handwork, no machines. The main tools were a brush, solution, and scissors. With the cutting my hands suffered, that's one of the reasons the doctor thinks I've got this problem with them now. The rubber was quite thick and it's caused ridges to appear on my hands.

'Sometimes they asked us to work till ten o'clock at night – the manager would tell us the planes were waiting at Weybridge to take off. We were all very patriotic and we did it. On occasions we worked seven days a week. But not the whole time. Our normal time was eight to six with half an hour lunch, and eight till one Saturday. One week's holiday a year. I started at fifteen shillings a week. Most of the women were older than me – their day consisted of working hard, going home, hoping there was a letter from their husband or fiancé. Any infidelity was very much frowned upon.

'I was in my teens when I went there. You weren't a teenager, you left school at fourteen a child, and in your teens you were treated like dirt. There wasn't this idea, now, that the young people are the ones who matter, you counted for nothing till you were about twenty. And this was also true in the family. You knew at work that you couldn't answer back. If you did answer back you'd get the sack, and you just accepted that you were young and inexperienced.

'People came from various parts of the country, lots from Ireland, Wales, Lancashire, Manchester, don't remember any from Scotland. I know that distance lends enchantment but we never had any of this North–South divide. It was talking to people from Durham and various places that made me want to go there. We were a very motley crowd. We had girls from Eton college who had been in service, Windsor Castle, people who had never worked before. Occasionally there'd be a crack about an accent, but it was nothing like the nastiness that seems to exist today. I find it all very sad.

'We had the Slough social centre – that was a wonderful outlet, a huge complex. If you worked on the trading estate it was cheaper for you to be a member. There was billiards, dancing, badminton, skating and swimming. Troops used to come over

153

from Windsor, the guards, so there were always lots of partners. You could get something to eat very glamorous like beans on toast or Welsh rarebit if you were lucky. We had industrial concerts for a shilling and *Music While You Work*. These marches were played and it was usually fast to help you to work faster.

'Our work had to be inspected by the AID inspectors. I don't know how they were recruited because they were so incompetent. No seams of latex could overlap, there had to be about a two-inch difference in case a bullet penetrated. These things were worked out very carefully. Each coat had to be inspected and stamped but the inspectors didn't know what they were looking for! We had to tell them. We were really concerned because we wanted to do a good job. We knew men's lives depended on it, and we didn't think it was right.

'From time to time handsome young airmen would come and jump on a table and tell us what a wonderful job we were doing. It was supposed to boost morale but I think it was a curiosity factor really. We also had Princess Marina come to see us and she was very nice, took a great deal of interest. But in the Slough paper it said a surprise visit was made by Princess Marina. Well, weeks ahead everything was being cleaned and polished, and we had flowers in the canteen so we knew something was happening.

'Our London died with the bombing. Our house was so badly damaged we got frightened and wanted to go away. This is my home – or it was (*showing photos, the house decked up in bunting for a church ceremony*). This was the last village procession before the house was bombed. It was like a fête, the band would come round, ice-cream sellers were there, people would decorate the houses on the route and your friends would line the pavements. They were small terraces, you can see how small the houses were, how close, this house and the house next to it. We moved out because there was a time bomb in the back. The air-raid shelter was hit and these people here (*standing in front of their houses*) were all killed.

'My family worked in the docks, my father's father and his father – they were ship's blacksmiths. At that time they walked across fields to go to the docks. My aunt used to tell me they carried red handkerchiefs with their dinner inside. When people moved from the little houses into flats, somehow it changed, people became more suspicious. There was a dignity among the working-class people which doesn't exist in the suburbs over in the West. People weren't on Christian-name terms, it was always Mrs Walker or whatever. You waited for your friends outside – you never walked in each other's homes, but my grandmother would wash and lay anybody out. Most houses were small terraced houses with two families in so people shared a scullery and an outside lavatory. You had to respect each other's privacy, it was very special, but the caring and sharing was very strong.

'I love this time of year because we used to go hop-picking then. That was our holiday. Early in the year you wrote to the farm where you were going to see if you would be accepted. When the letters came back, the various kids down the streets would be asking, "Have you heard yet? Have you?" We started running errands and saving up things like tins of condensed milk, packets of tea, then when the hops were ready the farmer would write, usually some time in August, and the excitement down the road about going to various farms! It gave me a love of the country I've never lost.

'Originally we went by lorry but when we got posher we went by coach. The men didn't go – they might come down at the weekend. There was some lovely people there, gypsies, people from Sussex, but they kept to their own meadow. They had tents and we had huts. People sat round the fire at night. My grandmother used to tell ghost stories, and the women made plum duff on the open fires. We had to collect faggots to light them. We slept in corrugated huts and my grandmother used to wall-paper them with flour and have a curtain up. The floor was white limed, just earth, and there was a wooden base with straw loops so you took your own palliasse, filled it up with straw. But we did enjoy it, we did enjoy it!

'It was hard work. We used to have cold tea in a pot which we took out and drank from a tin lid and that tea tasted like nectar!

In the morning the hops were heavy with dew, and they're very rough, your hands got very black. We used newspapers to eat our sandwiches, cheese sandwiches, and we'd go round to the oast house to get charcoals to clean our hands. On Sundays we walked three miles from the farm to mass. One Sunday, when we came out, the sirens went. When we got back all the huts were empty. They were all hiding up in the woods because they thought the Germans were coming over.

'You never went up West, you never came over to this part of London. The City of London was our world, our horizon. My husband lived in Poplar and we lived in Plaistow – Poplar's not as good as Plaistow! In the old East End families the grandmother was the pivot. It was like a series of villages.

'All of us left. My mother and father and I lived with my grandmother. We all moved, my sister and my two aunts – my aunt from Poplar, they also came. My brother-in-law said, "My sister lives in Slough, she'll put us up!" so we just went there. She opened the door and thirteen of us slept on the living-room floor. She didn't turn a hair.

'We had to start looking for digs. We moved around to different places where we could find rooms. It was pretty rough really. My grandmother got a house so my mother and father, my aunt and myself all moved in. My grandfather sat there with his huge armchair and his spittoon which he took great delight in – copper it was. He got a job in a car park. A lot of the bosses were reduced to bikes and if he didn't get a tip he'd throw the bike down! He was a real East Ender. He used to go to sea originally and then he became a stevedore. He was very generous – if he had it. He had an accident in the docks – he was picked up and dropped into the hold. It took a long time but he got about £300 compensation, and by the time he got the money practically all of it was owed to the bookmaker. It had all gone on fourpenny and sixpenny bets!

'At the end of the war I was extremely tired. Extremely tired. I was only twenty. On one occasion I was feeling very ill. We had a resident nurse, it was compulsory, and she said to me, "I'll have to take you home!" I had flu very badly, and when I say flu, not the kind we often say when we've got a touch of cold, I was too ill to go upstairs. I just lay on the couch. I couldn't lift my head up so it must have been pretty bad. My father always thought that it was wrong the hours we worked, especially being so young. I remember the tiredness and the women complaining terribly about their legs because of the standing and the long long walks to and from work.'

*Wanda Hart* also worked in Slough, at a factory which made propellers, shell-cases and pistons for many of the leading aircraft companies.

'I liked the factory. I was fourteen and I drifted into the print-room. I was the first girl to work there. They'd always had boys straight from school before – they'd considered it was a boys' job.

'Took me quite a while to learn. I don't know if you've ever seen a printing machine that prints on tracers, have you? It whizzes round ever so fast, big roll of yellow paper, and it goes in through rollers, going at a terrific speed. It lights up green, like a photocopier, which takes the photograph on to the blueprint. You've got to cut across the paper with a razor and when you started it all got jammed up. I got all creases like a concertina, but after a while you just go whoosh! like that. You don't think you're ever going to master it, but I got quite quick on that.

'It was all a bit secret, you didn't really know what you were doing things for. Everybody was doing bits, but you didn't really know how it was going to work out. They had a teleprinter sort of chuntering away. That's how they communicated with the other branches – Redditch, High Wycombe – because it was secret work. Everybody was on their guard a bit. If they saw somebody who was strange. People were very aware.

'We had security on the gates. When you were in, you were in! You couldn't get out. You had to get a pass scrutinized. Bit like a prison. "Where are you going? How long are you going to be?"

157

And *that* was my little pass! (*Gives me a rubber pass-holder, with a chain and a disc attached.*)

'Each week you used to have a different-coloured card to put in there with your name so that they knew you were working there. Nobody else could get a pass and get in because the colour changed each week – pink, green. You couldn't use last week's card because they'd be immediately suspicious. Every week had a different colour. The card came in your wage packet. And the number on the disc is your trench number – which is thirteen! (*Laughs.*) They called 'em trenches – air-raid shelters. Brick-built, you went down steps to them. I went in to have a look but I never went in because of an air raid.

'The Germans knew there was a big place at Slough, at the trading estate, that's why they had all the balloons at Langley, to safeguard the place from the air. We had the paraffin smoke-screen too. I used to wake up in the morning, all black round here (*her mouth and nose*). They say smoking's bad for you but when you think of that – black fog! Your clothes used to get all dirty, and your underwear, you know, the white – it went a grey colour. And it didn't come out when you washed. It was when there was moonlight. We used to dread a moon.

'I had this braid in my hair – I thought if the Germans invaded I had my hair like a Fräulein! I thought being a blonde, I'd be all right with the Germans. And Wanda's my name – a German-Slavic name – I thought I'll be all right. I had my hair up in plaits, you know, I'm Wanda, fair – we didn't know if they were going to beat us, did we, then! They could have done. If it hadn't been for the atom bomb we probably wouldn't have won. It was only the atom bomb really, wasn't it, that finished the war?

'We used to do quite long hours, Saturdays and Sundays too. I started at twelve and sixpence a week and then I got five shillings extra because I worked Saturday afternoon. If I didn't do that I was supposed to do Sunday morning – I got five shillings for that! I gave it to my mother and she used to give me two and six back, pocket money. She wasn't very philanthropic, my mother, bit Victorian. It was also rushy work, you know, everything was wanted yesterday. They told me afterwards that because there was a girl in the print-room they should put a stool in. No. They wouldn't allow it.'

'*No stool?*'

'No. Because I'd be sitting down. I was standing from half past eight in the morning till six o'clock at night. Yes. They wouldn't let me sit down, would they? We did get a break in the morning – they'd bring you tea round on a trolley but you'd carry on working, just sip your tea while you were working. I suppose they might have thought that being a girl you might have your off days, but no. That was that. Today, would they allow that? Goodness! When I look back – but we didn't really think anything of it. But I never asked for a stool!'

'*Who did?*'

'I suppose the welfare office. It was lovely having the clinic there because they dealt with quite bad injuries. I used to get flu a lot, real flu, not a mild cold. When the heating went off you had to sit there with your coat and gloves on, so you could type. Sit there with a scarf on, coat, a pixie hat! I used to cycle to work – everybody cycled – no cars – bit like Holland – racks everywhere for bikes. I remember I used to cycle to work feeling *ghastly*! I'd go down the clinic and the doctor would see me, give me a hot cup of Bovril or Oxo, take my temperature, certificate and send me home. That was all right but you had to get there. No cars to take you, go on your bike, and your temperature – hot and cold!

'High Duty Alloys was very noisy. They had their own generators. What a noise! Dreadful! And at the side of them was what they called the stamp-shop which had these massive hammers – wham! The largest one could be heard for about three miles' radius at night. So you had noise, you had dirt – your ears got blocked with hard wax. You woke up in the morning and picked it out to get it clear – they were always dragging us down the clinic to have that done. And black dust – you couldn't *see* across that foundry! When I look back – no masks, safety glasses, or anything! You used to get black – your nostrils used to get dirty (*indicates black stains on her lips*). You know, my brother and father – we were always trucking down to the clinic!

'They had a works canteen and a staff canteen. I was in the staff canteen but I preferred the works'! I didn't like snobbery, I didn't like it. I used to play the piano – I still do – and the BBC came down to audition, a talent show. There was tap-dancers! It seems a bit camp now when you look back! If you could play a piano you were wanted everywhere then. Oh, can you play the piano! I played "Nola" – what a piece to play! (*Laughs.*) Oh, I thought I was so clever playing on this piano! "Nola"! If I'd played some wartime song it would have been better. "When the Light Go On!" or "We'll Meet Again!" I don't think anything came of that! There wasn't enough talent!

'I belonged to a concert party and we used to go to entertain the Americans. They were *marvellous*! They're always very enthusiastic, aren't they? Enthuse over nothing at all! Oh, great audiences they were. I had a boy-friend then and he was a singer – he could take off Frank Sinatra. "You'd be so nice to come back to!" – and they really roared! I used to accompany him. They'd come and pick us up by lorry and I don't know to this day where we went. Of course they'd doughnuts! Oh, doughnuts! Lovely they were – and cigarettes. They gave us a coupon for five cigarettes each week enclosed in our wage packet. Any new girl started, the older men used to be after her for the voucher. They thought you were a bit naïve, you know. New girl, I'll get her! We all smoked. Everybody smoked. Relax – first thing they do is give you a cigarette. It was always a cigarette when you were in trouble.

'After a while they wanted a typist in the rate-fixing. They were all men in there, about twelve of them. They used to go to all the different departments. When I went for the interview they warned me, you'll probably hear strong language, but that didn't bother me. I just turned a deaf ear and did my job, and I remained there until I left, which was after the war. Things had eased a bit then. During the war it was all go! Nobody stopped to talk, chat or strike. No pettiness, we just used to knuckle down. Bit different to how it is today! They used to go out with the clipboard, do the timing, come back and then it'd all be typed up. It was all tables.'

*'Were they popular?'*

'No, no! Gosh no! They used to boo them right from the time when they appeared. They were the most unpopular department because the workers knew when they came out they was going to have to go faster, do more work, and they didn't get more money. They used to fix the rate for an hour and they were only talking about ha'pennies, farthings then!'

*'They must have been brave men –'*

'They could look after themselves. They had to. As soon as they altered the rate so the men had to do more, in came the representatives. That was when the rumpus used to start, that was why they warned me before I started there'd be a lot of blue language about, and there was! Oh yes! Really heated arguments. They would argue the toss that they couldn't do that! You know, *you* don't know anything about it because you're not doing the job! Which was true really. It's like if you're running and some-body says you can run faster – you think you know what you're capable of, don't you?'

*'What was the outcome? Who won?'*

'Oh the ratefixers. Yes.'

*'Did their unpopularity spread to the office staff?'*

'Um, I don't think I did so badly because I was a young lady. If I'd been an old lady I might have copped it! But being young I got away with it. And I used to mingle with the factory workers. A lot of the office wouldn't, they were a bit class – they used to think they were a bit above them. But I didn't, I liked the workers. The girls used to go about in pairs there! The men'd get hold of

161

your hand and say, "Put it in my pocket!" – it upset some of them, but I just used to laugh it off, I was a bit broad-minded I think. I wasn't brought up broad-minded but I turned out to be. But it used to frighten some of the girls. You had to be on your guard. It was mostly older men did things like that. Very young men didn't. Well, they seemed to be older to me then – I suppose they were about forty perhaps. When you're a teenager, thirty's old, isn't it?

'We had scandals there. Pregnancies. We used to say, she's getting a bit fat! And she's not married! Their husbands were away in the forces. Lot of hungry females about. They got pregnant and they had to go through with it – you didn't get abortions in those days. Only back streets. Get on the old gin bottle, hot baths. We all knew what to do.

'These men were only working there because they were on war work, or else they'd have been in the forces, wouldn't they? I mean, really, a lot of people used to call them cowards because they worked there. There were quite a few fights. My husband was in the army and he hated them. Well, I said, somebody had to do the war work. But some of them did try to avoid the call-up by working in an aircraft factory. My husband still has that attitude today.

'When you read today that there's something new, they think they're doing something different – all these articles in the *Sun* about how I lost my virginity at fourteen. The young ones say, oh, let's get a flat somewhere, we'll go on the game. We used to discuss it forty years ago, especially at factories like that.

'I think there were quite a few prossies there. They were in the piston bay and inspection. Blondes – they all had to be blondes then, if you were a gangster's moll (*laughs*). They had to wear their hair in a turban, no hair flowing because of the machinery. Turban it was, or snoods. The prossies were bottle blondes. I used to look at them dressing themselves up – I wasn't but I used to like to think I could be one. It was what my mother disagreed with – she said I looked like a tart. That was what I *did* want to look like! You know, things were so miserable and dowdy. The coats I wore were made out of blankets, army blankets, that was the coat I used to wear to work. My mother was a dressmaker and she made my best coat out of grey blankets, *grey*! Put all red buttons down the front. And knitted red gloves.

'I had to get away. I thought I'd go back when I was twenty-one. That was so I could live my own life. That's what I did. Yep. I'll be better off. Late teens. I thought, I get it at work and I get it at home – I'll get out of it. Although it was worse really, it made me stand on my two feet. When I went back it was, "Oh! You've changed! You've got hard!" I didn't really get hard, I got tougher. I learned to stand on my own two feet.

'The factory's just been pulled down. It didn't close down, it was pulled down. Last week when we drove past we said, "Oho! High Duty Alloys has gone!" Do-It-Yourself going up. Until then it was just as it was when I left. It's sad because it's memories that have gone, you know. An era. There was patriotism. They'd never put up with the conditions today! They'd collapse! They couldn't stand it! They couldn't go without their food, their drink, their sweets, could they? I don't think they'd survive today. *I* could, but I don't think these young ones could, do you?'

As it became apparent that the war would be a long one, and all resources would have to be mobilized, the aircraft industry drew in subcomponents manufacturers all over the country. Women who had never worked before sought jobs making planes to help the war effort. *Mrs Becker* was the wife of an airman who was killed early in the war. She went to live with her parents in a small country town in the Midlands.

'I suppose, like all widows, I hadn't been trained for anything. My parents had lived abroad, I was sent home to boarding school and I went back to the Middle East where we lived. No one ever thought I would need a job, which I didn't! I married and that was that. And then I suddenly found myself a widow! I said I've got to have a job, to earn some money.

'There was an advertisement in the old local paper saying they wanted to make up a night-shift of part-time voluntary workers at Westbourne Engineering, a factory in the town. My husband had always been regular air force so that was what I wanted to do. I called and saw the managing director of the firm. We chatted a little bit and I said I want to do this, something for the war. Oh, the weeks went by and I heard nothing so I called again. He said he hadn't enough volunteers to make up a shift. I was very disappointed.

'Then he sent for me one day and offered me the job of being a personnel officer in charge of the women. I said, "I can't do this. I haven't a clue!"

'But he said, "I know you can do it!"

'Well, the war effort urged me on and I agreed.

'Jock (*the managing director*) was a compulsive worker and if he had an idea at two in the morning he wanted to do it. My parents used to get furious. He would ring the house and say, "Would you send Mrs Becker round at once, I've just had a brilliant idea!" My mother used to get very angry and say, "She's fast asleep!"

' "Well, wake her up! I'm awake!"

'You wouldn't do it for a lot of people, would you, but immediately Mummy came into my bedroom and said, "Shall I say you're not going round?" I'd say, "Of course I'm going round!" He had that effect on people. Over the years I was with him he seemed to be able to get the right people or the right atmosphere.

'He never went on to the shop floor without his hat on. He used to wear a black Homburg and if he was going on to the shop floor he always put it on. Perhaps it's a tradition of owners, they always go around with their hats on?

'The firm was a family affair! We all knew each other well. People like myself who had nothing to do with the shop floor – except I was welfare so I was always walking around – we all knew one another and respected one another. I suppose it was unique. It was my only experience of a factory but I can't imagine – I suppose smaller ones were like that, you're not a number, you're a name, everybody knows you. Now I've been away from the town but when I come back people come up to me and I know their faces so well. Of course they're Westbourne Engineering, we can go back, and we're so pleased to see each other, it really is lovely. Quite uplifting. We were a family in every sense of the word.

'We had some excellent engineers there, there's no doubt – wonderful, wonderful engineers! Give them a lathe and they could turn out anything – go and get their blueprint – whereas these days they just press buttons. As for me, I used to be a jack of all trades really. I did all the wages, I was in charge of the canteen, I engaged labour and kept all personnel records. Anyone coming for an interview, I would do the interviewing.

'I was about twenty-six, I suppose. I had no idea I could do it. I remember because I thought I looked too young I used to screw my hair up. I used to wear it in a roll in those days and I'd roll it up tightly because I was dealing with men. Well, first of all I handled the women, and then Jock sent me to Nottingham University. I did three long weekend courses on personnel management, and that was the only training I had! (*Laughs*.) I was awfully lucky, I don't know what it was but I was good on assessing men and quite often if I said a man was going to be useful, it turned out that I was right.

'The women had no engineering experience, but they are very adaptable. It was wonderful, really terrific! They were making very small aircraft components. They were on the mills, and I had to make sure – women will have bits of hair out of their hats, so I used to be on the shop floor a lot, looking for that sort of thing. Women will have scarves and things and it was very dangerous.

'Another worrying thing was seeing that they wore goggles on jobs because of swarf flying off at different angles. And with the men, making sure they were using the guards that were provided – if you hadn't got the guard on you can usually work faster. The women were bad about guards because it shortened their bonuses. Also people hesitate to come up to the office to see you, if they've got a problem, but if you're walking by a machine a man will say, "Oh, have you got a moment to spare?" and you might be able to help him.

'Sometimes there were *private* things – I've had husbands come to me who were in the army or the air force. The neighbours had told them their wife was misbehaving, and they'd come to me for help, if I could help them sort it out. It was all very sad.

'I did have awful problems with the married women on shifts – nobody wanted the two to ten shift. They had families and it was very very difficult. At the last minute you'd get notes, you know, saying they couldn't come. All the machines were linked to one another and it meant your production was going to be less in the morning. I could send out – I had one or two strings to my bow, people who couldn't work permanently but who would come in.

'We had this marvellous feeling, it's never been the same since. People wanted to do things. We'd do the full day in the factory, and then I was an ambulance driver – that meant directly the sirens went I was out on foot to collect my ambulance. Fire-watching two nights a week, up and down this avenue, all through the night, till the next person came out. When you think what we did, we never thought that it was anything that we would grumble about. My father was in the Home Guard and on Sundays I was his driver so I was doing something then as well. I used to drive him to the rifle ranges. We had no lives of our own. Everything we did was something for the war effort. But it was wonderful because of this spirit of co-operation.

'I had some women directed from one of the canal villages, from the barges. Sarah Owen was one of them, an enormous huge person, she looked like a gypsy, they'd got a Romany look about them. She used to tighten up the chucks and things, and no one – no *man* could undo it. They were always saying, "Sarah's tightened this chuck!" Enormous woman – very strong and powerful – she was used to doing the locks, she could do them almost with one hand. She would undo something – a chap was struggling with two hands to undo it. They were a nice family.

'We had quite a few of these barge people – couldn't read or write – yet they knew to a penny if they had the wrong amount on their cards. It was an extraordinary business. They seemed to have an instinct, they could tell, you know. They would come to me and say this isn't right and tell you where it wasn't right, if they thought that it had been worked out incorrectly.

'In this family, Sarah had an albino daughter, very weak-eyed, and very fair hair. She was thought not to be "all there". Sarah said to me, "You send her out of the house and she never finds her way anywhere, she's always falling over everything." The girl was about, oh, eleven, and I felt very sorry for her. I used to have half an hour spare in the afternoon and I thought I'd try to teach her to read. The poor thing was always shunned and sent off into corners. D'you know what her problem was? She couldn't see! She was practically blind. And they hadn't discovered this. They thought that she was mental. I sent her to the chap who dealt with eyes at that time, we got her glasses and she was no longer mental at all. She'd just been pushed to one side. I thought this had happened in other families, this problem, where the children had got a disability like that and people think they're mental. They were such nice people. I was very fond of them. They were used to an outdoor life, all the time, and suddenly to find themselves in a factory – it must have been terrible for them.'

One of the women who went to work in the factory was *Mrs Evie Stevens*. A tiny person, now in her mid-eighties, she sits in the front room of her bungalow, surrounded by photographs of her eleven children and of numerous grandchildren and great grand-children. Unlike Mrs Becker she had worked before, as a domestic servant when she was in her teens.

'Do you know I got married from Chartwell? Oh yes, I was Mr Churchill's maid! This was in 1923. I was lent to him because his parlourmaid had fell down the cellar steps. I had a great big bunch of keys on my belt, I was like a wardress, I was. You see I had the looking after of all the silver and so on, that was lying about. I had responsibility, all for six pound a month. And we worked for it then! Sometimes we used to go to bed at two in the morning when they'd had a party, and we used to get up again at six to make early morning tea and take upstairs. They wouldn't do it now, would they?

'Oh, he did used to get upset sometimes! He used to come home the worse for wear and I used to undress him and put him to bed! I was only nineteen! Oh, I enjoyed myself because they had a big staff there. He gave me five pound for a wedding present and the Rolls-Royce took me to church. His chauffeur was in pale grey, and he handed me into the car. He said, "Now Evie, there's one thing I should like!"

' "What's that, sir?"

' "If you start a family don't forget my birthday's the thirtieth of November!"

'I said, "You wait till I get the ring on my finger first!" and he laughed and pinched my cheek. He said, "Let us know from time to time how you're getting on!"

'We moved here and I got a cottage straight away, half a crown a week. My grandfather was one of the best hand-sewn men in Northamptonshire. He'd got his own little workshop and he employed three men. He used to make me a pair of boots fastening right up to the knee, for 4s. 6d., and they were solid leather. But the houses were really bad. They ought to have pulled them down and made a clean sweep.

'There was as many pubs as there was good houses! They opened at six o'clock in the morning till twelve o'clock at night and the beer was good at fourpence a pint. I used to go and round my grandad up on Saturday dinnertimes – I've been into six pubs before I found him – he'd be the worse for wear when we got him home. Unless he'd been in the Wagon and Horses. It had got four steps to it and he fell down 'em a good many times – he was sobered up when he got to the bottom.

'I've been through the hoop, I know what it's like. I'd a big family – I hardly dare tell you how many – eleven! My eldest son's sixty-two. We were having a shilling a week for them, at fourteen years old. That was to shoe 'em, clothe 'em and keep 'em! My husband was on the dole. When one job finished you couldn't drop into another one. He went on the land, he went down the hospital stone-breaking, I don't know where he didn't go. He got on the kerbstones. There was a plant started up down the railway station. He made *thousands*! I bet there's some of his kerbstones all over England.

'When they come to a finish he went up Borough Hill when they were putting the water mains in. He was working almost up to his waist in water and he had arthritis on the sciatic nerve so then he was in hospital. He was in there in steel splints for nearly three months. And we'd got a young family then. But he was a good worker.

'He went along to this farm along London Road, Thrupp Fields it was, and he'd never been near a horse. He was a Londoner and he was scared stiff! They put him on the horse rake. I started on a farm when I was thirteen, I learned to ride when I was fourteen years old. My husband, he didn't know how to put a spade in the ground when he come out of the navy! I learnt him to garden! And we had some of the finest stuff you ever see! Used to grow all us own cabbage plants, sprouts and cauliflower, and he had a great big piece of allotment up the road. We went up Good Friday, and I helped him put sixteen rows of potatoes in. When I come home I started labour and my daughter was born Easter Sunday morning. We've been through some hard times!

'We used to sit up nearly all night making trays to give our kids a bit of dinner the next day! We used to do it by candlelight. There was no gas in the old cottages. I said, "Oh, I'll go and get a job!" I had to work nights. My husband said I'd never stick it. Anyhow I did. I think it was sheer, you know, madness that made me carry on. Well, you can tell: my youngest son was two years old and I left him as a baby. It was hard work! I've gone in the top shop, as we called it, at seven o'clock and stayed there till nine at night. Our work used to have to go to Hatfield to be inspected – the lorries used to come and go every day.

'Westbourne Engineering was in its rude state when I first went there. We used to sit on the floor because we'd no canteen to have our break. I was here, there and everywhere: if they found me a job I had to go. The first machine I was on was a Bardon & Oliver and it was as long as that room. We were making bearings. There were no guards on the machines and of course we'd never heard of factory inspectors till this night one walked in. He was only a little feller. He said, "Get down!"

'I said, "I'm not on piece work! I can't afford to stop!" He said, "I demand you get down!" And who should come walking through but the boss in his dressing-gown. The side-door went into his house. "What are you doing here? Leave my workers alone. They've got a job on that's got to be in Hatfield tomorrow at six o'clock."

'The inspector said, "Do you realize if that woman was to slip, she'd be chewed up in those gears!" So he took me off that job and I went on the riveting. Making rivets. They were little machines and they used to make a terrible noise. When we were on nights there used to be some rows of cottages near by and the men used to say, "God help us! Westbourne's got two machines in there and they make a row just like a woman in labour!" They did! They made a terrible noise!

'Next I went on a flange machine. I was putting males in one end and females in the other – one had got a groove in and the other'd got a deep slot. I've got one of the staves I made outside to prove it! You must see that before you go! (*And she has: the metal pole supports her washing line.*) We had a bucket of sand at the side of us because it was stuff that fires ever so quick –'

'*Phosphorus?*'

'Yes. We'd to stand with this bucket of sand so that when it caught light we used to chuck the sand over it to deaden the flames.'

'*Did anybody get burnt?*'

'There was one or two slight accidents, but we nipped it in the bud before it got serious. Nobody was took to hospital. From t' top shop I went down Foundry Place. There was little granny shops all over the town. Whenever there was a place vacant Westbourne used to have it. That was in the anodizing. All this stuff had to be dipped in this fluid. It used to smell terrible! In case you got it on your body you used to have to wear gloves.

'Mr Tonks was our foreman – he used to stutter ever-so. He said, "Mrs Stevens, I got a new job for you. Come on, I'll show you what you've got to do." It was a semi-basement, you had to go down these six steps. We barely saw daylight, only the people walking about up above!

'I said, "I'm not working in here!"

'He said, "You refuse then?"

' "The smell's terrible!" Well, you know what cellulose paint is. That's why I've only got part of the lung, you see. We used to have to wear a mask every day! And they were *black* after we'd wore 'em for a few hours. Anyhow, I said, "I should think we're going to get a bonus for doing this, a'nt we?"

' "Oh," he says, "yes, a pint of milk a day to drink, and ten shillings a week extra on top of your wages, danger money."

'My husband come round and tried to get me out of there. I says, "No, I'll stop where I am. I like it now." I used to service my own machine, mix my own paint, and most of the components had three coats of paint on. Because that work had to go to Hatfield to be passed for OK. And I got full marks. Mr Tonks used to set these struts up by the wall, in sixes. He says, "Come on, have a go! I'll stop here with you!" He said, "It strikes me you're a dark horse, Mrs Stevens. You've done this job before!"

' "I haven't! I've never had hold of a paint gun in my hands!" Do you know, I think I could go back to that job now. There was no tears! The paint had to be used at a certain thickness, you see, it was yellow, grey and black. Had three coats on it. I had five girls working under me round there, working ever so hard. I had one or two men with me as well. Yeah. Two that had been wounded in the services.

'One, I used to have to go and find him. He was generally round the churchyard. He'd tramped the desert in the Desert Rats, got lost, and he'd been hit on the top of the head. It sent him – you know. His name was Bert. But he'd always do what I'd say. "Come on, Bert, sit down and have a fag!" We had to go outside because of the thinners, it was highly inflammable. I could talk to him like a child. He'd have a roam round and come back and he'd work! I've been through the hoops so I know what it's like.

'One day I come down the stairs and Mr Tonks said, "We've got a VIP coming. You'd better put a clean mask on!" The police were all coming by with this jeep. I said, "That's Winston Churchill!" He stopped, he got down, of course the police were all around. He knew me! He pinched me cheek and put his face up against mine.

'My youngest son but one was named after him. I kept having these children and my husband said, "I reckon old Churchill's going to be unlucky!" On my mother's birthday – that's her up there – the doctor came round. I said, "Oh, for God's sake get me out of this lot!" I had so much castor oil that night I thought I were gonna die. Anyhow my son made his first cry at quarter past five on Winston's birthday, so I thought I've obliged the old boy, I'll sit down and write to him. I got the old gynaecologist to sign it. And almost by return of post Winston's secretary sent me another five pound! That bought the pram! I had some change and one big pram. So I never forgot him. Now my son's married, got three daughters himself.'

*'When did you finish at Westbourne?'*

'Well you see, I'd been there roughly three years. My chest was ever so bad. Every year I had bronchitis, and two or three times I had pleurisy as well. The doctor said, "It's no good, that job's doing you no good, it'll kill you! I advise you to leave." Mrs Becker didn't want to part with me, she said, "We'll see if we can find you a light job."

'I said, "No, the doctor said definitely."

'Nowadays, if I don't have bronchitis before Christmas, I have it after! I've been in hospital two or three times with it. And then I suffer with my breathing. I didn't get the sack! Oh no! I threatened to leave ever so many times. I said to Mr Tonks – I put my gun down one day – I said. "I'm not stopping in here another minute!"

'"Oh," he said, "stop till tea-time!"

'Of course, the pain had worn off a bit then. And the others kept saying, "Don't leave, Mrs Stevens! Don't leave! We ain't gonna stop if you leave!"'

# 7

# COASTAL COMMAND

COASTAL COMMAND HAD THE TASK OF COMBATING LUFTWAFFE attacks on British shipping, and reducing the threat from U-boats and surface raiders in the North Sea and the Bay of Biscay. Its role was crucial during the Battle of the Atlantic, when the Germans made a serious and alarming attempt to cut Britain's supply lines. Unfortunately the Command was ill-equipped and tended to get aircraft like the Vickers Wildebeest which were obsolete before the war even started. *James Bailey* flew another outdated aeroplane, the Handley Page Hampden, in Coastal Command, for much of the war.

'When war broke, I joined the army. I went to the Royal Artillery School of Signals to train as a signaller motor-cyclist, drove a car, and was promptly sent to a horse unit! I used to get arrested every time I came home on leave. We weren't allowed out without riding breeches, spurs, and all the regalia. At that time so you couldn't differentiate between peacetime soldiers and army soldiers everybody had to wear battledress, you weren't allowed to go walking around in the old-time uniform with all the buttons and so forth. As soon as we hit London dressed like that, the redcaps (*military police*) grabbed us. In the end we used to carry a special pass.

'They were an Indian Army lot which had come back to be

174

mechanized. They'd got horses. Funnily enough I took to horses, I thoroughly enjoyed myself. But a signal came through to say you could transfer to aircrew. I immediately applied and got accepted, and then nobody would talk to me! I was transferring down! They wouldn't have minded if I'd gone in the navy but the air force was the most junior regiment. Most of our officers were peacetime regulars, pukka sahibs! I either qualified as a pilot or had to go back to the army.'

*'Do you think you might have had a hard time in the army if you'd failed the pilot's course?'*

'They would have crucified me! Every incentive to qualify! I was a fully trained signaller and rider and they weren't happy about losing qualified people to the air force.

'When I'd trained I was put on to Coastal Command. I flew the Hampden. It wasn't very easy for the instructor. He stood behind you and peered over your shoulder to see what you were doing but he couldn't take over – he'd got no access to the controls. There was no such thing as dual control. I don't think I would have cared to have instructed on that aircraft!

'We had George (*automatic pilot*) which was useful because we used to do a trip down the Bay of Biscay which was somewhere about maximum endurance, about seven hours. It was a biggish aircraft with a fighter cockpit – once you were in there, you'd no chance of moving! It was handy to have something to eat now and again, and there's nothing worse than messing about with flasks pouring yourself a cup of coffee and at the same time trying to fly the aircraft! And also calls to nature.

'The Hampden had overload tanks which I was never happy about. We carried a crew of four and one of the gunners had to switch over for you – it was not under the pilot's control. Sometimes they got in a bit of a muddle. I used to make sure that we'd got plenty of height in case they switched off the tanks before they switched on the other ones. You'd get an airlock so you needed that bit of height to go down and wait for them to pick up again.

'There was a very active German U-boat base somewhere round Brest and they used to come out hunting. They knew our planes because there was nobody else going down the Bay apart from some old Whitleys which were relatively easy pickings. We used to get some very eager beavers coming out from Brest hunting. You got the odd scare – you'd see an aircraft – have I been picked up by the pack of wolves? Fortunately I never was.

'Flying there was a battle of wits. In the early days people spotted submarines, but the Germans soon cottoned on. They knew roughly the range of aircraft and they just kept submerged till they got across that range. The odd one was caught up on the surface but they were very few and far between. We achieved our objective. We didn't necessarily sink any submarines but we kept them submerged, which interfered with their anti-shipping patrols. If we hadn't been down there it would have been dead easy for the Germans to remain on the surface most of the time.

'The casualty rate was quite high. People were shot down. The biggest problem was dropping a torp. You've got to do it at about seventy to eighty feet high, absolutely straight and level. I used to go down till the navigator called up to say he could see the slip-stream on the water. Your torp runs at forty-five knots and you dropped from two miles out – you were at the ship long before your torp was. So they'd got plenty of time to shoot you down before your torp blew them up! If you immediately turned away you'd present a lovely target. The answer was to continue straight, dead in line, which is frightening for a person on a boat. You gave them a very small silhouette to fire at. That was the theory, but you did lose an awful lot of aircraft. It was finally decided that the Hampden was not the aircraft for the job – it was too big and not sufficiently manoeuvrable.

'When I went up to Turnberry to torpedo school, I learned that to fly low like that you needed to be properly trained. There's an awful lot more to it than a bit of devilry. I realized the appalling risks I'd been taking. You don't get any sense of speed unless you're low-flying. When you're way up there to all intents and purposes the aircraft is standing still, it's only when you get down low that you get a little bit of a thrill out of it! That's why everybody did it!

'On night flying you were going out looking for a specific target. They'd identified somewhere and you were sent to see if you could find it which wasn't all that easy. If the Germans knew anything was about they would anchor up. We used Wellingtons. They did a longer run – they used to go right out across the North Sea down the Dutch and Norwegian coasts. They didn't actually attack the ships – the idea was to call up the Beaufighters. It was supposed to be co-ordinated – you went round behind the ships – tried to sneak between them and the shore. They were obviously as close to the shore as they could possibly make it. You got round behind them and dropped a string of flares and hopefully, just as you dropped these flares, the Beaufighters would arrive and see their target beautifully illuminated. They came in and strafed them with cannon. Like all those sort of things, it needed an awful lot of co-ordination. You'd to get your signal right, the Beaufighters had to be absolutely ready to take off, they mustn't make any navigational errors. If you dropped your flares too soon – they dropped on parachutes – by the time the Beaufighters got there, your flares had gone and the target was no longer illuminated. So again it was probably more a deterrent than actually sinking ships.

'Flare-dropping was hair-raising. We used to have the flares inside and they were quite big. You lifted one up and dropped it down the tube. As it went down you pulled the pin out. I had visions of the bloke pulling the pin out and the bloody thing getting stuck in the chute! We didn't carry bombs on that trip so the bomb-bay was an overload petrol tank. If one of those flares had gone off, there was a fuel tank right alongside.

'Probably flare-dropping on a drawing board sounded marvellous. The ships would listen in to our radio and when they heard us scramble they would make a bee-line for the shore. It depended how far out they were – if you could get there in time you could pick them up because you could see the wake. They'd spot a ship breaking out and vector us on to it, and if the ship made a run for it they did make themselves quite a nice target. That didn't last very long because they suddenly tumbled to it so the obvious thing was to anchor up. Then they were very difficult to find. About the only way, once they'd switched off and were stationary, was to get them in the moon-path. It's like a great big searchlight shining down on the water.

'I'd the greatest admiration for the Germans, they were very professional – it was a bit of a battle of wits. We would fly when there was a moon up and we could get them in the moon-path, so they started to set dummies – they put a boat out and had little E-boats all round it, which didn't show up on the radar. If you went in, they had a little row of boats all the way round, they didn't know where you were but they knew you were up in the middle somewhere and a cone of fire came up! So next week you'd try something else.

'As time got on the occasions for meeting each other in combat became fewer – they became quite clever at dodging us, we became quite clever at keeping out of the traps they set for us. At the same time it did bottle the Channel up, it stopped them getting the stuff through, which is what it was all about.

'A Wellington could take an awful lot of holes and still remain airborne, which was a comfortable thought. We were flying out mainly across the North Sea, loaded up with flares, and our main fear was flak from boats. If you got a bit too close to the shore you'd pick up flak from there too.

'We had a very mysterious experience one night. We saw a red ball hanging in the sky, God knows what it was, for all I know I might have seen a flying saucer! One of the crew called up, "What's that over there?" It was a great big red glow and it just stayed level with us. We sat and watched, it was fascinating. Then I realized, "For God's sake look out on the dark side! Because whatever that is that's attracting our attention, you've got a blighter coming in on the other side!" I suppose it was there between ten and fifteen minutes. Then all of a sudden (*whistles*) it disappeared. We didn't say a lot about it because they'd probably have said, "How many did you have before you went up?" Even in those days there were all sorts of experimental aircraft. The Germans were pretty shrewd – they used to think up some smart ideas. Our main reaction was that it was some sort of German decoy.

'I completed my tour after the invasion of the Continent. They used to come back staggering through the air full of contraband! I sat there chewing my fingernails – I wasn't allowed to go. I couldn't help feeling I finished my tour a couple of months too soon. Oh, there were crates of it! Everybody was scrounging around for rations – cigarettes, coffee – a bag of coffee was worth its weight in gold. Later in the war the Americans used to come back laden with antique furniture and all sorts of things. We'd got aircraft going to and fro all the time and there was no customs or anything like that.

'I enjoyed service life and I was lucky that I had a very fair existence. I moved around a lot – never stayed in the same place very long. Before I went in the services I could ride a bicycle, when I was in the services I learnt to ride a horse, drive a motor cycle and a car, fly an aeroplane, and sail a boat! When I was with horses we were back in the 1914 war, all of my equipment was dated 1915. All covered in grease which we had to clean off. We were still using flags and maps for signalling. We did advance to field telephone sets, and we used to gallop along laying cables. They started using a type of radio but it was a hell of a job. You'd got to spend half an hour tuning it in. In effect it was a damn sight quicker to climb up a tree with a lamp and signal with the lamp. When we went on to the horses we couldn't take the radio sets anywhere. When you think of going from that to flying something like the Hurricane, which I did in Scotland! When I look back on it I think, "Good God, I was lucky," but at the time you don't realize it. I was dead lucky, believe you me, I think that surviving was as much luck as skill!' (*Laughs.*)

# 8

# GROUND CREW

To KEEP WAR PLANES IN THE AIR REQUIRED LARGE NUMBERS of ground-based personnel. The RAF had its own apprentice school which provided a core of skilled workers but the enormous demands of wartime brought large numbers of men from a wide range of industries and occupations into the RAF. Their relations with the men who flew the planes was very close: aircrew cannot speak too highly of the work they did, the long hours they put in, the energy and attentiveness with which they responded to emergencies. Often ground crew would be waiting in the middle of the night for 'their' aircraft to return from an operation over the Continent.

Many ground crew served right through the war, putting in six or seven years' service. Many who joined up in 1939 went through the frenzy and chaos of the Battle of Britain, a period they remember now as one of constant work, sudden postings from station to station, rushed meals and lack of sleep; culminating in fatigue and exhaustion. *Harry Old* finished his training course during the last week of peacetime and on 4 September 1939 was posted to his first squadron, based at Debden.

'It was pretty hairy there with the hours that we were working. Up until the time I left – I was posted from there on the twenty-ninth of December – I had eight nights in bed, that's all.

180

We were averaging out at about seven or eight scrambles a day.

'The rest of the time we used to eat and sleep in the hangar because we were a day and night fighter squadron with Blenheims and Hurricanes. We just did not get away. We never even got our clothes off! We were allowed twenty minutes to go and get a bath, a wash and a shave, and that was it, per day. Food was pretty bad too. In the end the MO insisted that we had a forty-eight-hour-pass every eight days. We used to go home. We *had* to come off the station then. When we returned you just went back into the routine.

'Another hazard there was at night. We had the LDV (*Local Defence Volunteers*) – forerunners of the Home Guard – doing guard duties. Quite elderly people, World War One veterans. Their attitude was to fire first and ask afterwards. If you were moving around at night away from the hangar – it was all blacked out – you could almost certainly count on getting a quick "halt who-goes-there!" – BANG!! I had two quite near ones, bullets whistling! Thank God they were bad shots!

'After that I was posted to Filton, as ground staff. It was fairly lively because we got some of the first air raids down there – heavy ones too. Filton was then part of the Bristol Aircraft Company and the Germans were over nearly every night when the weather was fit, looking for it. Bristol did catch a very bad battering.

'I was there the morning after one of the very heavy raids and got yanked in to help the civil defence people, the police and the fire brigade – what there were of them – a lot had apparently been injured and killed. One of the surface air-raid shelters had had a near-miss and it had blown the walls in. The concrete roof had come down and there were fifty-two people inside, or the remains of them. It was not a very pleasant experience. They just grabbed anybody to help lift the roof off.'

'*They were all dead?*'

'All dead. Mainly women and children.

'We also had quite a lot of fifth-column activity. We were doing all our own guards – there was no RAF regiment or anything like that in those days. I was on guard one night, Jerry was over the top, and a light flashed! I took a shot at it and made a kind of challenge, but I missed.

'A few nights later we were on another guard post. They were very worried even at that time about parachutists, and there was another light – yellow, green and red lights – triangle of them waving, quite bright too. This was within the fire zone of this little post I had. I asked permission to open fire but was told no. It was a good job they stopped us because unknown to us a Royal Artillery mobile anti-aircraft battery had moved in there. Somebody opened up with a machine-gun and when they picked this chappie up he'd got twenty-six rounds through him! Local man again.

'Every time there was an air raid over on the Patchway side of the aerodrome a window used to open and the curtains flap letting a lot of light out. We complained about it and asked if we could plaster this place but they'd never let us open up. Another night the same thing happened. A battery of Bofors gunners decided they didn't like it. One of them fired one round, put it straight through the window at about a thousand yards, and blew the house apart. That stopped the trouble there, though I think there was a bit of a row over it.

'After that I was posted again, to Cardiff airport, where we were re-equipped with military aircraft – brand new Blenheims. We did an acceptance check on them. I don't know what made me do it, but I took the bag off the oxygen connection just to have a look and found that the whole thing had been smeared with grease round the inside, a big blob of grease! Well, oxygen, even at low pressure, with grease, reacts somewhat violently! We found that all the aircraft had been done the same way. It was a deliberate sabotage. There was an inquiry on that but they never found the culprit.'

'*Would it have been somebody on the station?*'

'No, this would have been done at St Athan or at the factory. The aircraft as far as I can make out were flown from wherever they were manufactured to the maintenance unit, where they were given a check and so forth, and then out to the squadrons. We had the RAF investigation branch down more or less the same day and they questioned all our people, and satisfied themselves that it wasn't done at our end.

'We had a very heavy balloon barrage down there – seventy or eighty balloons – and one night we had quite a heavy raid. They had all the balloons up and then a sudden thunderstorm broke and you could see the lightning going from balloon cable to balloon cable! They were coming down and catching fire and dropping in fives and sixes – we were counting them – it was almost like daylight!

'Fortunately the cloud base was fairly low and the Germans were above it so they couldn't get a clear visual. The balloon operators were sitting on the winches, and when they got struck they either got badly burned or killed.

'The following morning we had about five or six cables strewn across the aerodrome and we thought this is going to be interesting, I wonder how they're going to get these in? I don't know what length of cable they carried but several thousands of feet anyway. Then to our astonishment, without any warning to anybody, these cables all suddenly started moving!

'Luckily we'd cleared 'em off our aircraft. They just started the winches up and hauled the cables in – they were taking roofs off houses and goodness only knows what! It was absolute chaos! I didn't hear of anyone getting killed but if you were standing close – they started them off slowly but there was an immense amount of power there.

'Another thing we had which I've never seen in any of the books – an invasion scare! We had a big fire-bell and were briefed that if that was rung, we were to disperse immediately. We said, Well, where do we go?

'Just disappear! Disperse!

'About one o'clock one morning there was this frantic ringing of the bell, gunfire and so forth, so everybody dispersed. I cleared off for a few hours, disappeared into a coppice, made myself comfortable and had a sleep. The firing died down and nothing else happened so about midday the following day I decided I'd go back.

'People were drifting back, though some of them had taken it very literally and gone home, to London and places like that! Then we heard rumours – I had this information second-hand – that a load of German bodies had been washed up on the beach around Burnham and Minehead and that way, and they reckoned a barge-load of Germans had attempted a landing. There was certainly a heck of a lot of gunfire that night but whether they intended to come there or whether they inadvertently picked the wrong place to land, I don't know.'

*'What was the purpose of you all scattering?'*

'Our total camp armament comprised two rifles and a hundred rounds of ammunition. One rifle and a bandolier of fifty rounds was kept in the guardroom, and the aerodrome guard had the other one. They used to walk round, one man carrying the rifle, one carrying the ammunition (*laughs*), so that was our total defence armament! We had nothing – no guns, nothing at all, absolutely nothing. At that particular time, after Dunkirk, even our 1896 rifles had been taken away from us and issued to the army. I suppose we were considered the *least* necessary to have any weapons so the only thing we could do was leave the aircraft and disperse. They were all civilian aircraft.

'When we'd been there for a couple of weeks we had a fairly heavy raid one night with a lot of incendiaries on the aerodrome. We were all running around picking up these incendiaries and chucking them away from the aircraft. We had a mixture of aircraft then, both military and civilian, it was a sort of change-over period. I saw one burning and went to run for it but my CO got to it before I did, picked it up to throw and it was an explosive – it blew him to pieces! You know, it was just one of those things – if I'd been two or three seconds earlier I'd have had it! It was a very sad loss because he was a very good man and everybody liked him.

184

'That's when some of our first Polish pilots arrived. They were quite a bunch! They were ex-Polish-air-force pilots, extremely good, but they had one main purpose in life – to kill Germans. I see their point. Most of them had pretty horrific experiences with the Germans. They'd nearly all seen action in the Polish air force, seen the atrocities the Germans had committed against the civil population and they'd had a heck of a time getting out, over to this country – you could understand their attitude.

'When we moved to Gatwick a Polish pilot flew us down on one of the old Rapides. At that time a lot of aircraft hadn't got radio or couldn't use radio so they used to have coloured Verey lights to identify themselves. These colours were changed about three times a day and one of the jobs of the ground crew was to find out what the actual colours were. The pilot used to load the Verey light pistol before he took off with the colour current for that particular time of the day, but this pilot obviously hadn't bothered.

'We were flying over Gloucestershire when to our astonishment anti-aircraft shells were suddenly bursting alongside! The pilot's English was almost non-existent – as it was with most of them – I remember a chappie hammering on his shoulders saying "Fire your Verey light! Fire your Verey light!" So he just slaps one in the gun and pulls the trigger, but they still didn't stop firing. Luckily, gunners being what they were, we weren't in an awful lot of danger but nevertheless there's always the lucky one. Eventually, after we'd fired about three different colours, they stopped – either we were out of range or we'd fired the right one! We came in, landed at Gatwick.

'In those days Gatwick just had the beehive, the big central terminal building and a strip of concrete running out. No runways. It used to be all marshy ground there. We landed and stopped so near the end of the runway we had to push the aircraft back. We got it out of the way because we had Blenheims following. They all landed quite nicely, ran off the end of this runway and bogged themselves down. We ended up with three almost new aircraft sitting on the ground, *in* the ground, and we wanted to get them out because we were fairly experienced in moving them.

'On a Blenheim under no circumstances were you allowed to pull backwards on the undercarriage, you had to pull *forwards* otherwise the undercarriage would crash. But the maintenance unit people turned up with two tractors and a steel cable. The flight sergeant in charge said, "All right, hook on, pull it out, no bother!"

'I said to him, "For goodness' sake don't tow them backwards otherwise you'll foul the undercarriages!" I was told in no uncertain terms where to go, so we sat there and watched him wreck all three aircraft! (*Laughs.*) They were write-offs. He pulled 'em all out, folded 'em up, dropped the lot, like that! Three brand-new aircraft!

'The Poles were a funny bunch actually. We used to get along (*he searches for the right word*) *reasonably* well but there was no real love lost between us. We certainly respected them for their fighting ability and their guts – they had tremendous guts – but then they had every incentive to behave that way.

'When we moved up to Northolt where we operated for about two or three months we had the Polish 303 Fighter Squadron there. Again they were a complete law unto themselves, nobody could control them. They'd taken them off the main dispersal area and dispersed them on the west side of Northolt in a sort of wood. They had just one track. They had dispersal pans coming off that track. When they got a scramble which they did very frequently because it was busy at the time, somebody used to come out with an old Polish hunting horn. Everybody else used bells for a scramble but they had a chappie who came out with this old Polish hunting horn and as soon as you heard that – and you could hear it all over the aerodrome – you immediately got out of the way!

'They didn't bother with the runways, they used to come out of this taxi track, tail up, straight across the aerodrome and off! Regardless of wind direction or anything. I've seen some of the hairiest take-offs the whole time I was in the service from there.

186

They came straight across the runway and God help anything that happened to be landing when they got a scramble!

'The thing that 303 could *not* live down – they were doing some practice formation flying over the aerodrome and they were told to remain within a certain distance. While they were up there a Heinkel came in underneath them, machine-gunned us and they never saw it! The first indication they had was when they fired the aerodrome defence – that was rockets with long wire cables attached to them. They were supposed to wrap round the plane and rip it to shreds. I don't know whether they did have any success with it. But they were too late firing them. The Heinkel was through.

'At the time our Naafi was in a brand new infants' school with large windows, which had been converted for RAF use. I was sitting in there facing one of these windows, and there was a pal of mine sitting on a chair at the side. I heard a noise and thought, what on earth's that? And suddenly realized, subconsciously I suppose, that an attack was coming off. I remember seeing the window disintegrate and I just went sideways out of my chair, grabbed the other chappie and took him with me, and we ended up on the floor. Miraculously nobody was hurt.

'I got up and had a look at the chair I'd been sitting in and there was a bullet hole right through the back! Cor, what a souvenir! I was busy trying to break the back off because, you know, this is a souvenir, can't be missed! And darn me, a service policeman came in, saw me doing this, and I got done for wilful destruction of government property!

'You know, you've got to hand it to Jerry! It was an absolutely suicidal attack with the squadron up top, coming in underneath it. I don't suppose he knew it was 303. A message didn't go up to them that we were being attacked, because the flying control tower also took a bit of a battering. This Heinkel went inland, turned round and apparently got away! He kept low level and there was no report of him being shot down.

'You've never seen anything like it when 303 did get the message! They were circling and all of a sudden they must have pulled boost over-rides and they were off! When they came back nobody had got anything. He'd got away.

'It was rather amusing there, every aircraft that came in was met by a First World War armoured car. Solid tyres, huge dustbin turret, and a Vickers .303 machine-gun, driven by the Coldstream Guards. It used to come out of a shed on a kind of tarmac, drive down to the edge of the grass – they daren't take it on the grass, otherwise it would have sunk and they'd never have found it. It was so heavy that it had developed ruts in the tarmac: the driver used to sit there like this (*with his arms folded*) and it used to go chuff-chuff-chuff-chuff!

'The turret would swing and follow whatever aircraft was coming in, and when they were satisfied that the aircraft was friendly, it used to go chuff-chuff-chuff back in! They did this seven or eight times a day sometimes. It was just like one of these penny-in-the-slot machines where you pushed a penny in and the thing comes out then goes back in again. I don't think it ever fired a shot in anger. It certainly didn't fire when this Heinkel came in.

'Northolt was protected by the Coldstream Guards and there was no love lost between them and the Poles. I'd been out to the cinema one night and I heard the rattle of rifle and machine-gun fire – what the heck's going on? I wasn't very far from the entrance gate and all merry hell let loose there! There was Guards and the Poles having a proper fire fight. The Guards had stopped drunken Poles coming in. They'd knocked one of the guardsmen out, grabbed his rifle and when the others came running up they opened fire on them. I think they wounded two guardsmen. The Guards being what they were, they opened up and a five-minute fight went on until the Poles ran out of ammunition! Nothing was ever said about it but I gather that a couple of Poles and one of the Guards were either wounded or killed – I can't remember exactly now but it was all very much hushed up. There was a general clamp-down after that on both Poles and Guards.

'We had some very unfortunate incidents with the aircraft. We went down to Old Sarum where we were operating along the sea with Lysanders. They were very good in the hands of a good pilot but they were completely unforgiving if you did anything wrong. There was an awful lot of people killed in them.

'One of the Lysander's biggest faults was it had a fully adjustable tailplane and you had to trim before take-off – the standing instructions were that immediately you landed you always put it back to the take-off position. Well, pilots being what they were, they used to forget. On one occasion I was driving a tractor across the aerodrome and I saw this Lysander taking off – I could see that he'd got his tailplane set wrongly! I'd a chap with me and he stood up waving his arms about trying to attract the pilot's attention – it's a horrible feeling! But he obviously didn't see us, nor did his gunner. He took off and as soon as he came off the ground he must have realized what was happening: the thing just went straight up like that (*almost vertically*), stalled, came in and dropped.

'I went across to see if there was anything we could do. It crashed just outside the hangar. The pilot was dead – he was burning – and the gunner was trying to get out. We went in and grabbed him and tried to help him. We did actually get him out but his left leg was off. Amazingly, he said, "Oh, has anybody got a cigarette?" I don't smoke, never have done. The other chap said, "Yes, here you are!" He took a couple of puffs and just dropped back dead, just like that.

'The fire engine was only a matter of fifty or sixty yards away but they couldn't get it started. I'm sure that chappie could have been saved. That was the first time I've experienced the smell of burning bodies. Afterwards we staggered up to the dining hall where it was stew for dinner – that was the last straw!

'By this time they were getting very very short of aircrew. The losses were very heavy and there was a general demand sent round to all units. They had to obtain so many volunteers. I was getting heartily fed up so I thought I'll try and get on to aircrew. I volunteered and within two days a posting came through to St Athan, on the flight engineer's course.

'We had the choice of what aircraft we went on. I decided on

Stirlings because the Halifaxes had Merlin engines and I wasn't keen on them. I'd worked on most engines by this time and the Bristol engines were more reliable and less prone to fires. I had about six weeks' training down there. Passed out and I was posted to Three Group.

'Whilst I was waiting for crewing, I was coming down to tea one afternoon and the door opened. Six chaps walked in, in flying gear, with rolled-up parachutes which they dumped in the corner. Apparently they'd been flying in a Wellington and the engine had dropped out. They baled out. A few weeks later – it wasn't as long as that – ten days later, the same thing happened. They had a Scotch-Canadian rear gunner and he said, "I've just seen a prop go by, just give us a yes or no, is it ours?"

' "Yes, it's taken half our tailplane with it! Everybody out!" So they all went out and got away with it again. Of course when it came to my turn to be crewed up, that was the crew I got!

'I'd always suffered from airsickness right from the very first time I flew. I was continuously airsick and when we went cross country or anything like that they had several times to carry me out the aircraft, I was incapable of walking. The medical people were quite interested because they hadn't come across a case quite the same. I had a medical officer fly with me on several occasions, to observe, and it wasn't anything that I was putting on, I was actually dead keen. I *liked* the flying!

'I was taken off aircrew. It was an experience that I wouldn't have missed, but I was extremely fortunate that my health didn't permit flying. The old Stirling was a pretty unforgiving aircraft, though it was very robust. I remember one crash when the aircraft landed, one undercarriage leg folded up, it rolled, the wings came off, the tail came off, and the fuselage was just rolling along the ground, completely intact.

'I was in charge of the duty crew at the time – what are we going to find in this one? We got there at the same time as the fire engine. The door opened, just as we got there, and the whole crew walked out, and *there* was the wings and engines and tail! The fuselage was intact, it had just rolled along like a cigar. They were bruised but nobody had got any bones broken.

'The rest of my war was overseas postings. I went to South Africa, seconded to the South African Air Force. Tremendous amount of political problems! Afrikaners were basically pro-Nazi. We had a lot of sabotage on aircraft. I used to go round and do spot checks on them. You'd find control cables half cut through and all that sort of business. You had to go out in twos or more because they used to hate our guts! I was out there for about a year. But I must tell you about a couple of peculiar things that happened in England during the war.

'I was very friendly with an observer, and when he came to us he was the only survivor of a crashed crew. We were doing quite a large number of operations from the conversion unit, especially for thousand-bomber raids – they used up every available aircraft. Crews who were still under training used to go on these operations – quite good chaps had done three or four before they completed their training!

'As he was a spare bod he used to get yanked in for ops with all different crews – he was a very happy-go-lucky type. Matter of fact, we had the Press come round one day. They just grabbed anybody who was sitting around, told them to get their flying kit on and walk out to a Stirling and they took photographs of them. The photo has been on calendars and everything and he's in it – we used to pull his leg unmercifully about it. Well, he got called up for an op one night, came back and said to me, "There's a letter here, would you post it tomorrow?"

'"Yes, all right."

'"And here's some money. Take the lads out and buy them a pint."

'"What the hell are you talking about?"

'He said, "I shan't be coming back off this one."

'Nobody knew what the target was, only the aircrew – no ground crew or anybody ever knew that. It was a very closely guarded secret, so I said, "Is it a bad one?"

'"No. But I shan't be coming back." I had an old wrist-watch, paid about five shillings for it, and he'd got one of the Omega

191

aircrew watches. He said, "You've always liked these watches, let's change them." I thought, goodness, no, maybe he had to rely on it. If anything did happen I'd feel I might have been responsible. So I didn't.

'Anyway, he went and didn't come back. I know you hear about these things, premonitions, but it's absolutely true, he *knew* before he went. He was normally a couldn't-care-less type, nothing would bother him, but suddenly – and it wasn't a bad op either – it wasn't Hamburg or anything like that, where they shot them coming back.

'We always used to get stray animals round airfields. One of the aircrew, a pilot there, some little dog took a liking to him. A sort of cross-bred wire-haired terrier. They made him a little flying suit, heavily padded coat, and this dog used to come out with them. It was strictly against regulations. On occasion, if the weather was going to be very bad, they wouldn't take him, but as far as I know that dog had done about eighteen or nineteen operations.

'When he didn't fly with them, he used to wait in the crew-room with us. We used to draw rations for him, his supper and all the rest of it. The uncanny thing was, when an aircraft was on circuit they used to call in over the phone and the ground crew'd go out and meet it. This pilot normally flew the same aircraft, whilst we had probably about twenty-four in the squadron. You could hear them coming in – there'd probably be four or five on circuit together. Then all of a sudden the dog would get up, scratch at the door, we'd let it out and the crew used to go out with him. He *knew* when that aircraft came on – I know this sounds like something out of a story book, but it's absolutely true, we never needed a phone call to tell us that aircraft was on circuit!

'He used to go out there, the ground crew with him. He'd trot alongside them in the dark, and sit down and wait till the aircraft taxied in. As soon as the pilot got out the dog'd take a running jump – he was only small – he'd catch him and the old thing used to make a fuss of him – it was quite a standing joke.

'One night they didn't take him with them – it was a bit of a sticky one apparently. He stayed in the crew-room and we got him his supper. He wouldn't eat it which was most unusual. He was nearly always ready for it. We had a dish there for him and whatever rations we'd got he used to share. We used to ask the cook for a bit for the dog. He wouldn't eat it! He was *different*. Several people commented on it because he was just lying in front of the fire – he was completely lifeless. Anyway the aircraft started coming in and normally he sat and put his ears up. And he just lay there. Anyway, to cut a long story short, this particular night the crew didn't come back. Whether they'd been taken prisoner or killed I never found out, but the dog waited till the last aircraft had come in and then he got up, walked out, and we never saw him again. We spent *days* searching all around, we were at Melbourne, well out in the wilds there, but we never found that dog. We asked all the local farmers and the pubs and so forth, never did find him. He disappeared completely. Just vanished.'

When American forces arrived in England, some RAF ground crews were seconded to serve with them. *Dick Ashley* was among them. 'I had to make a few notes, just to refresh my memory. It's so many years back!' He has books of notes he made when he was on courses in the RAF, beautifully illustrated and coloured, and carefully preserved. Both he and his wife are very proud of them. 'He should have been a graphic designer,' Mrs Ashley says, 'but the opportunity didn't exist to go to art college then – not for people like us.' Framed water-colour drawings by her husband adorn the walls. Physically he looks very unlike the traditional concept of 'the artist', being almost Pickwickian in appearance, ruddy-complexioned, with long fair side-whiskers and a professional gardener's hands.

*Mrs Ashley:* 'You've got to be quick to catch these men, you know. They're all popping off! There's so many that have died! Which I put down to their war service! The people we knew – when you get down to sixty, seventy – so many of them have died. It seems more than coincidence.'

*Mr Ashley:* 'But it was a nice life! Oh yes, I live in the past, I'm afraid. I thoroughly enjoyed it, absolutely. When I went into the RAF they gave me a mechanic's training – '

*Mrs Ashley:* 'You've got your books there! Don't forget your books!'

*Mr Ashley:* 'That's my what do you call it? *Pièce de résistance!*' (*He shows me crayoned drawings of aero-engines.*) 'That's the Merlin and that's the Sabre. The whole training was very very thorough. Straight through from elementary. I was always interested in mechanics – '

'*Did you have a technical education?*'

*Mr Ashley:* 'I went to a business college – Pitman's College! (*great shouts of laughter from both of them*) – honestly, I've often thought of writing a book myself! The education was wasted on me, I'm afraid, because I'm an outdoor man. Dad kept horses, broke them in and trained them and I went through all that, out in Essex.'

*Mrs Ashley:* 'You were a bit of a tearaway then, weren't you?'

*Mr Ashley:* 'I'm afraid I was. But I did the course, typewriting, shorthand, and came out with a certificate so I got a jolly good job in London at a store selling ladies' fur coats and dresses. I started in the packing department and moved up into the fur department as a salesman.

'When I went into the RAF the pay was quite good but not good enough – I was a family man – so when they asked for volunteers to work in a factory and operate a mobile workshop, I wrote in.'

*Mrs Ashley:* 'I've still got the love-letters, dear boy, and we went through them. Dick was saying how pleased they were with his work on the lathe so they were giving him another three pound a week! Even the amounts of money you were earning you'd put down. Some weeks you got four pounds a week and some weeks you got six pounds. Was that where you burnt your hands?'

*Mr Ashley:* 'Oh, the RAF made a hero of me there. The workshop caught alight one day. I was working underneath a plane in a hangar and there was planes everywhere. I managed to put it out but I burnt my hands pretty badly. They put that blue stuff on my hands, didn't they? But you forget the bad parts! (*Laughs.*) We used to go out right across the country repairing urgent jobs when the aircraft was across a runway, or even down on a beach.

'At one time I was on an American station. I was there for a long time, having their food and everything – we got marvellous food there! The PX you know, that's their Naafi. Chicken, doughnuts, big bowls of cream on the table, you help yourself. Fruit juice. Cigarettes. Big cartons of them, as many as you like. And steak too. We were working on Fortresses, billeted in these Nissen huts, and the Americans invited our crew round there. What struck me directly I went in, they were most charming these chaps, they were so nice, but they were all reading comics! *Dandy* and *Beano* and all those type of comics! That struck me. I shall never forget that.'

*'Why didn't they have their own people to repair the Flying Fortresses?'*

*Mr Ashley:* 'They were very short-handed. It was that stage of the war when they wanted every Fortress ready for going on these bombing raids. Daylight raids. They used to go off and then if they lost their nerve they used to come back. They wouldn't listen! We told them it wasn't safe to go! They had their own ideas and of course Jerry got used to them. They thought the Flying Fortresses were so well armed with all these guns, no fighters could get near them, but they started bringing out the fighters with the rockets, and they'd shoot them down out of the sky! It's a horrible death too, coming down in flames.

'The trouble is on these American stations I got to know all the Americans personally. They were very friendly. There was no loggerheads at all. We were at home then and we used to have them up for meals. We didn't have any problem at all there.

'Their mechanics just maintained the aircraft while it was flying, but we had to do the dismantling. And take the bodies out of the crashed ones. I shouldn't be telling you this! It's bloodthirsty! When there was a crashed aircraft, particularly these Fortresses – daylight raids they were shot down all over the place and they were burnt out often before you could get to them – we had to go in and dismantle them, take them to pieces. The bodies were still there. They had taken some away but – I remember one thing – I was cast as a bit soft! (*Laughs.*) One of the crew, one of my five men, came up to me with a thing in his hands and said, "Here you are, Dick! You can salvage this!" (*Laughs.*) One of the crew had been burnt to a cinder and all that was left of him was the bottom, his bottom!'

*Mrs Ashley:* 'Oh! I don't remember that!'

*Mr Ashley:* 'I didn't tell you.'

*'They put it in to give you a shock?'*

*Mr Ashley:* 'That's right. Oh yes, they wanted me to toughen up. Oh, many a thing like that. I was all right after that. That was more or less my initiation in the – the tricks! (*Spluttering laugh.*) Oh, you had to be tough there! Especially on this salvage work. There was occasions when aircraft would be taking off or landing – on one occasion they were landing and Jerry had followed it in. They shot it up and it caught alight. It was just back from a raid too. That upset me. I knew this American crew. It caught alight and you could hear them screaming – it was a hundred-octane petrol which is very strong. It went whoosh! like that. They couldn't get out. It was impossible to get near the thing. It had still got some ammo on as well, shooting off all over the place. But it was terrible, those screams and shots, knowing that they were the crew you'd gone drinking with! But it was a good life. You forgot everything when you were with these fellows.

'On the salvage work you had to be very careful. We used to dismantle doodle-bugs and put them on what we called in the air force a Queen Mary – a terrific long trailing thing. We'd take the wings off – there was only short stubby wings on the doodle-bug – take those off and put the body on there, but the Germans had a nasty habit of fixing bombs and things all over. There was one little chap that we knew, little Irish lad, so high to a grasshopper, and we were working on a crashed Messerschmitt – could have been a doodle-bug – we were on everything that was – but they had put a booby-trap in this aircraft. He was dismantling some radar effort they'd got in this plane and it blew up!'

'*Killed him?*'

*Mr Ashley:* Yes. He was a hell of a mess. Another thing that I used to hate, they put a very toxic acid of some kind into the aluminium on their latest model Spitfire. We were provided with these big long gloves with strips of metal going right through them so you wouldn't cut your hands, but sometimes you couldn't do delicate work with them on. You'd take them off and you'd get cut with this Dural and you'd pretty well have gone!'

'*It was poison?*'

*Mr Ashley:* 'Yes. The metal was poison. So few people realized that. Because it was hushed up so much.'

*Mrs Ashley:* 'He still has nightmares, you know. We put it down to his experience in the war. They say like the Jews for instance have nightmares when they're older rather than when they're younger.'

'*Are they nightmares about the war?*'

*Mr Ashley:* 'Oh absolutely. It didn't seem to affect me at the time though, did it?'

*Mrs Ashley:* 'I should say you've only been having them for the last fifteen years. I don't think you had them when you were younger.'

*Mr Ashley:* 'No, I was tough then. I boxed for the air force. I've got soft in my old age. I'm seventy-four you know.'

The RAF served in many parts of the world and ground crew travelled great distances as part of their work. Most had never left England before. In conditions of war their journeys could be very dangerous. *Peter Jago* left his job in the family drapery firm in south London, and his wife and young family, to join the RAF as an aero-engine fitter. 'I was suffering from home sickness, living in digs up in a loft with no furniture but camp beds, and being bullied, though in civilian life I was an employer myself. It was a horrible depressing feeling. But you have to come to terms with it because you're stuck with the service. Otherwise it makes life intolerable.

'In the RAF I did a fitters' course which was very condensed. We were told that what the normal apprentices used to take four years on we did in about eight months! I remember there was an instructor there and every day when we went into the workshop he used to get us all lined up. An airscrew was bolted up on the wall for instruction and he got us to salute it! We all thought it was a bit of a giggle but he wiped the grins off our faces. He showed us some photographs. There were chaps with their heads cut in half and their arms chopped off – they'd walked into an airscrew when someone was about to start it or they didn't realize how close there were. It's always stuck in my mind since – he said, "You're grinning now but without a doubt in your career in the RAF you'll see someone injured like that!"

'I was then sent to my first operational posting at Hornchurch. There were some wonderful chaps there, the kind that made your bed for you when you came back off leave late at night so all you had to do was step right into it. Most of them had been in the air force during peacetime and there was a wonderful spirit. And some characters.

'I was introduced to Spitfires there and became very interested in them. Firms all over southern England were doing Spitfires and the *Daily Sketch* or *Daily Graphic* set up a scheme to see who could do an engine change the quickest. Our particular mob had this idea for putting new engines in. I don't know long it took us but we won. It was a wonderful engine.'

198

*'What were Spitfires like to repair?'*

'Oh, really like Meccano. Very straightforward. I was very interested in the engineering. I loved the work and so did a lot of the other fellows. When the break time came and the Naafi wagon came round with tea, the accepted thing was, somebody would pick something out of a Spitfire engine part from one of the trays in the stores – where did that come from? And we all knew, even if it was a pin this size. We were very proud of our knowledge.'

*'So you'd be working under considerable pressure?'*

'Yes, that was our life, we were working all hours of the day there. The officers were bringing food round to us. When you just couldn't keep your eyes open any more you used to kip out on a pile of blankets in one corner of the hangar. A lot of the work was airframe repairs. I had a pal who was as keen on the airframes as I was on the engines. He taught me how to repair the airframe and I taught him how to repair engines and the two of us used to work together. Usually it was bullet holes in the airframe – some of those kites came back from a sweep looking more like colanders than aircraft! One day a pilot came down into the hangar and said to our chief there – it was after a bombing raid – "Get somebody up on the roof, there's a dead body on there!" Goodness knows how long it had been there! It must have been blown up during a bombing raid.

'At that time, the Battle of Britain was on and we were getting reports on the radio that London was being bashed up. I remember breaking out of camp on quite a few occasions on Sunday when we were not working, and trying to hitch-hike my way back to London to see how things had gone on. My wife and family were in Dulwich. The Elephant and Castle is only about five miles from Dulwich and on one occasion I got that far and just couldn't get any further, walking or any other way. Buildings were demolished and lying across the road. The police wouldn't let you go any further! I thought, if further along is like this is here, everything's gone.

'I also went on a course at de Havilland airscrews, Stag Lane. I was a corporal then – the lowest rank there – with all ranks right up to senior officers. At the end of the course we had to take an exam. I was very keen, interested in the subject, and I thought I'd done pretty well. But when the instructor gave me my marks he made a bit of a face. I said, "How do these marks stand with everybody else?" With a bit of a grin, he said, "Well, you're bottom."

'I said, "Oh! I thought I would have done better than that!"

'He said, "Don't worry about it. The highest marks go to the highest ranks, and they're all scaled down – that saves an awful lot of arguments! In fact you passed well but the highest rank gets the highest mark." I admit I can see now that if I as a corporal got higher marks than some wing commander, somebody's head might have rolled!

'From there I got posted abroad. We didn't know where but the big theory was Trincomalee, Ceylon. The troopship, the *Windsor Castle*, left Glasgow in March 1942. I'll never forget the nights. We were crammed together under the decks so tightly that we were even sleeping on the stairs leading up to the deck. I didn't eat for three days – all I could do was vomit bile and blood. I was completely disinterested in what was going to happen to me and wanted only to die quickly. This wasn't seasickness – it was homesickness. We reached the Med and one night we were torpedoed and sunk. I got picked up by a destroyer, with quite a few other fellows. We had over two thousand aboard, the weight making the decks awash at every turn.

'We landed at Algiers. We weren't billeted anywhere, we just wandered on the beach and tried to sleep on some corrugated iron, with no padding whatsoever. I don't think they knew what to do with us. We were doing nothing, just sitting around the place.

'While we were in Algiers we were billeted in the Casbah! It was reputed to be the world's worst slum. Brothels were legal and well attended, by sailors mostly. Oddly enough, we were almost regarded by the natives as fellow occupants. When we first went there we had to go around at least six at a time, armed with revolvers, in case of trouble, but when we got accepted we used to wander through the Casbah on our own.

'Whilst I was there, the RAF decided to develop a tri-fuelling squadron, using Napier Sabre engines. I was pretty keen on the mechanical side so they sent me on a course in England, at Napier's in Acton. We flew home – I've got an idea it was a Lancaster. We were in the bomb hold, most frightening thing because there's one bomb door which opens like that and we were just standing around on it. There were ten of us inside there. I can remember one of the crew looking down during the flight and asking, "Are you all right down there?"

'I said, "We're all right but there's a pipe here dripping petrol like mad and filling up a slot at the bottom!"

'In flight the bomb doors were shuddering and opening two or three inches at the bottom – you could see right down, very frightening. Very cold too. We were so high up we could just about see shipping in the Med.

'Back in Algiers we were on real hard tack as far as food was concerned, but when we got to England, to Napier's, there were breaks mid-morning, lunchtime and mid-afternoon. A trolley used to come round *loaded* with food – I suppose because it was munition work – but they had whatever they wanted there! Bacon sandwiches, cold sausage rolls, everything! I used to buy some of this stuff and take it home. We'd never seen anything like it!

'When I returned to Algiers I was more or less put in charge of a gang of ten and they started up a new hangar out at Maison Blanche for producing Sabres. It was just a big bare hangar, with a lot of packing cases and crates and all the materials for an overhead gantry which was going to run on rails down both sides. That was all stacked in the middle of the floor waiting for a gang to come out from England and erect it. After we'd been there about a month nobody came and we couldn't find out about it. I said to these nine other chaps we'd erect it ourselves. It was a twenty-ton gantry. We got some extra native labourers, balanced it on blocks and gradually raised it, and we got the thing erected. When the gang did come out from England they just couldn't believe that we'd done it without any cranes and derricks.

'I have some photos of the Sabre. It was an abortion of an engine. The Merlin had six cylinders, the Sabre twenty-four, and none of the studs, nuts and bolts were accessible – you couldn't even see them! You were feeling around corners and you'd got weirdly contorted spanners to get at them, giving it half a turn then choosing another spanner and giving it another bit of a turn! Oh, it was shocking!

'When the engine came from the works it was almost solid with inhibitor grease. Everything inside was smeared with this stuff before they assembled it. Shocking sort of thing. I developed a proper oil tank and this cleaned all the stuff out without any dismantling. It worked very well. I put them into Typhoons and the engine then had a cotton cartridge starter. You got a thing very much like a six-chamber revolver, with a chamber about that diameter. You loaded it up and when you pulled the trigger it used to fire a pellet, but it also produced a lot of gas at very high pressure – it was a very sudden push. When you were in there and you fired it, inevitably one clutch didn't start it off so you fired all six. If it still hadn't started you got out quick because the whole engine was in flames! It was obviously a rushed job, they hadn't worked out all the problems.

'What happened then was just typical RAF muddle. We stripped engines and reassembled them over and over again. Not one engine was assembled in a serviceable state, so in other words ten of us had been completely wasting our time for eighteen months. I calculate that amounted to forty thousand lost man-hours. Then the war finished in Europe and all these engines which had been overhauled and wrapped up in packing cases were taken to the docks and dumped in the sea! Hundreds of them. There was no use for them and I don't suppose they could have sold them for what it would have cost to get them back to England.'

'*How long were you out there?*'

'Two years. (*He shows me a portfolio of photographs of his service in Algiers and Egypt.*) That little chap (*an Algerian boy, grinning at the camera and clutching a bottle of beer*) was our servant. He used to cost us in wages the equivalent of six shillings a fortnight. I don't know how old he was, about six I should think. He used to wake me up in the sergeants' mess with a cup of tea, and that was fairly early in the morning, then clean up the room, and at night-time he'd still be there.'

'*Did he have family or was he an orphan?*'

'An orphan, I think. He was glad to get in there because the conditions in Algiers for the natives were pretty grim. If he could get to the swill bin, that was worth his while. Meals were prepared in the mess, the swill went into a big forty-gallon drum and these natives used to wipe it round, get any food they could out of there. The poverty was very bad.

'When we were billeted in the Casbah, you could hear a noise at night and it was the natives going through all the dustbins that had been put out to be emptied. They'd be turning these dustbins upside down on the pavement just to find a fishbone or something. In fact some disease, I think it was cholera, broke out whilst we were there and we weren't allowed to mix with the Arabs at all, you had to go straight into the workshops. You could see dead natives lying around on the streets, nobody would bother to touch them.'

'*When did you come out of the RAF?*'

'There was no work to do, everything had been packed up but I couldn't get released because there was no other flight sergeant to take my place. I went to see the CO about it and he said, "We've got to have a replacement here."

'I said, "I'm not doing anything so if you want me I'm down on the beach!" I was building a hut down there. Which wasn't the way for a flight sergeant to talk to a commanding officer, but I was time-expired, he couldn't do anything really, and he accepted the position. For about another two months I was on the beach building boats and just hanging around till my number did come up and I left.'

*'What was your worst experience during the war?'*

'Oh, being torpedoed! It was very crowded on the ship and the hammocks were slung so close together that as the ship heeled, one hammock would rub against the other. I remember feeling, oh, fed up with this. It was very close and fuggy under there and for several nights after lights out, I'd taken my hammock down and gone to sleep upstairs on the companionway, sitting on the stairs and sleeping there all night. I don't why I'd gone back again to my hammock but the night after I'd stopped sleeping on the stairs, this bomb – or torpedo – hit and that's just where it hit!

'There was a tremendous bang and almost immediately the ship heeled right over. We were right down at the bottom of the ship, but the crew were all scurrying around unscrewing big brass plates in the floor and turning cocks and eventually they righted the ship so that the gunwale was just about level with the water on one side.'

*'You took to the boats?'*

'It wasn't very well organized. There was a load of boat stations but nobody had said what should be done in the event of an accident. These rafts were piled up on the deck and thrown over and the next thing we saw was they were floating way back there because the ship was still moving! Apparently you have to tie them on to the rail before you throw them over. I dare say half a dozen or so were lost.'

*'Were many people killed?'*

'Oh yes, quite a few. The stairway from the tourist deck down to the after-hatch had been blown away at the bottom. Two soldiers gave a frightful yell when they got to the end of the ladder and fell off into the dark hole beneath. The water was cold and it seemed very eerie in the dark. I remember thinking I mustn't get drawn into that hole in the ship's side! Then a body floated past and his boots really scared me – they looked like a dorsal fin!

'I landed on the raft and there was quite a big contingent of elderly army types on there as well as us RAF chaps. In those days they called us the Brylcreem Boys. The raft was overloaded. Quite a lot of chaps were floating around, either hurt in the explosion or drowned. They recognized them as their pals and they were pulling them on the raft even though they were dead.

'Eventually, instead of hanging on to the raft, which was about this depth in the water with ropes all round it, we were almost holding the raft up, keeping it afloat! I said to these army types, "It's no good saving him even if he is your mate! It's no good trying to keep him on the raft, it'll just make it worse for the rest of us!" They all turned on me – "RAF! You get off!" So when I saw another raft with fewer chaps on I left my raft and tried to swim off to it. It's easy enough when you're looking down on the sea from a ship but when you're in the water, whilst you're in one trough of the sea, you'd get a swell up here. As soon as I'd got a few yards away I couldn't find this other raft! I got rid of my life-jacket and I could swim very well but when I struck out for this other raft I never did find it, even though I knew it was over there somewhere!

'A destroyer had turned up by that time but we thought they weren't going to bother with us. The destroyer didn't quite know whether there was a sub about or what had done the damage and they were dropping depth charges all around. Eventually they came back and went round with a searchlight picking up odd bods on their own first and dealing with the chaps on the rafts afterwards so I was probably one of the first to be picked up. I was spotted by the destroyer's searchlight beam and the crew threw me a rope but I was so cold by this time I could only hold on till I had dragged my waist out of the water, then I kept slipping back again. My fingers were so cold I couldn't manage the vertical climb up to the deck!

'Eventually two sailors clambered down and hauled me up between them. It didn't worry me at the time. There was no panic, definitely no panic. Fellows at that age are funny. They're wisecracking. I remember someone saying you shouldn't be here, you haven't got your swim-suit on!

'The sailors brought us some steaming hot coffee – I suppose this is part of the routine – get some steaming hot coffee down. The first thing I did was find my way to the galley. I was only in underclothes and I rinsed these out under a tap – I didn't like them being in salty water. Isn't it funny? When I think of it now I get cold shivers! But at the time, being all fellows together, it didn't seem to worry me so much.

'By that time they were picking up dozens and dozens of fellows and they were all dropping down on the deck. As I say, there were these big jars of hot coffee around. I recognized one chappie who was in our lot, in the RAF. I was trying to fold his hands round the coffee and warm him up a bit and he just died in my arms. Shock, I suppose. But another fellow who'd had quite a big chunk torn out of his leg in the explosion – they'd hauled him up and put him on the deck – was quite cheerful and happy! I heard from him afterwards, he got over it all right. Some people die of shock and others can take it.

'When I came back to England at the end of the war, it took a lot of settling down. You missed all the camaraderie, the chaps that you worked with. Thinking of it now I realize it must be very strong in the mining industry. It's probably why they stick together, all working in danger together, it probably builds up quite a spirit. Getting back to civvy street, it's such a complete change, it's almost like homesickness in reverse. All this is why it's interesting talking to you, this is a part of my life which *I* feel was important but nobody else does who hasn't been through an experience like it. People since the war – they say oh, I can't be bothered with all that – so you don't tend ever to mention it. I've found it very interesting getting all this off my chest. I've never spoken to anybody like this before.'

206

# 9

# SHOT UP, BALED OUT, CAPTURED!

BOMBER COMMAND SUFFERED MORE LOSSES PROPORTION-ately than any other branch of the service. Over 47,000 aircrew died on operations and another 8,000 were lost in accidents. Nearly 10,000 more became prisoners, but if the plane was shot up an airman had only a one-in-five chance of baling out, landing safely, and becoming a prisoner. *Alan Mellor* was flight engineer on a Halifax that was badly damaged over Berlin in January 1944.

'They threw everything up at us there and shot us to bits. We didn't have enough fuel to make it home, though we flew on for a good three and a half hours. But the Halifax really was a good aircraft. She could take a lot of damage. We had no starboard elevator, half a rudder, and half the port elevator was gone, but we managed to get it down, to crash-land. She was far superior to the Lancaster, far superior. It's always been a sore point with me. When I saw your letter in the local paper I thought I'd get in touch with you. You know, it was often given out on the news that so many Lancasters took part in a raid but actually it was Halifaxes – the Halifax was left out of things and as a crew member you actually felt, well, robbed.

'I volunteered for the RAF – joined on my nineteenth birthday which was the eleventh of November 1939. My papers came through on a Friday and I picked 'em up: my mother and father didn't know, I hadn't told 'em. When I spoke to my father about going in the RAF – years before the war started I wanted to go in the RAF – oh no! So I was a bit apprehensive about telling them. I was going up on the Monday morning and it was the Sunday night before I told them.'

'*Did you tell them you were on bombers?*'

'Oh yes, they knew I was on bombers.

'The RAF never dictated who you were going to fly with. You were all put in a room, like a social occasion, drinks and talk. You were told to go round and sort yourselves out. There was no time limit. You weren't rushed into it. Probably take two or three days. I remember a chap, pilot by the name of Wade, I'll never forget his name, came up to me and said, "Would you like to be my flight engineer?"

'I thought he's all right but I said, "Well, I haven't had a chance to look around yet!" (*Laughs.*) I don't know why. He got shot down on his first op and killed. I'll never forget that, I suppose that's how I remember his name.

'I walked around and I saw Rob. He was a real tall thin gangling sort of bloke, he seemed as though he hadn't anything in him at all, but we were attracted to each other straight away. We became great friends. And George the wireless operator, a London fellow, we got on like that!' (*Snaps his finger.*)

*Mrs Mellor:* 'He was best man at my wedding. They still keep in touch, those two.'

*Alan:* 'When you worked it out, you'd put a whole crew together, all with basically a few hours' training. If the pilot had six hours, that would have been a lot. Your wireless operator probably had more experience as far as wireless is concerned. Gunners didn't, navigators might have, but not under operational training. Very very difficult. How can I explain it to you? It's like you go to school in the RAF, you're taught things by the book. You go from your training unit to your operational training unit, they say the same things, do it by the book. You go from there to your operational unit and the first words that the chief engineer says is forget what you've been told. Forget everything about it, it doesn't apply, and that's right.

'We flew the Mark Is – we used to get a lot of tail flutter with them. Then they changed to the Mark III and oh, a tremendous difference! Full bomb-load with the original ones, you used the whole of the runway and struggled to get off but with the Mark III you took off as though you didn't have anything on board at all!'

*'How many trips did you do before you were shot down?'*

'Er, fifty-nine.'

*'So you did a second tour?'*

'Yes.'

*'And out of that fifty-nine can you remember approximately how often you were hit?'*

'I was' (*counts them*) 'oh, about twenty times, I suppose, about twenty times.'

*'Were you superstitious?'*

'I used to have a very favourite tune at that particular time, which was "Begin the Beguine". Whenever I heard it and we used to go out on operations we always had a rough time. It got so bad in the end that they used to rush to the wireless to turn it off so that I didn't hear it, that's how bad it was. I got very superstitious about that. Still am. And Q for Queenie was a jinx aircraft because so many of them – *every* Q for Queenie – was shot down. They tried to do away with Q. Crews would carry mascots and wouldn't fly without them. Very superstitious. My pilot always used to tap on the door before he went in, like that' (*taps on the table*). 'I don't care what crew member it was they were always superstitious. The fear is always there, like everything else, if you're in the trenches or you're in the front line, you've still got the fear.

209

'You flew out in three waves and the last of the three used to get most of the fighter attention. The inexperienced crews used to be in the first wave, and the more experienced you got the further you were pushed back, into the third wave. Which we ended up in. The third wave all the time.

'You see, the German defence was extremely good. Their searchlights for a start, in a box, and each box contained a hundred searchlights or so. You just used to get the one beam roving around but as soon as it touched you, the rest used to come on and you were coned. If you were coned you were very lucky to get out. We got coned once, only once, but it was a hell of a job to get out –'

*'What did you do to get out of it?'*

'We dived straight down, got maximum speed and pulled out on the way. But you're very lucky to get away. You don't know where you are, you can't see a thing, they're so blinding and so powerful. They fire up the beam and then it's like going into the target. Obviously you've got to fly one direct route so it's like a dead straight line, and they know once you start your bombing run that's the way you come in and that's the way you're going out. To avoid collision you've got to fly in that particular line. Once they find your stream, which way it's going – they used to fly above and drop flares, one there, one there, on each corner, on either side of the line, so it's like a street. Once they'd lit up the sky they'd hang there and fighters used to come in, you're on a straight level course and can't deviate, not during a bombing run. The defence was quite good.'

*'How did you cope with flak?'*

'What they told you to do was weave, and light flak didn't bother you because it was well below you – sent purely and simply to keep you up, not to bring you down. If you were down low enough they'd have a go at you to bring you down. With the heavy flak, if there's a large group of aircraft, then they couldn't predict you, not with accuracy, so they used to fire up what they called a box barrage, cover a certain area of the sky. The only thing you could do was weave, which is what they used to tell you to do, or you could weave without straining the pilot simply by the movement of the gun turrets. By moving them you'd cause the aircraft to weave. A bomber can hold its own against a fighter, irrespective of being slower – being slower helps, because you can turn inside him and provided you've got a good gunner giving you the correct instructions then the pilot'll be all right.'

'*There was a blind spot on the Halifax –*'

'Yeah, underneath. They would come up underneath you. We had what they called Monica but we never used it because it drove you mad. But one night we did have it on and we could hear this pip-pip-pip and it was increasing, getting nearer and nearer but we couldn't see a bloody thing! We were flying just underneath the cloud, and all of a sudden the cloud disappeared and there was a JU88 homing in on us, right above us – he couldn't have been twenty feet up! The mid-upper gunner said, "Shall I have a go at him?"

'The skipper said, "No, leave it! See what happens! Don't give our position away – we don't know how many of them there are knocking about, might be more than one!" And just at that moment a Mosquito came up and chased him away. Good old Mozzie!'

'*Did you always fly the same plane or did you take any?*'

'Oh no, we had our own! It was J and we used to have a big portrait of Jane out of the *Daily Mirror* on the nose! We always called it J-Jane and of course they didn't like that, specially after the Americans came in – it had to be J-Jick. They used to say, you mean J-Jick – don't forget J-Jick! Just because the Americans used Jick as their call sign we had to conform, so there wasn't any confusion but we wouldn't have it – we were always J-Jane, and we would never knuckle under!

'I had three crashes through engine trouble, engine failure or an engine knocked out. One of them was quite funny. We were running short of fuel, coming back from Milan, and apart from that we were jumped by a fighter. The bomb doors fell open. We couldn't close them, not even with the emergency. On the Messier system on the Halifax you could pump them back up, but even that had gone and we weren't sure whether our undercarriage was going to come down or not. We could smell burning rubber and we didn't have a clue what it was – we searched the plane from one end to the other because it was very strong! But we couldn't find anything. The fumes were really unbearable.

'Anyway we crept back and got as far as Middle Wallop: we had to call up for an emergency landing. We put the under-carriage down and got three green lights so we were all right. As soon as we touched down we knew what it was. The wheels and the undercarriage just folded up – the tyres had burned right through. The belly skidded across the airfield – lot of dust and smoke – we went to get out as quick as possible, in case she caught fire – but all the bolts had been shot through! We couldn't open the door! My wireless operator – "Oh," he said, "I want to have a pee!" A natural reaction, to be truthful! I said to him, "Go through the hole in the door!" I remember saying it, you know! And he did. At the same time, unbeknown to us, a Waaf had been going round the perimeter in a van, came tearing over and tried to open the door of the aircraft from the outside – she was covered! We all wanted to stay in the aircraft after that! It wasn't me, girl, it wasn't me!

'I was on operations until the twenty-ninth of January 1944, when we were hit over Berlin. We found we'd lost the H2s equip-ment, in the big blister underneath. That had gone, leaving a complete hole in the floor. The rear turret had gone. The rear-turret gunner was blown inside the aircraft and the only wound he had was the shrapnel through his hand, and both the zips of his flying boots were skin deep in his legs – as though he had a zip in his leg.

'We crashed in Holland, a place called Enkuizen if I remember rightly. We tried to set the aircraft on fire but it didn't burn. We went along the dykes. The banks were very steep, we walked along them for miles. We wanted to cross the road and there was a curved fence with a greenhouse on the corner which went back a hell of a long way. We couldn't see through it, couldn't see a soul anywhere, so we crossed the road and walked straight into them – four Dutch policemen and two German officers. One of the Germans spoke perfect English and he said, "For you the war is over!" *I* wouldn't say it but he said it.

'They handed us over to the Luftwaffe who took us to Amsterdam where they marched us through the city to the old naval barracks. While we were going along the people in the trams were giving us the victory sign.

'They put us in a dungeon, you couldn't say it was a cell, it was a dungeon. It had a big massive door as wide as this kitchen, and a little tiny grill. Every five minutes the grill used to open and they'd shout, "Roosevelt gangster!" (*Laughs.*) *"Roosevelt Terrorfliege!"* They used to shout that through the window and slam the thing shut again.

'Then they took us into Germany proper. We got on a lorry with four Americans and a massive contingent of guards and they put us in the train. A sergeant's sitting up against the window here, I'm next to him, my pilot was sitting next to me, another two guards, and three guards opposite. The door opened and a sailor tried to get in. We asked him if he was looking for the *Scharnhorst* because it was sunk Christmas Day 1943, wasn't it? I thought he was going to do us an injury, I really did!

'We had to change trains at Zwolle and that was the first indication I had of how the Dutch were really frightened of the Germans. It was a massive station, something like King's Cross, and it was a busy time of day: the train pulled up and these guards formed a circle round us with their guns pointing out, not in! We were the prisoners but the guns were pointing out and that platform was cleared like that! With the officer in the lead they marched us down the subway and there was an old lady going down. They knocked her straight away down the steps, didn't bother to ask her to get out of the way or go round her, just knocked her out of the way, and that was that.

'They put us on the other train which took us into Germany proper, to Frankfurt to the interrogation centre. That was the last I saw of anybody for a fortnight. They put me in a very narrow cell, between three foot and four foot wide, but very long, about as long as this kitchen and half as long again. It had very hot bars running across all the way through, which they turned right up, hot and cold treatment. They'd turn it up till it got so you took your clothes off, and then they'd turn it right down so you shivered. You don't know where to lie except on the floor, and the only way you could get a drink was they had a sort of lever up on the wall by the door. If you pulled it down it dropped a metal plate outside and the guard used to come. You'd say I want to go to the toilet and they'd let you out and that's the only way you could get a drink. They never brought you anything.

'After two days of that a German officer came in. He spoke perfect English and wanted me to sign the form for the Red Cross – well, we were warned about that – it had details you were not supposed to answer so I refused. They took me into a massive room with a German officer sitting at a desk and *he* spoke very good English too. He asked my name and I told him. Number, and I told him that. He opened a book and for two or three minutes turned the pages over. "Oh yes," he said, "we've been expecting you for a long while!" And he told me more about myself than *I* knew! "Oh yes," he said, "you come from Moray Road, Finsbury Park?"

'I said, "Yes, that's right."

'"You went to Montem Street School?"

'"That's right."

'"You became a wall and floor tiler?"

'"That's right!"

'"Well," he said, "I lived in Blackstock Road for years!"

'Then he said, "You belong to the no-petrol squadron." No petrol? I didn't know what he was talking about so I didn't answer. It struck me afterwards that the letters of our squadron were NP – it didn't register at the time. He wanted to know what engines were we using? Because that was the new one – it was the

214

first time it had been on operations. I didn't answer, didn't answer at all. He said, "You will tell me. If you want to go to prison camp," he said, "you'll tell me." Anyway I still didn't answer and he started, he went mad! What he said I don't know because he spoke German and I didn't – but as you see 'em in the films was exactly the way he performed.

'Then he quietened down, went out of the room and came back with the *Daily Mirror*, and a packet of Player's cigarettes. He offered me a cigarette. I thought I'm not going to refuse that! He said, "You will tell me what it is, we will find out, we will find out!" He went back to the book again and told me where I'd been trained, the marks I'd got off the course, everything. Eventually they threw me back in the cell.

'After a fortnight of this, I was shoved out and went to Stalag Luft III, where the Great Escape took place. But they saw us as troublemakers, which I was, unfortunately, I don't know why, and sent us to Stalag Luft IV, up near Memel in Latvia. We hadn't been there very long when the Russians started to advance and they evacuated us. Well, including the French, Polish and American prisoners of war I suppose there must have been twenty thousand of us, so we were split into two groups and the ten thousand I was with went to Memel, on board a coal barge called the *Instaberg*. We sailed down the Baltic, all loaded in the hold, ten thousand of us in one hold, you can imagine, we were sitting on each other, literally one on top of the other. There were no facilities for anything so they used to shove hoses down every morning.

'Eventually we got to Swinemünde and we'd no sooner landed than they marched us off, the whole width of Swinemünde which is I think forty-eight kilometres, a fair hook especially with no food. Then into Germany proper and we were on what they called over here the Black March. We had the SS with us, and if you dropped out through sickness or anything the SS just used to shoot them. There weren't many of us left when we were picked up, out of the ten thousand, there were very few left. I think there was about one thousand seven hundred of us left.'

*'The others had died?'*

'Mm, mm. Something like that. I did know the actual figures but I can't remember them now. We continued on that march until we were finally picked up by the Sixth Airborne Division. I had dysentery very bad. We'd nowhere to go, we just kept going in circles, but we happened to stay in one place for about ten days and my wireless operator managed to get some milk and a loaf of bread. I think that saved me because I didn' even have the strength to crawl in the end. You get so weak, you begin not to care.

'We managed to get away early one morning. We knew the front wasn't so far off. It was just beginning to get daylight and we heard what we thought were tanks so we hid. I was looking through the bottom of the hedge – we were on a slight rise – and down the bottom field there was another row of hedges and I could see a red hat going along. I thought that can't be a German! I took a chance and ran down there and it was the Sixth Airborne Division. They said, "We can't stop, we've got to get to Kolberg before the Russians, but commandeer any German vehicle you can lay your hands on! We'll give you as much petrol, all the food you want, and make your way to Lüneburg!" So we were more or less left to our own devices. We managed to get a motor bike and with that and a car and a lorry, we eventually reached Lüneburg – it took us about two and a half days.'

*Mrs Mellor:* 'Really, the way he looked when he come home, he weighed just under four stone. He couldn't even pick up his overcoat. He looked like Jesus.'

*Alan:* 'I was met, mind you, the RAF met me at King's Cross and offered to drive me home in a van. I said no, I've looked forward to walking out of Finsbury Park tube station, that's the way I'm going. I came out the Wells Terrace end and there's a pub on the corner. A conductor was standing outside and he said, "Cor blimey, mate!" I was dragging my bag – all I had in it was an overcoat, a vest, a pair of pants, a pair of socks and a shirt,

216

that's all I had in it! But I couldn't carry it, I was dragging it. He said, "Cor blimey, mate, you look rough! You look as though you could do with a drink!"

'I said, "Thanks all the same, mate, I couldn't even touch it at the moment!" I walked up the road, passed my sister and she didn't recognize me.'

*Mrs Mellor:* 'But he had a beard. His hair was jet black, very dark, almost to the point where he looked foreign. Where it had grown, his hair was down here, and he had a beard. He was so thin in here (*his cheeks*) that I always said he looked as though he'd come off the cross, so nobody would have recognized him. Probably only his mother, nobody else.'

*Alan:* 'The funny part about it was, I wasn't supposed to be on the operation that we got shot down on! I wasn't supposed to be on it at all. We were due home on leave – we'd had one or two very bad operations – well, we had several come to that! It was an all-English crew when we started, but the rear gunner went off his head and screamed to be let out the aircraft one night. We had to come off the runway and wait while they sent us out a replacement. He was subsequently court-martialled and we had to go to his court martial. He was reduced in the ranks and convicted of Lack of Moral Fibre, which was a terrible thing! Now looking back on it it was a thing that should never – the word should never have existed! I think that that sort of thing should be scrubbed if anybody's got that on their record. He'd done five operations up to that particular time.

'Then a fortnight after that, we had an English navigator and he decided that he just wanted to get out of the aircraft! We were over Germany at the time and he just wanted to get out! We had to tie him down and restrain him. He was also court-martialled but got away with it on medical grounds. We had two Canadians after that, rear gunner and navigator, both very good, so we got on all right together again.

'This particular night we went in to get our leave passes and they said, "Oh no, you've got to stay, two crews haven't returned to base. If they get back in time to get bombed up you can go, but if they don't –'' So there were two crews standing by, mine and another, and one crew got back! We tossed up and lost so we had to take the place of the crew that didn't get back. We went to briefing and found it was Berlin – oh, Christ, no! Not again!'

'*You'd been there already?*'

'Yes, twice before. It was a bad operation, a bad place. The defence was very hot, very strong, apart from the fact that you had a long journey over enemy-occupied territory. You'd got fighters coming at you all the time and you've got them all the way back. When we set off I went down to change over my tanks and the fuses blew! We carried three spare fuses and I put every one in and the last one held – if it hadn't we'd have had to come back! It held. It just seemed as though it was – coincidence!

'When we got to the target it was well alight. We had a master-bomber and our call sign was Ravens. We must have been absolutely spot on time because they called up and said, "Hello ravens! Hello ravens! Ignore reds, ignore reds, bomb greens, bomb greens!" We were making our bombing run on the reds and we changed course and we'd no sooner changed than WHOOMPH! Anti-aircraft shells!

'Next thing I remember was a brilliant white flash and then a terrific explosion. I looked and the target was up there (*up above him*), so I knew I was upside-down. I looked out through the astrodome and the wing was alight, so we immediately pressed the fire extinguishers – it went out. There was a terrific wind, everything was blowing about, things were flying about all over the place, negative Gee! Bloody great accumulators floating past you, but finally it got straight and we tried to get everything heavy into the nose, because that was the trouble. That was how we sat. To hold the nose down everybody had to move forward, to try and keep the weight there because we were continually going up.

'That's how we came back right the way across Germany till

we got to Texel. It was coming daylight then and they really pumped everything at us, you could see it going in through the floor and out through the top. They look as if they come up ever so slow until they get to you, they were very accurate with them, and then we had no choice. My parachute was useless, all shot to pieces, in little bits. My pilot said take his but by that time we were only about two hundred and fifty feet – no chance.'

*'Did you ever think that you might get shot down?'*

'Oh yeah! Not first of all. It's like everything else – the first four or five, even though we'd had rough trips, it didn't seem to register. But after that, that's when it registers, and then you're all nervous. The worst time was before take-off because you go out to the aircraft an hour before and sit there and wait and all you're praying for is for them to scrub it! (*Laughs.*) To be truthful. But once you start, I suppose it's training, you just get down to doing what you've got to do. Your life depends on it anyway. It just becomes routine. I'm not going to say you're still not scared. Especially the high moments of tension. On the last one, definitely, I had a premonition, this was it.'

*Mrs Mellor:* 'My mother-in-law knew!'

*Alan:* 'It's funny, we were due home on leave and I sent a telegram to say expect me at three o'clock in the morning and I didn't have a chance to cancel it. Once operations are on you're not allowed to make a phone call or any communication whatsoever. Anyway, I got hit at exactly three o'clock in the morning, dead on three, and at three o'clock in the morning my mother woke my father up and said, "Alan's downstairs, go and let him in!" I used to throw a stone up at the window. He said, "No, I can't hear anything!" When my father didn't get up, she got up, went to the window and saw me standing at the gate. Went down to let me in and I wasn't there! She looked and couldn't make it out, came back upstairs and told my father, and he just told her, "Silly cow! Go back to sleep!" (*Laughs.*) And the next morning they received the RAF telegram – I've got them here somewhere –

219

saying shot down on operations, your son was reported missing, you know.

'About six months later they had a letter from a woman some-where up north saying that on such-and-such a radio she'd heard my name mentioned as a prisoner of war, and that was the first indication they knew that I was a prisoner of war!

'When I came home they met us at the aircraft. Heads of the different services were all there, air vice-marshals, marshals, admirals and God-knows-what, shaking hands with everybody as they came off the plane. I went to a rehabilitation centre near Rugby which was supposed to equip you for civilian life. I hated the bloody place so I didn't stay – I walked out and nobody missed me. I used to go back and collect my money, wages for a fortnight and come home again, and nobody said a word.

'One day I went there and the CO said, "I haven't seen you for a while, where have you been?" I didn't tell him! He said, "Have you made up your mind what you want to do?"

' "To be truthful I think I'll stay in the RAF."

' "Well, I don't know," he said, "there's so many – I don't know what the situation is."

' "I think that's what I'll do."

'They sent me home on indefinite leave and I was at home, oh, a good two months. They didn't know what to do with me. I was sitting around. They'd so many and they didn't know what to do with them. I was so bored!

'Now it makes you feel very bitter, all the things they do, but I wouldn't have missed it. The friends I made.. The camaraderie was great, it's a different world! A different world! It's how the world *should* be without wars! Everybody helped one another, it's a different life. Unless you've experienced it there's no way you can possibly understand it. We used to have some terrific times! Really great. I had a great bunch of fellows which I wouldn't have missed for the world. Nostalgia! I certainly wouldn't forget it. They take the mickey out of me and say, "Oh Dad!" '

*Mrs Mellor:* 'He won't go in a ship, or on the water, or in a boat of any kind. He will not go near the water.'

*Alan:* 'No I won't.'

*Mrs Mellor:* 'It's about the only thing I can say really, apart from the lumps and bumps he's got. He will not go near a boat.'

*Alan:* 'I didn't like to talk about the war first of all, but now, it doesn't bother me. One time I wouldn't. Just after the war, no.'

*'Because of the prison camp experiences?'*

'I think so. I didn't want to talk about anything like that to be truthful – I had an extreme hatred of the Germans. I'm still not particularly fond of them. I don't think I've detested anybody so much in my life.'

*'Have you flown since the war?'*

'The first one I was very apprehensive about. It's hard to explain. Not to the extent that I didn't want to get in it, I was looking forward to it and yet not. But once I was off I felt great, I was back to normal. If I go away on holiday the best part is the flight there and the flight back. In a sense ninety per cent of it is lost, but if the window's there and I'm by the window, I'm great! And I don't regret any part of that. I love flying, I really do. I'm happy up there.'

*Bill Sixsmith* was also shot down, in a Spitfire over Italy towards the end of the war. He has prepared for my visit with photos of his RAF career arranged in neat piles on the coffee-table near where we sit. From time to time he refers to his log-book, checking the entries against the photographs. 'That's Reg and me, we joined up together and trained in Rhodesia. He turned out to be the best pilot and I was the worst. I got lost on a cross-country, force-landed in Bechuanaland, got ill and caused the RAF no end of trouble. The upshot of it was, they sent the best ones home

221

and the worst ones up to the Middle East. So like ten thousand other pilots Reg never flew again and I did about seventy ops in North Africa and Italy.'

*'You look very young. How old were you?'*

'Eighteen. The first time I went in a fighter I looked at the pilot and what a shock! He was no more than twenty and I was seventeen or eighteen. Same age, nearly. My father was in the First World War as a pilot and he was over in France after eight hours! I went on ops after about three hundred! It's a hell of a difference. First World War, you go over there in eight hours, you just didn't live.

'Most wonderful atmosphere in the RAF, in desert air force. Our flight commanders and CO were just like the boys. No difficulties with regard to rank – you called everybody by their Christian name. My first night the CO came up. "Dawn patrol tomorrow! Barber, Griff, Paddy," etc. They're either writing letters, playing cards or reading. They hardly even looked at him – OK, OK – just a brief sign, yes, all right, OK. Well, that took about two minutes and off he toddled. Next morning those who had to fly the dawn patrol, went. I thought, I'll never be able to do that! I was scared!

'The following afternoon, the flight commander said, "We're just going on a recce, would you like to come?" *Like* to come, mind you! Off we went, four of us. We just flew around getting the feel of things. About four days later, the CO came up and said, "Paddy, Sixsmith, Jock, dawn patrol tomorrow!" – and I was just like the others. It didn't affect me one little bit. Just a sign to say, yes I've heard it, OK. You did a dawn patrol and a dusk patrol. But in the middle of them you did the ops!

'We were dive-bombing, all the time. There was no aerial warfare, just dive-bombing, or escorting Marauders up to northern Italy. We went on average once a day, sometimes four Spitfires, sometimes six. We would bomb specific targets – Faenza, different places, or something important like Nazi headquarters, an explosive dump, barges in the Po River. Anything that moved got done. They showed us photographs and said that's what you gotta hit and that's what we hit!

'Everybody had a five-hundred-pound bomb underneath. The leader would say, OK, line abreast, so you'd all get in a big long line – a long way apart. All this business you see on television about close formation is rubbish, because close formation means you're playing with the throttle the whole time trying to keep your place. That uses petrol. You can't afford to use petrol in a Spitfire because they'll only fly for about an hour. You've got to be there and back. You flew so you could see everybody. I mean loose.

'I flew as number two to the wing commander, about that fence away from him. Underneath him and about that fence away.'

*'Looks close enough to me!'*

'Yeah, but you're not on the throttle all the time. If he goes as far as the garages it doesn't matter, so long as you're looking out for him. We get to the target line astern and he would say, "Will you all identify the target!"

'You go round and say, "Yes, I've got it!" Once he's satisfied everybody knows what the target is he says, "We're going in next time round!" We go round again, you just turn over and go straight down, using the machine-gun sight as the bomb-sight. When you get within about two hundred feet you let it go – providing you're not slipping and sliding! You're having to trim the aircraft like mad to keep going straight because it's doing about four hundred to five hundred miles an hour. As you go down you're going faster and faster. If you get the slightest bit of skid the bomb could land two miles away, but if it's not skidding you'll hit the target!

'Down we go, bomb the target, straight up again. You start at twelve thousand, you finish at twelve thousand. You just form up again and home you go!

'Anti-aircraft fire was a big hazard. Faenza was known as flak alley. We often went through it. They used to sling up some stuff and you'd get these great black plumes on either side of you –

223

boom! boom! boom! It sounds brave but at the time you got so used to it you never thought anything of it. It won't hit me! That's where Griff got put on fire. He crash-landed, fortunately on our side of the line.

'We liked flying, oh God yes! Dusk patrol, dawn patrol or anything else that cropped up, wonderful! Come into the crew-room, on desert air forces, CO might say, "I want four pilots to bomb barges in the Po River." They'd come out of the brickwork. If there was one person in the crew-room at that time, before you knew where you were there's twenty! But if he said, "I want somebody to test-fly O for Orange!" – whoosh! Gone! Nobody wanted to test-fly anything. Ops, yes. Test-flight, no. So funny! Just flying, oh! Rubbish! But bomb on board, let's go! Wonderful.

'Funny thing, I never knew what the tour of operations was! I did about fifty-five hours' ops. Since most of them lasted about thirty-five to forty minutes I suppose that means about seventy operations altogether. They didn't think it was possible to put a bomb on a Spitfire but there was nothing else for the air force to do unless they put the bombs on so there we were, dive-bombing like mad! And it was great.

'One time four of us went, supposed to bomb a target. We were on the runway and word came through it was cancelled but because we'd got bombs on they said go and get rid them. We went over and it was a question of finding something to drop them on. We found a little tiny bridge *miles* from anywhere, just a little tiny bridge over a stream. Jock said, "We'll bomb that bridge down there!" Line astern, down we go, blow the bridge to smithereens, come up like this, not taking evasive action, not doing anything because there's nothing there. Suddenly Jock's lost his tail! Direct hit on his tail! He just spun in. He didn't get out. We used to lose about one pilot every fortnight, three weeks, something like that.

'Then I went, got hit in a bomb dive, either going down or coming up, I don't know which. I didn't feel it, but suddenly all the oil fell out and the engine stopped. I said, "My engine's cut, I'm going home." Nobody answered. The radios on those

Spitfires – well! When you got on the runway you said to the tower, "OK to take off?" They'd say, "Yes," and by the time you got into the air it wasn't working!

'I was at seven and a half thousand feet and a Spitfire glides a mile per thousand feet. I was very close to the front line and if I can glide seven miles from this point, I should just about creep over the line. I flew nice and straight, picked out me field which is what you should do, pick out a nice field so you can land. Wheels up of course. I got to five hundred feet and oh! the ammunition, tracer and Christ knows what else! Coming up this side of me, coming up that side of me! I zigzagged away and lost my field. By that time I'd gone down fast. When I approached the ground I was doing about two hundred miles an hour. You can't crash-land a Spitfire at that speed – I was hoping and praying the thing would stop. Finally I saw this field coming up in the distance and it had a sort of forest before it. I thought I'll run along the top of the forest, slow it down and just plop into the field. Which I did.

'I got on to the ground, the whole thing smashed up, propeller and all the rest of it. I just sat there. I could hear gunfire all around me but I couldn't see anything. Then these three Italian peasants came out of this house towards me, very gingerly. I tried to open the hood but it had stuck. I was very lucky it hadn't caught fire – mind you, Spitfires very rarely did. These Italians eventually got the hood back. I tried to get out and couldn't – my legs were paralysed! When you're strapped in you just can't move! I didn't think they were broken – mind you, I didn't know. But I couldn't get out, that was sure. They lifted me out. I put an arm round one and an arm round the other and they took me into this house. I thought I've made it! Italian peasants, I've made it, I've got over!

'They took me through the door, along the passage, into this room, and twenty German officers were sitting down to dinner! Oh God! I couldn't believe it. It was just like the Führer had arrived. "Nice to see you! Well done! Do you want lunch?" (It was half past one, lunchtime.) Can you imagine? I couldn't have

225

faced baked beans under any circumstances. "Would you like a drink?" I thought I better have some wine, it might perk me up a bit. I was as sick as a dog immediately. Down came the German doctor, looked me over, felt me. "It's all right, it's only shock. Don't worry about it."

'I was with them for some time, then they moved me into a room. "Now, got to leave you here, turn the radio on so you can listen to the British news. Don't try and escape because there's a guard on the door. The Canadian tank corps are only two hundred yards away but don't do it!" I could hear the planes going over the top. I thought, God! they'll be back in the mess! We all had to leave so much money – thirty pounds – your mess bill always had to be covered. If you didn't come back, party in the mess that night! I've no doubt they celebrated my departure in the usual way.

'After about an hour the area commander sent for me. Bloody great room he had. He's sitting at a desk writing his papers, didn't lift his head or anything. "Don't you salute senior officers?"

' "No sir, I'm not properly dressed, I haven't got my cap on. In the air force we don't salute officers if we don't have our caps on."

'He got over that and said he wanted to ask me some questions.

' "I can only give you my name, number and rank!"

' "I want to know about your squadron!"

' "Look, put yourself in my position. If I had captured you how much would you tell me? You wouldn't tell me more than your name, rank and number!" He accepted it! Wouldn't ask me any more! It worked so well that time I used it every other time I got clobbered.

'About nine o'clock at night, two enormous German military police came to transport me up north. I got in this jeep, they sat in front, and off we went. Absolutely total darkness. The jeep had these dimmed headlights so you couldn't see it from the air. We'd gone about five or ten miles when they stopped. Country road, total darkness, absolutely quiet. The driver got out, went pit-pat pit-pat into the distance. I thought, I know what's going to

226

happen, he's going to circle round behind and shoot me! I just waited, then all of a sudden I heard pit-pat pit-pat – he got back into the driving seat. He'd got lost, gone to look at a signpost!

'They put me in a truck full of German soldiers. There's always a little seat in the back where they put the tool box. All the German soldiers moved away from that so I could sit down. Most of them came and talked to me. "Don't want to fight the English, this war's all wrong, why don't the English and the Germans join together and fight the Russians!" That's what they wanted. Didn't want to fight us. I found that all over the place. The German army, the Wehrmacht, they just couldn't do enough for me! Treated me like a prince. When I was captured we'd been dive-bombing 'em morning, noon and night, you'd have thought they'd be a bit hostile! Not a bit. When I first got caught, I said to this German officer, "You could see I'd got no engine, I was coming in to land! Why the hell all the tracer?"

'He said, "I'm sorry about that but you were going straight for the commander's house!" When he told me why, I said, "All right, I forgive you!" How they didn't hit me I don't know. They were right on the end of the wings, both sides. Why they couldn't hit the bit in the middle I don't know.

'I finished up at Verona, the interrogation centre. Four of us altogether, myself, two pilots and a gunner. We stayed a few days till we were given three German soldiers armed to the teeth, to take us to Frankfurt. I suppose it's a thousand miles and we walked – twenty-odd miles at a time, the whole of the Brenner Pass. At the end of it we got into a train, about fifty prisoners of war. No room to sit down. I was looking through a crack in the carriage and saw three American fighters! They're going to have this train! I said to the guards, "Better stop the train, get us out!" They did. We ran for our lives down the bank, into the field. These American aircraft blew the whole train to pieces, absolutely. Three German soldiers were killed and we thought that they would take reprisals on us. But they didn't.

'Now we walked, about six RAF and ninety Americans. I'd got flying boots on – there were two types you could have. Lace-up shoe with a kind of puttee attached to it, up your leg, or suede flying boots, and of course I had them, didn't I? They've got fur inside – lovely they were. You can imagine what walking a thousand miles in them did! It's like walking in slippers. My feet were absolutely red-raw.

'We'd got no food, no nothing. My feet were so bad I couldn't walk any more. Two Americans carried me to the camp. I was very lucky. The week previously another air-force boy had come in with the same trouble. They'd sent him on the sixty-mile walk to Nuremberg and he died on the way. When your heels are open it's very very dangerous. When I came in with much the same problem they decided to look after me.

'You stayed three days normally. Get fed, kitted up, Red Cross parcel, then you were ready for your sixty-mile walk to Nuremberg. But I stayed for sixteen days, and on the sixteenth, about four o'clock in the morning, *Raus! raus! raus!* Patton was getting close! They moved us all out and we walked day and night into Germany carrying a Red Cross parcel. We had a hundred and fifty guards, walking along this tree-covered road which was miles, straight as a die, miles in front of you, pouring with rain. Suddenly they'd say halt! You'd sit down on the grassy bank, go straight to sleep. You didn't know whether you were there for an hour or two hours, or two seconds – it felt like two seconds. It was still dark and pouring with rain, you were soaking wet. Up you got and walked on again.

'Eventually, one afternoon, I saw a spotting aircraft over the top of us. What's he doing there? We were walking through this village. Round the corner came tanks, flame-throwers on them, whoo-oosh! Setting everything on fire! We ran behind the houses and waited for the first tank to go past. Great white star on it, fantastic! We rushed out – it's us! It's us! Wha-ah-ah! Very stupid, but fortunately they knew we were there. Some Germans told them there's a POW column ten miles ahead. It was Patton's tank corps – I love that man! We all ran out, they gave us chocolate and cigarettes – you know what the Americans are like. They put the tanks in a big circle and us in the middle for that night. First thing in the morning we had coffee, pancakes, doughnuts, eggs and bacon, everything you can think of. We were all incredibly fit throughout this time. I was thirteen weeks a prisoner, and never got to a prison camp.

'Filthy dirty, hadn't washed or shaved for weeks, terrible. Kept dirty specially for the German public to see us dishevelled but it didn't upset us at all. It was the most remarkable thirteen weeks. Far more exciting than flying. Very lucky to have had it really.

'The Americans emptied out an ammunition truck, put us in it and sent us back to Paris, to RAF headquarters. Went up to the entrance of this place, guards on the door, walked through, officer was there, "What do you want?"

'"We're returned prisoners of war!"

'"Come in! Where are you from? God! I've got to tell the flight commander! Hang on there, hang on!"

'Flight commander comes in –

'"We're just back from Germany –"

'"Oh! Hold on a minute! Get the AOC!"

'They wanted to know if we had been ill-treated, and if we *had*, who had done it. Well, I'd never been ill-treated.

'Innsbruck, this roundabout, about six roads leading off it, the whole area flattened, absolutely flattened. Rubble piled up where the houses were, six avenues just junk piled up. People recognized us and started to collect. Our German soldiers put us against a wall, stood around us with their guns at the ready while the crowd grew and grew and grew. They started throwing housebricks and hit one of the boys, cut his head open. Then they tried to come in to get us but these Germans made it quite clear they'd shoot 'em.

'Two hundred yards down the road, an SS hotel, SS soldiers on the steps, encouraging the population to come in and get us. Our guards had to take us to a prison and put us in there for the night. Turned out the Americans had pattern-bombed the area the night before and blew up a children's hospital. Crowd thought we had done it, especially as we were aircrew. Had we been captured by the SS they'd have done us straight away but the Wehrmacht were fantastic.

'I stayed at RAF headquarters about two days, was sent on leave. This photo's my friend Paddy. When I got shot down he wrote to my mother I was OK. Before he got the reply from my mother he'd been shot down in flames and killed. I understand they lost about twelve pilots in twelve days! Yeah. The Good Lord sits on my shoulder because if I hadn't had mine when I did I might have had it later! My mother and father were told I was missing, but they didn't know anything else.

'When I came out I got a job as a collector of insurance. Terrible! Awful! I went out with the chief salesman – I couldn't *believe* what he did and what he said! He used to sign up everybody he spoke to – they couldn't resist him! On the Wednesday we used to go cold-knocking on the doors. We'd all meet down in Kilburn and the chief salesman would give us a road each and we'd go down this road – lies! Absolute sheer lies! "This street's been specially designated for a special policy this week. If you take advantage of it, fine. If you don't you won't be able to do it next week. Now Mrs Harris and Mrs Smith up the road, they've taken it, what do you think?" We'd finish up with about twenty of 'em. And if anybody did break a leg that was the last thing we wanted to know! That meant paperwork! We just wanted the money, that was all. I could sell insurance to women like falling off a log but when the old man came home at night he threw it out!

'The areas we went to I wouldn't go near now. Harlesden. Shepherd's Bush. I used to go in and collect about thirty-five pounds a week, in shillings and two bobs. You'd never come out *alive* of Harlesden now!

'I don't believe it now myself, you know. I think to myself, did I do that? It seems a bit of a dream really. People get the impression that you're super brave. Nothing to do with it. I'm the biggest coward under the sun! It's the training. Plus it will never happen to you, whatever happens to somebody else. Safe as houses. I was lucky because there was no German aircraft in the sky. We weren't Battle of Britain stuff. What we were doing was exciting but it wasn't dangerous, apart from anti-aircraft fire. Nobody lost their nerve or went berserk. Nobody.

'I was lucky. The navy wouldn't suit me, nor the army. Thought of shoving a bayonet into somebody's not my idea of fighting a war! But if you're in an aeroplane on your own it's real gentlemanly stuff, isn't it? You're shooting at something, you don't know what it is, you're dropping bombs on something and you don't know what that is, and if you kill somebody you don't know about it – it's all good fun really. You don't get too close to what you've damaged. It's all very reasonable and nice. You go back to the mess after you've killed somebody and have a jolly good dinner, play cards in the mess that night, and write home to Mum and say, "I've had a smashing day today! We went on an op and we blew this place to smithereens, it was smashing!" You post it and mother reads it and she says, "Old Billy is doing well!" If you wrote home and said, "I'm in the army and I've just stuck a bayonet in some German!", that's horrible, it really is. I couldn't do that. No, I had a smashing war. I wouldn't have missed it for anything.'

In 1944 *Phil Pearson* was bomb-aimer in a special-duties crew flying Stirling bombers, delivering supplies to the Resistance in France.

'Good old Stirling! Nobody's ever heard of it! But *I think* it was a marvellous aircraft! I went into the RAF in 1941. I volunteered –'

*Eileen Pearson:* 'They told him to go home and wait!'

*Phil:* 'I kept on wiring them and eventually they said if I wired them any more, they wouldn't call me up at all!'

'*Choosy!*'

*Phil:* 'They were being funny. As a kid I didn't realize it. I thought, my God, I'll never get in! This is awful! That kept me quiet.'

*Eileen:* 'One is very silly at seventeen and eighteen. It's a dreadful thing to say but I can remember when war was declared thinking, oh! goody! After the first scare in 1938 and there wasn't a war, I was disappointed! It's dreadful, but I think most young people think that it's all rather exciting. Couple of years of it and you went off the idea!'

*Phil:* 'I was posted to the States for training, to Georgia in the South. We were made very welcome. We liked the coloured lads because we weren't used to coloured people here – we treated them differently to what the Yanks did, especially the Southerners. I know we always got best service in the mess – whatever we asked for. We used to eat like horses. You'd call a waiter up and say you wanted some more eggs – they didn't go and get you an egg, they came back with a great tray full of fried eggs! I suppose the rest went into the dustbin. It was awful when I think of it – terrible! Or a piece of melon which was about that size and about that wide – you couldn't get your face into it. When I came back I had a kitbag full of cigarettes and silk stockings and chocolate –'

*Eileen:* 'Lemons, nylons.'

*Phil:* 'But I flunked the course there, so I remustered as a bomb-aimer in Canada and did my training out there. Came back in June '43. We crewed up just before we went on the Wimpeys (*the Wellington bomber*). We all went into the briefing room or whatever it was, and at that time we hadn't met engineers or gunners. They came in for the first time. Navigators, bomb-aimers and pilots had been together up to then. They arrived and we were told, well, mill around, talk to one another, and sort of just select.'

*'Can you remember what it was that caused you to choose the other members of the crew?'*

*Phil:* 'I don't know really how one cottoned on to one another. You just went round and nattered to people. Are you crewed up? No, I'm not. Well, what about it? I think it was quite a good way of doing it because at least it was your choice. To me, the crew was the most important thing altogether. If one bloke did one thing there would be someone else to back him up, you know. We were an all-British crew, but the squadron was made up of Aussies, South Africans, New Zealanders, Canadians – we all got on well together.'

'*Did you get a lot of losses there?*'

*Phil:* 'Yes, I suppose we did. I can only really remember two particular ones. A new crew came into our billet – our billets were for two crews, fourteen men. This crew was in our billet and they took off – it might have been their first op because we went down and watched them go. They slewed off the runway, went across the grass, pulled up over the tops of trees, went round – we saw them going round – and then there was a great explosion! They went straight into the deck. The other one was a crew that went over to France and crashed. We heard the Germans captured one of them and shot him! By that time the invasion had started and our blokes were classed as saboteurs because we were dropping stuff to the Resistance.

'Our first op was a nickel on Wellingtons – a nickel was a leaflet run, just a training flight at the OTU. You took leaflets over and dropped them somewhere in France just to get used to gunfire and so on. When we were on special duties we did two bombing raids in France on rocket sites and we went with the main force.

'Once we were used as a decoy for the main force, going up to Bremen. We got recalled when we were still out there in broad daylight. All we were told was that if you went with the main force, you just kept your head down and watched the stuff going down past you, which it did. They didn't use Stirlings normally by the time I was flying. But it was ideal for the job we were doing. I think the landing speed was about eighty-five – and the cruising speed about one hundred and thirty.

'Special Operations was taking provisions over to France. Last night we were watching a film on TV and it shows them coming

233

over dropping stuff to the Resistance. There was a bloody great fleet of aircraft in semi-formation and it was barely night-time anyway. That's what we were on, my squadron at Tattenham dropping stuff to the Resistance, but you went over singly, one aircraft, not *shoals* of aircraft. You only did it in moonlight periods because it was low-level, so the rest of the month you were stooging around. You went across to France and then dropped down quickly, low-level to your spot, pulled up, dropped the load, and then hell for leather out of it!

'My own job – a lot of it – was map-reading and navigation. If you fly near enough to the deck you pick up all the points. You could literally follow a river, the Seine or Somme or whatever, you could actually follow the river along whereas with the main force you had a definite route to go. Although we had a definite route it was obviously possible to vary because we'd got no other aircraft with us. Our black-out was pretty good, but in France I don't think they'd ever heard of black-out – well, they had, but a lot of these little villages, I'm not going to say they were lit up like London but at night you could pick 'em out. If you got a moon in front of you it was almost daylight. It wasn't so good when the moon was behind you, but when the moon was in front it was so easy – the rivers almost looked black except when the moon caught them and they flashed. Towns – you could pick it all out really – fields, bushes.

'The Resistance lit bonfires and we were told before we went what the code letter would be. They used Aldis lamps, or torches, or whatever they had over there, that flashed. You'd come over, they'd light the fires when they heard the aircraft, you'd climb up, ready to drop the stuff. You were told how the bonfires were lit. If they're a straight line of three or four, or a cross or something – you'd be told what the recognition letter was and once you got that you'd unload. If you didn't get the letter of recognition you'd take it back.'

*'Did you ever get spotted by an enemy plane?'*

'No, no, I don't think we did. We were low enough that it

wouldn't have been very easy for fighters to shoot us down. It would be mainly from the ground.

'We had a super padre on that squadron. He used to stand at the end of the runway, late at night and it was cold! He was always there when we came back, with rum and coffee, pouring it out. I never knew him not to be there, whatever time it was.

'The first time we took off, on the first op, an electrician came out in his wagon. They'd done all the tricks, but he used to come out to make sure everything was OK. We were out on the pad waiting to take off and he said, "Oh my God, I must have a leak!" or words to that effect. So he did, on the tail-wheel of the aircraft. The next time he came round he said, "Oh, for luck!" This became a thing. He always came round. But this last op, we said, "We'll see you this evening, don't forget, it's our last op, don't forget!"

' "No!"

'He was getting married to one of the WAAF and he went into Cambridge or Newmarket, to buy bits and pieces. We were hanging around at the pad waiting for him to come and he never came! He got back, we understood afterwards, about half an hour later so we took off without him having pee'd on the tail-wheel.'

*'You felt that was bad luck?'*

'Well yes, it was, because we got shot down that night. We got it firmly fixed in our minds. As it was our last op we took a load of empty bottles up with us, because we understood – don't know if it's true or not – if you throw a bottle out from a great height, as it comes down it whistles like a bomb. Our rear gunner loaded up the turret with empty beer bottles and as we went over he tossed them out, just for the hell of it. It was over France, a bit unfair because they were on our side, and on the way back we got shot down. We probably woke the gun crew up – they caught us on the way back. It was only light flak but we were down low on the deck flying at eight hundred feet. They shot the two starboard engines, they caught alight, the flames were all on one side of the aircraft. On the Stirling it's dual control, it took both

Jock and me all our strength to hold the thing up, and she literally ploughed into the ground, but very smoothly.

'We had canisters of some sort, with a spike at the end. If you crashed and the aircraft wasn't alight you could bang 'em into the side of the fuselage and they would burn. Jock and I climbed out of the top along the other wing and by the time we left it was alight. We found out afterwards that Jerry, because they got there so quickly, put it out, and hauled the thing away.

'The rest of the crew went down the back and jumped out there. We ran in one direction and they ran in the other. We heard dogs barking and all I know is that the other five got captured almost immediately, but Jock and I managed to get away with it. We were over there for three and a half months.

'We spent the first three nights hiding out in woods. We'd had first-class training on escape. Went to Feltwell in Suffolk which was near us and did an escape course there, for about three days, and they gave you all the rules of things you should or shouldn't do. Finally they took you out in crew buses into the countryside and dropped you off, one at a time. Your job was to get back to camp, to a given point in the camp without being caught. They did teach you a lot, simple things that were quite true. Never go to knock at a door for help, unless one of you stays hidden and one goes – you can both get caught.

'On Sunday I remember we walked further because we heard the church bells going. We sat in some woods and we could see the church. We thought we ought to be able to get some help there but decided it was a bit too dicey. Once or twice we knocked at a farm – Jock usually went and I stayed hidden in case he was jumped upon so I'd come to his help. They didn't offer any help at all. It wasn't because they were anti-British, they were frightened. Our uniform, when you think about it, looked much of a muchness with the German uniform. We'd still got flying boots on.

'We were walking eastwards, going towards Vervins – we knew there were Resistance up there so we might be able to contact them. On the Sunday we spent the night in a haystack, got inside

236

it, got bitten to blazes! In the morning we got out and shook all the filth and wet off us. We were in a little clearing and we were woken up by a woman with a pail. She turned out to be Polish, don't ask me how we found that out. She could hardly speak any French, nor could we! She came down and milked the cows in the field and she did give us a drink of milk – don't ever drink warm milk straight out of the cow, it's horrible!

'She told us to go back and wait in the clearing and she would bring help. Shortly after, two blokes arrived, didn't speak to us. Jock and I sat in the middle of this little clearing, only about this big (*twenty-five feet across*) with a tree in the middle. We sat with our backs to the tree and these two blokes went round and round this clearing, with sickles pretending to chop. They were really watching us though we didn't realize at the time.

'Then a woman came to see us, a big woman, who'd lived in Jersey or Guernsey and could speak English. She told us she'd be back that evening with some clothes. She took our flying boots, gave me this old pair of boots tied up with string and Jock got a pair of shoes. We kept our trousers, she gave me an old jacket, and Jock an old zip cycling jacket, and caps! Bloody old caps! Took our flying sweaters which were jolly nice wool, whipped those, gave us a haversack each with a bottle of water and some bread, and then we pushed off.

'We'd got our escape kit with us, a plastic pack with a razor, a rubber water-bottle – you could tie it on to your belt and put it down inside your trousers so it couldn't be seen. Maps of the area on material which you could make into silk scarves – what else? Wakey-wakey pills which you could take if you were in a real emergency, odd things like that. Oh, I think there was also a bit of chocolate, nuts and raisins.

'This woman said, "Wait back in the clearing. A youngster will be along from the village later on this evening, you should follow him. He doesn't speak English but he'll make signs and you follow whatever he does and do exactly what he says." So, later on in the evening – it wasn't dark, about six or seven – this lad arrived and beckoned us and we followed him. We kept going,

237

oh, I don't know what time – it was night-time – and we came to a big country house with walls round it and gates. He motioned us to be quiet. We jumped into the ditch because we heard the clattering of boots, and then we heard guard-changing and German voices. We lay doggo in this ditch and he went *"Doucement!"* – which we did get – *"Doucement!"* He wriggled forward to go and get the lie of the land.

'We waited there for I should think an hour or more and he never came back. My belief is, rightly or wrongly, that that was deliberate. We didn't know who they were. We didn't know where we were, they'd got our clobber from us, they'd got no love for us, and they'd deliberately taken us out and dumped us right beside a German headquarters of some sort, wriggled off, and that was it. When it dawned on us this was probably what had happened, we turned in the ditch and well and truly shot off!

'Later, we saw an old girl picking up ears of corn. She was about sixty odd, seventy, a typical little French peasant woman. She'd got a barrow and was collecting all this greenery and putting it in. We went up and spoke to her and she realized what we were – we couldn't speak French, mind you. Well – Jock spoke better French than I did but I could listen to it better, that was how we worked it. Although it was only three days we were getting a bit desperate. I think we would almost have approached Hitler himself and asked for help. We thought, she couldn't lay us out! If she'd started hollering we could have run, but she didn't, she was very good, very good indeed.

'She made it clear that we were to follow her so we did with about twenty yards between. She took us back into Saint-Quentin and into her house. She gave us these super omelettes, French omelettes, which she did on a stove with broken twigs for heating, and she put us up in the front bedroom of the house. We stayed there I don't know how long. Shutters on the windows. And right opposite we used to hear the Jerries come – I imagine it was either a mess or a canteen. We used to look through the cracks in the shutters and watch them going by.

'The time we spent with her, I'm not sure how long it was,

about a week probably, the poor woman was trying to contact somebody who was in the Resistance! It must have been terribly difficult. Eventually she found a schoolmistress who spoke English and who soon put our minds at rest. She got us out. We had to follow a man in a white mac – it sounds like a film, but of course the films are made up of this! If he was stopped we weren't to do anything, we were to keep going and move on.

'He took us to the station – we were told that this would happen. When we got there we had to go and look at the timetable of the train. We hadn't a clue what all this was about. We just stood there looking at the timetables which we couldn't read. Two women came up to us, caught hold of our arms and they got tickets and took us on the train.

'We went to another town and there we were put up by Jean-Marc and Claude, who had a little girl named Françoise – I've met them since – we went over there after the war. We stayed with them for a week or so, but I think they decided it was a bit dangerous. Françoise might let it out so they moved us two or three doors away into a house owned by a chap named Gilles – no surnames obviously.

'The house consisted of a front bedroom, a front sitting room which we never went into and never saw, a back bedroom and a kitchen. At the back was a yard with a small barn at the bottom where they kept chickens. Gilles disappeared and left it to us. We had the house to ourselves, but Claude or one of her sisters used to come out and give us food, and we could take eggs from the chickens and so on. On our own, no worry. We were told exactly what would happen if there was banging on the front door – we had to leap out of the window – and which direction to go.

'They moved us several more times and on one occasion we were put up in a house for a short time. There was a husband and wife and we had the bedroom of their son who was about our age and a prisoner of war in Germany. By this time my socks – I'd got holes like that! We opened a drawer one night and inside were shirts and rolled up socks – loads of them. Everything. This son's. I said to Jock, "Look at this lot, my God!" This is dreadful really, when I think about it now. "I'm going to nick a pair of these socks because mine are absolutely ruined!" So I nicked a pair of socks.

'Well, eventually, we moved off from there, into the woods again with the Resistance. This big bloke arrived, not the chap whose house we were in, but a farmer. There was a lot of nattering amongst the crowd, and they kept looking over at us, natter-natter-natter! After a while one came over and made it quite clear I'd got the socks and later we learned – no kid! – the argument was to whether they should put a bullet in me! There I was being looked after by these people who were risking their necks, and their wives and kids, and I was stupid enough to pinch their socks! If I'd asked for a pair, they'd probably have given them me. But I pinched them. I didn't realize how close I was, but that was what the argument was about.

'At one time we had to run for our lives because the Germans were supposed to have surrounded the village – whether they did or not I don't know. We got into the woods and coming towards us we saw three figures. All five stopped dead. We heard they were speaking English – or American. They turned out to be a pilot, navigator and gunner. From then on the five of us stayed together.

'We hid up in a barn for a long time and people brought food to us every day. One of them took us out once on bicycles to get a breather. Cycling down the road, a Jerry truck passed. As it passed he's going like this at them (*giving them the V sign*) and Jock and I thought, what happens if they stop? There were all these blokes hanging out the back! You're conscious all the time that anything could happen.

'One day they decided to move us from the barn – it was probably getting a bit dicey to get food to us, or somebody had seen a lot of movement. Not being able to speak fluent French one didn't get the gist of it. All we knew was we'd been told by escape committees in England before we ever went flying that whatever happened, do what they told you, they know the lie of the land better than you do.

240

'The rest of the time we were outside, in the woods, but it was June, July, August. The weather was good so it was no hardship to roll up on the ground and sleep out there. We heard that Paris was liberated, the Resistance were getting excited and ready to break out, we heard that the Americans or the Allies had got through near to us. One of the Resistance blokes had pinched six bicycles so we pedalled hell-for-leather towards where we understood the Americans were.

'When we got to the American lines, they took the three Yanks off separately and shoved us in a wire compound for the night. There was one poor lone little German soldier in there – I shouldn't think he was much more than seventeen or eighteen – he was tickled to death to see us!

'Next day we were taken by jeep into Paris. Jock and I were wearing civvy clothes, old boots and things, so every time we stopped in any village, the villagers were shaking their fists – they thought we were Germans or collaborators because we'd got an armed guard in the jeep! Instead of getting fêted as we hoped, as heroes, they were threatening to kill us! It was rather funny.

'We came back to England in a motor torpedo-boat, little sharp-nosed funnel thing. I was scared to death because I thought, well, having got this far, with my luck I'm going to drown, when I'm just nearly home. I stayed up on deck all the time.

'I got back to Peacehaven and they whipped us through to London. I don't know which one it was, MI5, MI6, MI-I-don't-know-what, took us for a debriefing, still in these rags and tatters. Some corporal came up and said, "Well, we can't do anything about it tonight because we're all knocking off, it's five o'clock!" – war on, mind you! "You two make yourselves scarce and find somewhere to kip, and we'll see you back here tomorrow morning."

'Well, we'd got damn all, no money, nothing, so we made our way to the Strand Palace where the crew used to meet when on leave, and we met a whole crowd of our bods all on a night out! We were welcomed there, still in rags, boots tied up with string and dungaree trousers. They said, "Give the telegram a chance to get home to say that you're OK."'

*'What had they told you while Phil was in France?'*

*Eileen:* 'Just that he was missing. I'd already had the letters saying – I think the period was twelve weeks – if you didn't hear anything then they started paying you as a widow, and I'd had the forms to say what my widow's pension would be. I think the worrying part was that we heard from the rest of the crew. It was only Phil and Jock that we hadn't heard from so one just hadn't got a clue what was happening.'

*'You knew nothing until this particular day?'*

*Eileen:* 'No. I was expecting our first child and I'd got very fat in the meantime! It was rather funny because Phil had gone into the personnel office first and it was put over the Tannoy that I was wanted up there. I was living at the time with my grandmother and she'd gone away, so when I got in and this woman said to me, "Sit down, I've got something to tell you," I thought my grandmother had been taken ill. But she said, "Phil's in the other office!" I can remember opening the door and seeing him. The room was full of people. I rushed up to him and after we'd had a little bit of a kiss and a cuddle, we looked round and the room was empty. Everybody had scuttled out!'

*Phil:* 'At one point they were going to fly us back –'

*Eileen:* 'Another coincidence! I didn't like to bring this up!'

*Phil:* 'This was early on. They said they'd got it organized. The Resistance had got back to England on the radio and they said they would be sending an aircraft over to pick us up. That night or the following night, I'm not sure which. We got organized, and the load of Resistance men were armed to the teeth with sten guns and God knows what. They just marched along and no one seemed to worry – it was after dark and there were curfews. We got to the field that they were going to land in with the things ready to light up and they never came.'

*Eileen:* 'You must bear in mind that I was in the very early stages of pregnancy therefore a little bit queasy. It was either the Saturday or Sunday after Phil had been reported missing – I was absolutely convinced he would come home that night! I lay awake listening because I could always recognize his step coming down the road and my bedroom was in the front. Eventually I dropped asleep and the next morning, I just couldn't believe it. I couldn't stop myself crying because I couldn't believe that he hadn't come home! When I saw him afterwards I found that that was the night he should have come home, if this aircraft had landed. I've never been so convinced of anything in my life. I was so disappointed.'

*'Did you ever find out why they didn't come?'*

*Phil:* 'No. I should imagine there were more important things on at the moment. I went missing on the Saturday and D-Day was on the Tuesday so to pick up a couple of odd bods at such a time –

'When we got back to England I went up to the RAF nuthouse up in Scotland –'

*Eileen:* 'Rehabilitation centre –'

*Phil:* 'Anybody that was shot down, they went up there. We had psychoanalysing, had your teeth pulled and things, and we all acted daft deliberately. The CO who was as nuts as any of them had a car and invariably about half a dozen of us used to clamber all over the car, on the running boards, in the back, and he used to take us into town and dump us somewhere, and we went drinking.

'I didn't go on ops again after that. I was posted to Canada on Liberators to go to the Far East, but they lost my papers. They went to the bottom of the pile! I didn't want to go to the Far East!'

*Eileen:* 'No. I didn't fancy that at all. But the war ended before he could be sent. What was rather interesting, in 1965 we went out to France for a holiday and Phil got to the village. But he'd never been moved during daylight so it all looked different. We drove round and round this village and it is a real rural place. The French kept coming out and looking at us – I was getting really frightened! While he was there during the war, a woman gave him a pair of trousers which she said had belonged to her husband who was a prisoner of war. We stopped the car outside this woman's house and immediately – it only took her a couple of seconds to open the kitchen window and then she started shouting out, "Philippe! Philippe!" We went in and he met the husband whose trousers he wore! The whole family were there – it was a very drunken day that! We were taken all round. I thought they'd probably dealt with dozens of airmen, but for that particular village Phil and Jock were their big war story. We met the grandchildren and the aunts and the uncles – they cried over us and kept pouring out more wine! Wherever we went, a tray of wine! It was a fantastic holiday!'

# 10

# THE WAAF

THE WOMEN'S AUXILIARY AIR FORCE WAS RE-FORMED IN June 1939. In the First World War a women's auxiliary corps had demonstrated the invaluable role women could play in wartime. In the Second World War, too, women took on a wide variety of service jobs, releasing men for combat and ground support. Waaf on operational stations shared the risk of enemy attack with their male colleagues, and many served in dangerous theatres of war overseas. *Jeanne Truman* had tried to join one of the women's services at the very start of the war.

'I volunteered for the Wrens that first winter but they wouldn't have me because I had a French birth certificate. I went over to the WAAF and said, "Look, will *you* have me?"'

'They said, "Oh yes, we're not going to worry about a thing like that!" and they signed me on. All my family were volunteers, it was the normal thing to do. We were ten of us in this house, my father waiting to be called up, my brother-in-law, my two sisters and I. In fact there were some people who were very critical of any girl who wasn't in the forces and gave them white feathers!

'I was sent up to Darlington and arrived on this camp: there were forty of us in huts. You were told to undress and get into a dressing-gown and wait for a medical board. All day they seemed to come along and say you can dress now and have lunch, or you can dress now and have tea – I finally got into the medical board about nine o'clock at night!

'We slept in huge dormitories – very uncomfortable straw beds – it was a shock moving out from home and going into a place like that. Seven people out of the group were taken because they had lice in their hair! People used to pinch things, so the Naafi wouldn't give you a knife and fork until you had given your cap in exchange! I always remember this idea of giving your cap as a hostage to get your knife and fork. When you rinsed the knives and forks you had to dip them in filthy water. Those sort of things gave you a terrific shock at first. But I was only there for a fortnight, to teach us to march, that sort of thing.

'The uniforms fitted *fairly* well – not badly. The shoes were very uncomfortable until I became an officer and had my own. I was very cross when I started because they wouldn't give me a cap. They wanted me to wear a beret – I have a very small head – I was very very small. I said, "No, I'm going to have a cap, and I'll put cotton wool all round it!" Which I did. They also wanted to classify me as a cook because according to them I wasn't five foot. Anyone who wasn't had to be a cook! Luckily the medical people were friendly and said I was five foot one and a half! I couldn't understand why if you were a cook you were smaller.

'My first posting was to Bomber Command headquarters, to the Press section. I was very fortunate indeed. I had languages and had been interested in writing, and I was working with very interesting people. We used to have the PROs – the public relations officers – of the five groups of Bomber Command ringing up with their stories as soon as they got in from the raids. I had headphones and used to take down their story. The officers would come and grab the paper out of my typewriter, go and edit it, and then I would dictate it to the Air Ministry. We also had to get the communiqués which were sent out – how many of our aircraft were missing, what had happened on the raid – which was quite exciting because we got the news of the raids first. I was allowed to see the films taken by the pilots. My PR officers did manage to get me on a trip to see what was going on. I had to file a blood – that said you exonerated the air force if you were shot down. Alas, they said no higher up.

'Brian Howard was my AC2. He was a corporal and used to make our tea. He used to tell me all about "My mamma! When we went to Nice –" and all this sort of thing. Extraordinary voice, he wandered round looking rather satanic, with *War and Peace* under his arm – very different from all the other AC2s. He was what they called the ACGD which was just the one who made the tea and coffee and carried messages.

'Then they decided to send me up to get a commission, medical board after medical board. I was sent to the Lake District. We had to do all this marching around with a horrible sergeant who was always yelling at me. I couldn't understand why till I realized that mine was the only name he could remember! They were trying to teach us to be well behaved, so apart from the technical lectures we had to sit and do embroidery and elocution and all this absolute nonsense!

'It was rather frightening because they didn't tell you whether you'd passed until the last morning at breakfast. I thought this was rather sadistic: you just waited and if they didn't come and call you for breakfast you knew you were out. They made us do a lot of discussion groups, in the form of a debate like in Parliament, and one person took a part marvellously. But she was political – we weren't interested in politics – and they RTU'd her (*returned to unit*). Very bad. She was Jewish and had something to do with the Zionists.

'I got through, partly due to the fact that my sister was on the same course. They didn't know. She had a different name to me. She'd help me with my embroidery. I got very bad chilblains with the cold there, standing out on these beastly fields, and she used to come and polish my buttons and do things to help me.

'They sent me to intelligence, to the Air Ministry to work in the department of DDIS, the Deputy-Director of Intelligence Security. We got all the first information, had all the secret papers, about Mulberry, the v1s and v2s, long before they turned up. When I used to go home on leave we spent our time under the dining-room table. I heard them that first night, and I thought those are the pilotless planes.

'Then I was asked to go into the special forces. I went off for training up to Scotland – great fun for young people. Three days of intelligence tests. You were taught morse, climbing up rocks, going for miles along hills and shooting guns, throwing grenades, and trying to blow up things. It was quite amusing going around in the dark with blackened faces. They were mostly men, only two of us were women. My other sister joined me but I wasn't allowed to tell her about it. We were sent to jump school and I didn't do very well because I hurt myself at the beginning.

'I was very keen to go to France – I was born and brought up there and consider myself as French as well as English. I got over on the thirteenth of September 1944, just after the Liberation. I worked as an intelligence officer at SHAEF and was also in charge of the information with maps. I went for intelligence briefings every morning, and then changed the maps. Anyone could go in to see how the advances were. What I found very odd was that an awful lot of the places, especially on the Russian front, had the same names and I thought I do hope I've moved them into the right places and not the wrong ones!

'The war was still on. When we arrived there were still posters on the walls telling you how good the Germans were with children and so on. The other thing was everybody hates *les flics* – the police – but now they were heroes because they led the Resistance in Paris!

'There were tremendous queues in shops. The Americans were received wonderfully at first, then they became unpopular because they were too well paid and used to get all the luxury goods. The prices went up. French people couldn't buy anything any more. It wasn't quite the same with the English because we were not paid as much and we had to have most of our pay deposited in England. We were only allowed ten pounds a month, so that didn't allow us to buy any extras, but we found a lot of things. We were able to get more clothes than in England, and things like silk stockings which we hadn't seen for years. Perfume too, but food was very very difficult. I went to the hairdresser's and heard in the next booth to me a woman proposing a ham in exchange for a perm! She was a country woman and would bring her ham in from the country! A lot of people had parcels sent in from relatives in the country where they still had plenty of food, butter, eggs.

'We were lucky because we were in army headquarters, well fed, and we could invite guests in. I invited my cousins and they'd come along and have a meal and a bath. They'd fared very badly because my uncle was English and he had to hide. They moved sixteen times. It was worse in a lot of ways in Paris than I expected. My cousin and I had been very close and organized a way of writing during the war, through a postal box in Lisbon. Only she had to be careful, even doing that, because everything was censored. She used a form of code – she would write, "Audrey came to see us the other day. The poor little thing seems rather thin, I don't think she's very well." Now Audrey was a friend married to an Italian, so she was saying that the Italians were there but they were rather shabby, not in very good shape. All her letters were a little bit like that. I used to say the same to her. "Michael's joined the same club as father" – she knew father had been in the army so she knew he'd enlisted.

'We posted the letters to a postal box in Lisbon – there were also Red Cross messages which came through sometimes. So we'd had a little information about them but I hadn't realized they'd been so very hard up for food. My cousin's my age but she's not very interested in food now – she said it was too important during the war, they talked of nothing else and thought of nothing else. They cycled for miles to get a cabbage which lasted two days. There was a black market everywhere: a lot of people couldn't have survived if they hadn't had that. They used to give us at the British Army office club in Paris what they called Bafs – special money used to buy things in the Naafi. When we had a new issue of Bafs they were being sold in the streets in Brussels the same morning on the black market.

'A lot of people who had received the Germans were now

249

receiving the heads of the Allies. They wanted to get well in with them. They were people who had very big houses, a lot of money, and wanted protection so they were very very very generous. A lot of people were taken in the purge, but I was told by somebody who was working in those offices, some of them paid to have their file put to the bottom of the pile. They knew that as time went on people would be less liable to find them. They'd say, oh, poor things, they shouldn't have ten years' prison, only two years.

'Theatres were still playing but they were not heated. There was no heating in a lot of places. I remember going to see *Le Soulier de Satin*, a four-hour programme, and I sat there with my army boots on, my battledress, plus my heavy top coat, and I was so cold by the time I got out the wing commander I was with said, "You're *green* in the face!", and gave me a brandy!

'I stayed there until January '46. I could have come out then but I thought, no, I'm damned, it's too cold. I signed on for another six months to come out in June. Actually I could still be in the air force now because they left me on full rations and pay and forgot about me! Completely forgot. I'd taken another job doing newspaper work on a paper called *France*. In some ways they were very thoughtless. If a man was killed, usually the commanding officer wrote and told the family, but some of them were very tactless. When my brother was dropped in France they sent his uniform back to my mother because he went in civilian clothes. My mother was in floods of tears, she thought he'd been killed! Luckily my sister realized that he was doing something and she said, "Look mother, I think he's all right." Later they did say he was OK.

'By the end of the war we hadn't got many clothes. If we were invited to a ball we had to go in uniform but that meant you were always as well dressed as anyone else, even the ones who spent a fortune. I was very lucky. I had a Canadian boy-friend – I still see him, he's got children and grandchildren, and his grandchildren come here – but he was shot down and was two years in prison camp. He left me all his coupons, a hundred and fifty! This was the greatest present anyone could have given me, and I bought some civilian clothes. Otherwise anything we'd had at the beginning of the war was worn out. You were only given ten coupons a year which was enough to buy you ten handkerchiefs. You couldn't even buy a pair of slippers with that.

'Another thing which a lot of men don't realize is the matter of trying to get cosmetics during the war. I was very lucky because I had cornered the market. I liked Nivea cream. At that time I didn't smoke and I used to exchange my cigarette ration for somebody either to mend my stockings or to give me Nivea cream!

'As soon as I got released definitely I went back and stayed in France for twenty years. I was a bit annoyed because I wanted to go to university – I hadn't been able to before – and they told us we were going to get the same advantages as the men. But after the war they said, "Oh no, we're letting the men go, because they'll want to build a whole career, but not the women!" One of the things we all complained at was doing the same job as a man, in the same office with the same expenses, and they were getting a third more than we were! We complained. What was their lovely story? We were given pyjamas and they weren't. We could have bought the pyjamas if they'd given us the extra money! When we were in the ranks the men got thruppence a day good-conduct pay and we only got tuppence! That was the one that annoyed me. I said why shouldn't we behave as well as them?'

*Rita Symons* was eighteen. 'I chose the WAAF because my brother, cousins and friends were in the RAF. I had to persuade my father to let me go. He had to sign – in those days you had to be twenty-one to do anything you wanted to do, eighteen wasn't thought of. He didn't want me to leave home. It was bad enough my brother being overseas. Most of the women were going up north doing munitions, they never got home, they were most unhappy. I said, "Well, at least if I go in the forces I can come home every three months." But when I went in, they stopped all leave!

'When I came out he was very proud of me and wanted me to walk about with him in my uniform all the time! He didn't want me to wear civilian clothes. He'd say, "Come and meet me from work and come in uniform." I went up there once in civvies and his face fell. After that I used to go up in uniform so he could show me off to everybody.'

'*What did you think of the uniform?*'

'Oh it was awful! You had to wear your cap straight, peaked cap, and you used to fold your skirt and put it under your mattress, to press it. Shirts with the separate collars, thick stockings, and the shoes were awful! I put these shoes on, went to walk, and they were so heavy compared to the shoes I'd been wearing that I just didn't move.

'I trained to be a teleprinter operator. I thought that's a good trade to come out with. We did our square-bashing and such-like at Wilmslow – it was six weeks, mostly square-bashing, and being kitted out in uniform. I'd been in girls' training corps at the youth club so I was used to square-bashing. We used to go into this big hangar for lectures. Big white screen, cinema screen in fact, and the woman would stand up and talk to you. You'd fall asleep because you were staring at all this white.

'We were in barracks, very clean because we had to keep them clean ourselves. We had kit inspections, marked all our own kit. Every morning you folded up your blankets and sheets, and then you had like your palliasse – that was your mattress – you laid one blanket this way, and then on top of that you put the other blankets and sheets, and then you had to bring it over, and your pillow went on top!'

'*You can still remember how to do it!*'

'Oh yes, yes, yes, and making your bed. They had to be made a certain way, hospital fashion. When you had a kit inspection your bed had to be stacked and your bedding laid out, your clothes laid out. They'd come along with a list and say two shirts, and you had to show you had *three* shirts, two there and one on. At Wilmslow we were in a big hut, forty-four of us, and most of them were Scots or Geordies, I was the only Londoner – from down this end. All their accents! In the end, I had to speak like they did so they could understand me! When I phoned home my mother said she couldn't understand a word I was saying. I became the storekeeper. Everybody in the hut who found any clothing that didn't belong to them would give it to me. When we had a kit parade they'd all come to me. Have you got a spare collar, I'm short of a collar, and I'd dish it out to them. I was the one that mothered everyone else. I was the youngest actually. I've always been an organizer. I organized them.

'When I was at High Wycombe, at Bomber Command, teleprinting was the most secretive means of communication there was. You would type on a machine here and it would come out elsewhere. Raids would be planned at headquarters and we would send out – some of it in code – signals to all the different Bomber Command stations, planning what they were to do. They would go off, do it, come back and report to their offices. The signal would come back to us telling us what had happened, and this would all be collated together.

'We also had two machines with Met reports and these would be coming through all day long. We had one machine that if an aeroplane had been seen to go down, the names of the crew would come up. If they were believed dead or prisoners of war, kin would be informed. That had to be monitored – we'd take it in turns to sit there. Very depressing really. Once it came up that the husband of the woman on the other side of the room had gone down, missing believed killed. The warrant officer who was in charge called her in and told her. But she wouldn't believe that he was dead. It took about fourteen to sixteen months, but it came through that he was a prisoner of war. And he came home eventually.'

*'Did you realize at this stage how heavy the losses were?'*

'Well, we had it all the time coming through so we knew. It was taken for granted, it wasn't taken as heavy. You didn't realize how bad it was, you just took it as it should be. You never realized it was as bad as it really was.

'There were men and women on my watch. I was in charge of

thirty-eight women. Some didn't want to work, some were lazy – same as you'd get anywhere with women because you're thrown together – different types of women. We had people who were well-to-do – Lady Somebody-or-other – and others that were, well, very common. One got married at Queen Anne's Gate, a very posh wedding which I went to, and yet I had other friends from the country who had never been to London in their lives till they came with me.

'We got paid about two pounds something a fortnight, very poor pay. Plus a few rations of cigarettes. The food was awful! I was very skinny when I first went in and they fed you on nothing but potatoes so I really put on weight. Once when I went on nights, only half the lights were on. We got a plate of soup and when I went to sit down there was dead wasps in it! I took it back and this sergeant in charge of the mess said, "It's all right, you can have another plate if you like." It used to be in a tea urn – you turned the tap on. I said, "It's come out of the same place, I don't want another plate!" That's why we took so much food back! I used to bring all this food from home, come back laden and everyone would be sitting up waiting for me, you're late! Where's the food?

'We were in an underground section – it looked like a door in the side of a small hillock. You walked in and everything was below ground. The ops room had a big map on one wall. Rumour had it that a Waaf officer on a ladder plotting an operation fell off and was killed! It was a very interesting job because you were at the hub of things. When VE day came through on a signal, we had to swear on a Bible that we wouldn't say anything until it was given out. We came off night duty and we used to go home straight away – we shouldn't really but we did – and we had this lift in a sports car. This chap was driving and some of us were sitting on the back. He was saying, "It seems as though it's going to be over soon, doesn't it?"

'We were saying, "Oh yes, we think so!" We couldn't say that we knew it was!

'At High Wycombe there was a young woman who had fallen

pregnant – we had a lot of that sort of thing going on. She lived with her father and stepmother. The RAF officer persuaded the chap to marry her. When she came back everybody gathered round her in the Naafi to find out how she'd got on. She said when she got home with him, her stepmother said we've only got two bedrooms, and if he's going to marry you anyway and you've slept together before you might as well sleep together now – the night before their wedding! Nowadays people don't think anything of that, but we thought it was *terrible*! Our ears pricked up – I'd never heard anything like it in my life. Another young woman, general duties woman, got pregnant and she gave the WAAF a list, one of *them*! Of course, being eighteen and naïve, mouths opened wide, didn't they?

'One day we went for a walk, eating cherries we'd bought. A beautiful car with a pennant pulled up. The driver said, "Would you like a lift?"

' "Yes please."

' "Get in."

(*Awed voice*) 'Bomber Harris was in the back! And we went all the way with the cherry stones held in our mouths – didn't know what to do, you know! He smiled at us and when we got out we saluted him – very nice! I appreciated it because you never got that, a lot of the officers were snobs. We had so many, you'd meet them coming through the woods, all different nationalities and services. Every so often an officer would complain we hadn't saluted and we'd be called in to a lecture to remind us we were "saluting the uniform not the person wearing it"! We got over this by forming single file through woods, spaced out, so the poor officer had to keep saluting, "up and down, up and down", while the women only had to salute the once. The officer soon began to look the other way and saluting died a natural death until the next time.

'When the war was finished everybody wanted to get home. After VJ day we all thought we were wasting our time. High Wycombe's only thirty miles from London, so all my free time I was coming back to Tottenham. One Waaf – to me very old, she was in her twenties – came from south London. She said, "I'm going to hitch home, would you like to come with me?" All leave had been cancelled. I said, "Do you know what you're doing?"

' "Oh yes, I've done it several times."

' "So what happens if we get stuck and we can't get back?"

' "We'll sleep in a haystack!"

'I thought, she knows what she's talking about, I'll go with her! The normal way to London was quite direct, but we wouldn't go that route. Two women had been picked up by SPs the week before, so she said we'll go on a roundabout route. The guns started to go – you could see the flashes. There was two little cottages and she was going to knock at the doors!

' "You can't do that! You can't wake people up at this time of night. Come on, what about this haystack?"

' "Oh, I've never done that before!"

'Now she told me! Anyway a truck came along with some Yanks in it, and they gave us a lift! We used to hitch-hike a lot. Don't forget that was during the war. People would stop and give you a lift quite happily. We always hitched in uniform.

'There was a different atmosphere everywhere you went, even in London. People put themselves out for you. They'd stop and give you a lift. We used to travel the same time on a different day every week and meet the same people, you'd travel along with them. You knew a lot about them and they'd look out for you. You wouldn't do that now, would you? I'm scared to go out in the street at night now!

'We're going back a long time, fifty years. It was a different world. At the start of the war I was evacuated to Norfolk. I was really fortunate because I was with a family who were very good to us. We were right out in the country. We had no running water, rainwater to wash in, a well for the water, a very old-fashioned country toilet, just a bucket. When we got there the teacher went in to tell her that we were Jewish, and when I came in she started looking in my head. I said to her, "I haven't got nits, you know, I come from a clean family!"

' "I'm looking for your horns!" Yes, she thought Jewish people had horns!'

256

'At High Wycombe I used to write poems for the women to send to their boy-friends. I used to write a lot of poetry. (*Shows me a typed paper.*) This is what we used to do when the CO wasn't looking:'

*Beware the Frenchman who is free*
*with virtuous girls like you and me,*
*he seems to have a hundred hands.*
*You'll know he never understands.*
*Any girl who says* oui oui
*will shortly after find that she*
*is what the French call* en famille!

*Beware the tough colonial bloke*
*who likes to have his little joke,*
*who when you're quite prepared to yield*
*will knock you senseless in a field.*
*For girls it really is not fun*
*when you come to find he's done*
*what you yourself have not begun!*

*REFUSE! should officers say honey,*
*would you like a lot of money!*
*Because the WAAF does not think it's nice*
*that service girls should have their price,*
*so if you're offered half a crown*
*accept the insult with a frown*
*but do not take it lying down.*

*The more you've heard you will I think*
*agree most trouble comes through drink,*
*and when you're tight you never know*
*whom you'll allow to have a go,*
*and afterwards comes nasty shocks*
*and one wonders what is in the docks.*
*Is the father Box or Cox?*

# 11

## ARMY CO-OPERATION

Army co-operation command had been set up in December 1940 to develop battlefield co-operation between the army and air force. Ideas developed were put into practice in North Africa and the Middle East. One of the Spitfire's great advantages was that it was capable of considerable remodelling. As a result it became and remained the leading British fighter plane throughout the war. But it could also be modified for special purposes and one of these was Army Co-operation, flying over enemy lines and photographing troop movements, strong points, and so on.

*George Arthur* went into the RAF directly from boarding school. 'We had one of these beat-ups! First of all, one week, an army officer arrived, then a naval bloke, then a man from the air force, all to drum up volunteers for the services when you left. I just decided I preferred the RAF to the other two. I joined in '41 and flew over here to start with but that winter was such a bugger they stopped all flying and sent us across to America. I went through the BFTS scheme, with American instructors. When they told us you lot are posted to Miami we all thought it was Miami, Florida, great! It turned out to be Miami, Oklahoma, dry!

'When we pulled in to Miami, the platform was lined with

258

people, American families. As you got off the train they would come forward and say, "Right, what's your name? We're So-and-so, we'll be your hosts for the time you're here!" It really was excellent! A lot of the people that were in Miami, Oklahoma, when we were there training later came over here in the American services, so I kept in touch with them for a long time afterwards.

'It was fairly liberal. Provided you put your flying time in it was pretty good as far as being off the camp was concerned. The American civilian instructors didn't want to fly at the weekends so usually you were off! They used pretty ripe language – very strict. If they told you to do a ninety-degree turn it had to be ninety degrees. It was no good doing ninety-two or ninety-three. Navigation-wise flying in America was silly. It's either north–south roads or east west, which is why the Americans were no good at navigation over here.'

*'At what point did you find you were going on to fighters?'*

'I must have been about six months ahead of when they decided they'd got too many pilots. When I joined there was a shortage and they were rushing us through. The whole training was nine months, which is quite a long time. When you consider that they had all those flyers in Canada and America and Rhodesia and South Africa, they were turning out pilots pretty rapidly. They'd already decided I was not going into Fighter Command but to Army Co-operation which meant a different sort of training.

'We were there about eight months, came back in the August of '42. Got sent on leave and then recalled after about four days and told, you're all off to North Africa to fly Hurricanes. We got out there in January '43 having done about five or six hours on Hurricanes.

'Blow me, when we got to North Africa the squadron hadn't got any Hurricanes, they'd got Spitfires! They pointed us towards a Spitfire and said, "We used to be a Hurricane squadron but we're now Spitfires so you'd better get in that thing and fly it!" We had to, there wasn't much choice. They had one Hurricane on the squadron to get us into it, and then it was Spitfire Vs.

'I went to North Africa, Sicily and Italy, so I did that tour. Got as far as Rome and I'd done a tour and a half then – they used to do it by number of trips and number of hours. We weren't supposed to do combat – in fact we were escorted by fighters in North Africa. We flew in pairs, reconnaissance. Where the Luftwaffe were still reasonably strong, if we were going say as far as Tunis, then we would have six fighters with us. They'd pick us up or we'd pick them up and they'd stay up top while we went down and did the reconnaissance bit. If fighters came into the area, we were told to beat a hasty retreat and let the buggers up top deal with them. The German air force in Italy was pretty non-existent, after Foggia, apart from when they made special efforts. Anzio, for example.

'I preferred the Spitfire to the Hurricane – it was a smoother aircraft. The Hurricane always had this tendency to do a bit of kangarooing on take-off if you weren't careful. Wasn't quite as fast and though the Hurricane pilots reckoned it was as manoeuvrable, I'm not sure that I thought it was. It was a bit heavier and more cumbersome. The Spitfire V at low level was extremely manoeuvrable, which is what we wanted for getting in and out down below. The army would say, "We're putting in an attack tomorrow, go and tell us what's there." We would go over and do a particular area and report any movements we'd seen. Convoys or groups of tanks or any German formations.'

*'And they would fire at you?'*

'They would! And hit you occasionally. I got shot down! I bloody well did! In North Africa, right at the end. The Germans got penned up into that little peninsula at Zagwar. They had all their troops there waiting to be taken off, and they took their anti-aircraft stuff as high up the mountains as they could. I was over there one day and they got me! I had to do a forced landing at a place called Pont du Far.

'I think it was my thirteenth trip (*checks with his log-book*). Well no, it was eleven or twelve, because I had two trips that day so it must obviously have been the second one. It was never proved that I needed to have done a forced landing. You can never tell. I wasn't on fire, but I got a great hole in my wing and one in the engine, and I suddenly had a stream of glycol – a whole stream of white smoke. We were a long way from base so I thought it was really rather wiser either to jump out or force-land. I didn't fancy jumping out so I force-landed.'

*'Had you had any training for jumping out?'*

'Well, yes, if you call it training. You stood in an aircraft hangar, on straps, and then you had to jump, which was bloody frightening I must say! I don't think I ever fancied jumping out, to be perfectly honest. There were two schools of thought about that. Some people would jump out at a drop of a hat, they'd rather jump than force-land. I took the opposite view, not because I particularly wanted to save the aircraft, but because I didn't fancy jumping!'

*'When you force-land, what exactly would you do?'*

'It's wheels up. I had no power – well, I had power but I throttled back because I thought the temperatures were going off the clock. I was the number two of the pair, and the number two in Army Co-operation is not really supposed to know exactly where he is. You are supposed to be looking after number one's tail. He does all the navigating and the reconnaissance, you keep him company and look after him. We were just coming away from Zaghouan when they got me, so we were headed more or less back towards the line. I thought it was too far so I told number one I'd been hit. We had a chat about it and he said, "What are you going to do?"

' "I'm going to force-land." He went off once he saw me beginning to go down.

'I picked a great big field – there was a farmhouse. I knew the direction was right, that it should be on our side of the lines. You just do a wheels-up landing. I got in all right, did a belly flop, and all was well except it was in the middle of no man's land. The French Nineteen Corps was to the south, the Germans were just up there, so I went and hid in the farmhouse. I was how old? Nineteen and a half, with a .38 pistol and no more idea than climb in the air what to do with the thing.

'I just waited till dusk. A German patrol came and looked at the aeroplane, came to the farmyard but didn't come any further, then disappeared. When it got a bit dark I set off down the road and a jeep came along, a French jeep, blowing the V-for-victory sign, collected me and took me back.

'When I got back to the squadron three days later all my kit had been divided up – the boys had taken everything! Telegrams had been sent home. The poor old Mum got a telegram saying *missing* – not missing believed killed but just missing in action. I had to go round everybody's tent and get back my gear! (*Laughs.*)

'The only other sort of excitement – I had to ditch a Hurricane in the Med. I had an engine failure while I was towing a drogue, just before we went across to Sicily. I had to ditch about four miles off, fortunately it was nice and calm. No one had had any instruction on how to ditch – we never expected to. I don't know what the right form is but on the way down I thought I know what I'm going to do. I got the thing going as slowly as possible, and put the flaps and the wheels down. When I was about fifty feet up I undid the straps, sort of cruised down on the seat. I thought I'll make the tail hit first, on the theory that if the tail hit the nose would go down and it would shoot me up the front. Sure enough it did! I'd undone my straps and was just waiting to be shot out. I swam about two strokes, looked round and there was nothing to be seen, the plane had gone!

'I swam for a while. The chap who was firing on the drogue followed me down and then whizzed back to base, picked up a dinghy, came back, spotted me and threw the dinghy at me. I swam to it, got in it and paddled ashore. I had a bit of a stiff neck for about two days and that was all.'

'*How was life on the squadron organized?*'

'We were in tents and there was a farmhouse which incorporated the main administration block. At that stage the Germans were still likely to come over and strafe the airfield so we were pretty well dispersed right round. We flew, if I remember rightly, day on, day off. Flight A one day, B flight the next. The total number of pilots on the formation was something like twenty-two, so you had ten or eleven on each flight.

'The day you were on you certainly did one trip and you might be called upon to do two, either at dawn or last light and one in between probably. At dawn you would go and sit in the aircraft on the end of the runway and wait until you could see to take off, then off you'd go. By the time you got over the lines you'd catch all the fires being lit for the troops' breakfasts on the other side so you could tell where they were! The last light one was just to see if they'd moved.

'You flew fairly low on these trips. The army would want you to look at an area almost immediately in front of them. The fighter boys who used to escort us would probably be above ten or fifteen thousand feet. We would go into the area at about eight and then go down. Number one would go really low to do the spotting on the roads. You came back and reported the number of vehicles you'd seen, or the amount of movement, if there was a concentration of troops or vehicles or whatever. You came back and reported, so you had to be reasonably low. You just went whizzing down as fast as you could, weaving your way through the area, and then out the other side, back up. You'd probably do two or three runs and then report back what you'd seen. So the army could decide which way to attack and how to go in. The ops in between would be just routine – the army wanted to know what was about. It could be any time during the day. If the army didn't have any requirements then we didn't fly. That wasn't very likely. They usually wanted us to do something.

'Our maps were pretty good. We had been trained in navigation. I don't suppose the fighter boys really knew much about navigation because they would go up high, do their bits and pieces and then they'd be given a course to steer back. Whereas we were told, there is your area, go and look at it, and you'd work out your own route there and back. When you first start navigating, you do it by railways, rivers and major landmarks. I didn't find it terribly difficult – you got lost a few times but you'd always know vaguely the direction you needed to go. The longest trips were from Sicily to Naples, over the sea, that's when we had to carry these extra tanks. That was always a bit dodgy with nothing to compare yourself with. You flew a course and hoped that you'd hit the coast just south of Naples.'

*'Did you have heavy losses?'*

'Not after North Africa, no. By the time I was operational, which was early '43, I don't think we lost more than about two. They came and strafed us once or twice – in fact the aircraft I was supposed to fly on my first op was set alight. But casualties from direct German action from that time on were negligible.'

*'Morale was pretty high?'*

'Oh yes! Great life! Great life it was! (*Laughs.*) Yes, I must admit, looking back on it, I really got in, and got involved on the ops side when the tide had turned. The Germans really hadn't got the aircraft then, after North Africa. Salerno was a bit hairy. The Eighth Army were going so fast that in September of '43 we had about six moves. We just lived with the aircraft, with a toothbrush, and every three or four days we had to move to keep up with them. Because the army were that far ahead, we had to have special ninety-gallon extra tanks which made the aircraft on take-off a bit dodgy, it upset the trim. You flew to the area on your reserve tank and dropped it when you got there, which made a nice whistling noise, made everyone duck a bit! Then you came back on full tanks virtually. They were long trips.

'The average trip was only about forty-five, fifty minutes which is why you had to do a hundred before it was considered a tour. Whereas in Bomber Command they did thirty ops but six hours a time! I'm jolly glad I wasn't in Bomber Command! I don't know who did the selection but thank God he did! (*Laughs.*) I don't think I'd have liked flying a heavy aircraft. I've never flown anything with more than one engine – I don't think I'd have liked it.

'On the Spitfire IXs we had cannon – one twenty-millimetre and a couple of machine-guns, I think. We fired them in anger occasionally on what we thought were enemy convoys. When you got back the airmen were always delighted to see the covers off the guns. They would have been disappointed if you didn't come back and say, "Oh, I've shot one down today!" or, "I've been involved in a fight!" They always wanted to know exactly what you'd done and what you'd hit. But it didn't happen terribly often. We were under orders not to use the guns unless we were (a) absolutely dead certain we were over the German lines and (b) we were being fired upon, or (c) we knew exactly what the hell we were firing at! The object of the exercise was the photographs and you had to get them back. The thing that was most likely to go wrong on these trips was your radio. The engine was very reliable.'

*'And social life?'*

'Oh, social life! Well, it was usually in the mess. There were always football matches against the airmen or the sergeants' mess. We'd make up teams and play another squadron at something. The evenings all seemed to sail by. We were in the mess, drinking beer, free (*laughs*). Oh no, the social side of it – the days you weren't flying you would all get in a truck and go off to the coast! Swim up at Bône. It was lovely! It was excellent! I reckoned I was in doing my ops just at the right time. Any earlier would have been highly dangerous, any later I would have been down the mines with Mr Bevin. I felt sorry for those chaps who went through all their flying training and came back to this country expecting to fly and were shoved down the coal-mines! I wouldn't have been very pleased about that, and I shouldn't think they were.'

*'Did people get superstitious on your squadron?'*

'No. Not that I remember. No, I wouldn't have said so,

probably because it was so different, you're only away forty-five minutes.'

'*Did you come across any instances of LMF?*'

'Only one on the squadron, only one chap went back. Well, you know, it was a case of he'd take off and then he'd come back: there'd be something the matter with the aeroplane. After a couple of times the CO got a report from the flight sergeant who said, "I've been right through the aeroplane and I'm very sorry to say there's nothing the matter with it!" The CO'd have the chap in and give him a chat and so on. It was kept pretty quiet too. I don't think it was publicized that he'd been sent back and LMF was attached to it, it was rather put that he'd just been posted to another unit.'

'*It seems to have varied enormously –*'

'I think it depended on the commanding officer. Some COs would probably have made a song and dance because of the way they felt. They would say, "I can't have people on my squadron who won't fly!" I don't think the trick cyclists – psychologists – of those days took it into account or would accept that in some cases – a good many cases – people felt they just couldn't fly any more. They wouldn't accept that they'd reached that point. To be known as LMF – many of them committed suicide, I would say. They were given all the shitty jobs.

'When the war ended there were problems in Trieste. Italy and Yugoslavia both reckoned that they wanted it so we had to fly border patrols just to show the flag. We were all coming out on release and so on, and I came out in December '46. I was a squadron leader by then.'

'*What were the duties of a squadron leader?*'

'When the war was over which is when I got it you had to keep the squadron in flying practice – you had to have a good adjutant, particularly from the administration point of view. Just keeping the boys in flying trim but not doing anything desperate. As the

CO it was really rather nice because you selected when you wanted to fly, so you picked the days when there were no clouds and it was nice and sunny.'

*'When you came out was it easy to settle down?'*

'No! Bloody difficult. Bloody difficult. You weren't particularly well paid in the air force in those days but with your overseas allowances and all the rest of it you weren't short, and I came out with money in the bank. It wasn't long before I hadn't fourpence to bless myself with. That was the most difficult bit. Having been a squadron leader in charge of two hundred people – I was what, only twenty-four. I joined my father's firm and there I was, an absolute sprog, in the packing department of a woollen merchant's – difficult! I only stayed there a year and then I got into the insurance racket which I've been in ever since.

'Back in England I stayed in the VR. We used to go once a fortnight on a Sunday and fly if the weather was all right. You'd fly from Woking to Shoreham, land and have tea, and fly back. Or you'd go to Bembridge and have tea, and fly back, it was just swanning about. Then you had to do a fortnight each year when you flew during the day and got pissed every night! Oh, it was lovely! No wonder the Air Ministry got browned off with it. You got paid in your RAF rank, pay and allowances for that fortnight, and you got paid at work as well – my firm thought I was a good lad to be in the VR! So they went on paying me, the air force were paying me, it was all very excellent.

'The last real flying I did was that Korean call-up which was '52–'53, when they called up the Z-men or the G-men or whatever it was. They gave us Spitfire XXIIs which were exceedingly powerful in comparison to the Vs and the IXs that I had flown. Finally I converted on to Vampires, I did a little Vampire trip. Fifteen hours and that was the end of the course. It was just three months' call-up if I remember rightly.

'The difference in outlook in comparison to a Spitfire is so tremendous – there's no nose in front of you. Literally the first take-off is seven or eight thousand feet just going up like a lift, before I got the wheels up – I wondered where the hell I was!'

'*You didn't go up on your own?*'

'Oh yes. Single-seaters. You went straight from a Spit XXII into a Vampire! You spent the morning with a blackboard and a lecturer telling you about it. He gave you an indication of what to expect, just warning you of the power in comparison to anything you'd flown before. You sit in the Vampire on the taxi-track waiting for it to take off, you gradually let the throttle forward, let the brakes off, there's a great big kick up the backside and bingo! you're off! Very very powerful in comparison to the Spitfire. Much more comfortable. The thing about the Spitfire and the Hurricane was they were pretty uncomfortable in the cockpit, very close fitting. For sheer speed this Vampire was quite frightening. And if the light went out, if the jet went out, you couldn't relight it, so either you got out or you force-landed. The fuel was right under the seat, virtually. Highly dangerous when I consider. Well, we didn't do very much. It was a very gentle course. I think the idea was they wanted to see whether pilots of 1945 could be converted to jets without breaking them all.'

'*And were you?*'

'We had one Vampire prang during the course. Landing was difficult initially because the angle was so different.

'Then in about 1952 they decided the VR was (a) much too big, (b) much too expensive. We went to one of these fortnight camps that you did and spent the time doing exams. They set them so they halved the strength of the VR at a single stroke! They just said you're not good enough for these days, none of you are good enough so you're out! The VR immediately got halved and we all got the bullet. I came out in '53. That was the end of it.'

The Spitfire was designed as a short-range fighter, for defence. Later Marks of the plane were adapted for ground attack, carrying bombs, and were used for dive-bombing in North Africa and

Italy. It flew in combat until the very last days of the war. Pilots joining the air force in 1944 and 1945 had been captivated as teenagers by the Spitfire's exploits in the Battle of Britain and, like *Louis Astor*, were determined to fly the plane as soon as they were old enough.

'At the beginning of the war, 1939, I was evacuated to Brentwood with the school. I was fifteen. I used to see the pilots fighting up in the sky in 1940. I was rather introspective – that may have been part of the reason why I wanted to go in for Spitfires, I don't know. I probably would have got in a lot easier if I'd joined on my seventeenth birthday, but my people were opposed to me joining that early. So they didn't call me up till just before I was nineteen.

'I wanted to fight, I knew I was going to have to fight, and I had a horrible feeling I was going to be hit by something I couldn't see. Which is what happened. I had thought that on fighters we could be in combat with each other, and maybe avoid that. But, contrary to a lot of people's expectations, the enemy put themselves where you can't see them, come in and shoot you in the back, which to me is not true fighting.

'We trained in Rhodesia. They were taking their time to a certain extent, because there were a lot of people on the course. Altogether we did three hundred and nine hours' flying including the twelve I'd done in England before we got our wings. This was in 1944.

'Rhodesia and South Africa were beautiful! Paradise. Like Switzerland. Everything there to buy! Shops were full. We had sugar! I bought an Omega watch for five pounds that was sucked off my wrist when I opened the plane in the desert. We went up to operational training at Ismailia. It took us five days to get from Salisbury to Egypt.

'First of all we went on to Hurricanes then we graduated on to Spitfires. It was so delicate! When I took off, there was so little movement by comparison to the Hurricane. You could almost turn it over on its back on take-off. The cockpit was very small and everything was there to hand, like a glove almost. I had an amount of low flying and circuits, forced landings, spinning and aerobatics, and cross-countries.

'We flew from Cairo to Italy, we were in Naples, and then we went to another Spitfire school because they didn't want us too early. I got up to squadron on the thirteenth of April 1945. We operated over Bologna and the areas around there flying Spitfire Vs, VIIIs and IXs. The ops were mainly short and a lot were on the other side. Couldn't have been more than twenty minutes each way. The danger was flak, not enemy fighters. We were low down. I was number two to the CO. When I went up there he used to introduce me round to his friends, this is my number two – I don't think I was!

'We were told at the end of the war to avoid the Messerschmitt jets which were very fast. There weren't any other planes around. We used to go over to the other side of the lines for about half an hour, maybe less than that, and dive-bomb a gun position or a house that was stopping the army. Or maybe guns there, a strong position. We used to dive-bomb – we carried two five-hundred-pound bombs. We'd go up to four thousand feet and dive, drop the bomb at two thousand and pull out. It was quite a makeshift way. You just pulled a bit of string and a bit of wire and that released the bomb.

'They issued us with a .38 Smith & Wesson revolver. We were told – or we'd heard rumours – that if we were caught with these on us the Germans would shoot us, so I didn't always carry mine with me.

'The first flight I had was thirty-five minutes on local flying (*he reads from the notes he made at the time in his log-book*). I went on an operation on the fifteenth of April for an hour and five minutes, bombing and strafing. The next day I did two trips, bombing and strafing, knocked over a cart. Two trips on the seventeenth, and two on the eighteenth, bombing, hit a house, strafed a haystack and left it burning. We used to come in low, we'd dive. I don't think we were low-flying as such. It might have been better if we had. It's better to go at a hundred feet, you're not so vulnerable as you are at a thousand. On the day I was shot down, four aircraft flew out at six thousand feet to bomb three field-guns. We had one near miss and three wides.

'I did thirteen trips altogether, eleven sorties, and on my thirteenth hour of operations I was shot down. The day before my twenty-first birthday. We dropped our bombs and we were on the second sortie run-in. I was hit by an eighteen-millimetre shell, which exploded on to the aircraft. It blew my glycol radiator off, I was pouring out petrol, I was pouring out smoke.

'Apparently I phoned up and said that I'd been hit, and they told me to turn to starboard. I didn't hear them. I crossed the line a little further down – I was quite all right then – crossed the line and continued on, getting lower all the time. I couldn't get any height to bale out, so I tried to make a crash-landing in a field. When I was up with Johnny – my squadron leader – last time he said I was getting lower, made an approach, and the right wing suddenly went down. I'd stalled; I crashed and somersaulted ten times. As it didn't catch on fire, the petrol must all have gone.

'My mother had written asking me what I wanted for my twenty-first birthday and in reply she got a telegram saying I was missing, believed crash-landed. I was unconscious for eight weeks, dangerously ill for three, and seriously ill for five. I had a penetrating wound over my right eyebrow and one or two small wounds on my body. It may have happened in the plane or it might have been shrapnel, I don't know.

'During my concussion I was so badly injured that they put "dangerous", they wouldn't touch me. I presume they must have fed me by tubes. They put stretchers to the side of the bed because I was very violent. Apparently I swore a lot. I was curled up like a little baby and the injury to my head triggered off the formation of bone in my elbows – they'd never seen anything like it. They found out that in my arms was a massive bone. This hand slipped when they took the plaster off and the median nerve was trapped – terrible pain! Even now it's just like pins and needles.

'When I recovered consciousness the only thing I can remember was trying to fight somebody and screaming that my arms were hurting. They found out that I had a focal brain injury and couldn't read properly. When they took the plaster off my arm it looked a mess and I fainted – well, the sight of it – they slapped me on the face and brought me round.

'I went to rehabilitation. They were very pleased with the speed and efficiency I got because it was the largest piece of bone they had ever seen – they hadn't really experienced this at all. I also went down to six stone, dropped down to six stone. They said, "What are you going to do now?"

'I said, "I'm going back on the squadron when I get better." They told me the war was finished. We had a very high casualty rate – three weeks we were given – an average of three weeks.'

'*Did you expect you might get shot down?*'

'It didn't occur to us. I had a little fear somewhere but I never felt fear, I just used to laugh at it. I never – obviously I must have been frightened when I was hit – I must have frozen up somehow, I should imagine –'

'*Were you wounded when you were hit?*'

'I don't know. I've got a few slight wounds, yes, but nothing very much as far as I can remember.'

'*Were you nervous before your thirteenth trip?*'

'No. It didn't occur to me. When I used to go in for the football pools I used to work on thirteen, it might be lucky for me now. It wasn't!'

'*How many days passed between you arriving on the squadron and getting shot down?*'

'Seven days, a week.'

'*And right at the end of the war too, the twentieth of April 1945! Did they give you any training how to use a parachute?*'

'No! No. If they'd given me some training on baling out I

272

might have – my squadron leader baled out twice so it obviously wasn't difficult. You would turn the plane upside-down, pull a pin out and drop.'

'*Did you have any problems with the Spitfire hood?*'

'We flew more or less with it open.'

'*And the guns?*'

'Four machine-guns, four cannon. They could be difficult – they didn't fire when you wanted.

'About the middle of July they took me home. My mother got several letters from the matron about my case, but for all this she didn't know I hadn't been scarred. When she saw me in hospital I was facing the other way, and I heard a voice saying, "Well, there he is!" I turned towards her and she said, "Oh thank God he's not scarred!"'

'I couldn't stand for very long, it's taken me a long time to get over that. Nobody could recognize that I was ill. I got discharged from hospital about the middle of June 1946, and the bank that I'd been in before the war accepted me on a temporary basis. But I broke down – I had a mental breakdown – they were going to discharge me out of the bank.

'I went to a local branch and the manager there took pity on me. He helped me out a lot, gave me a good training and I did all right. They put me on the permanent staff. I haven't been able to work full strength, but I've done routine jobs and managed to cope with it. I haven't claimed much time off. The doctor – they don't know about pills really. They know that they do you good, but they don't know the effects of them. Gradually I took more and more. In fact when I got early retirement when I was fifty-eight, I knew then that I was taking too many and it took me nearly a year to come off it.'

'*Did the RAF provide any kind of long-term assistance?*'

'Only money. They did visit me to ask if I needed anything – the social security, not the RAF. I was getting 100 per cent disability at the time, when I was invalided out. They said they wouldn't take me on permanent staff at the bank with a 100 per cent disability pension so my mother said, "Ask for another medical and see if you can get it reduced."

'They said, "How do you feel if we mark it down to seventy?" ' "Yes, that'll be all right." '

*From medical-history reports of Louis Astor:*

Had Spitfire crash 20 April 1945, in Italy. Age 21. Severe concussion and mental confusion developed, was disorientated socially, and in varying degrees of coma for eight weeks. Gradually became less violent. He can walk if helped.

7.8.45   This is a long-term case.

13.8.45   Neurologist's report:
He evidently had a very severe closed head injury with brain damage. Examination is not easy at present. He is improving slowly.

7.46   Report by Ministry medical officer:
Gets daily attacks of dizziness, sometimes three to four attacks in 24 hours, lasting a few minutes. Memory for recent events is poor. Easily tired. Speech deliberate and inclined to slur, but this is improving. Is unable to run. Gets attacks of diplopia.

24.6.52   Neurological examination:
He is mentally dull and slightly retarded. Has frequent headaches. There is no doubt that there is intellectual deterioration.
Additional remarks: No improvement.

1.6.55   Ministry Medical Board with neuropsychiatrist:
Appellant's statement: 'Under only slight pressure of work I am easily flustered and frequently lose my temper. My balance is still very unsteady, most especially after slight exertion. I can no longer do much reading beyond short

274

newspaper accounts and my ability to study has been ruined.
I also have a slow thought reaction and it is hard for me to
argue in conversation. The pain continued all this time and
I was suffering from nightmares. It seems that my endurance
is negligible, that I am living on the edge of my capabilities
and that normal effort taxes me too far.'

Report by neuropsychiatrist:
Tense and anxious. Unconfident. At times appears a trifle
perplexed. General mild deterioration in cerebration but not
amounting to any degree of dementia.
Additional remarks: No material change in his condition.

The Wellington bomber continued to be flown all through the
war, a testament to its durability and versatility. As a bomber on
operations over Europe it reached the end of its useful life in 1943,
but it had also proved to be adaptable for special duties. Versions
were made for Coastal Command, minelaying and reconnaissance. *Will Tomlinson* served as an air gunner in a Special Duties
squadron flying with the Second Tactical Air Force during the
invasion of the Continent. His plane was a Wellington adapted
for low-flying photo-reconnaissance. In 1945 he was nineteen
years old.

'As a young lad, I used to stand in the garden and watch the
bombers go over and my main ambition was to *be* there! I just
wanted to get the years behind me and hoped that the war lasted
long enough! It was all that filled my mind, though the girls did
go for that uniform, particularly if you had wings on!

'They were Mark XV Wellingtons, a beautiful aircraft, very
manoeuvrable. It was tremendously strong with that geodetic
construction. We used to come back with half the fuselage blown
off and gaping holes where another aircraft would probably have
broken in half!

'I wanted something to do with aircraft but I was too young
to join up so I went to work at Hawker's. I tried several times to

leave because I just wanted to move on somehow, getting nearer to the air force, but they wouldn't let me. The only thing you could leave for was to go into aircrew – they wouldn't release you for the army or navy. In those days you were directed to a job.

'I remember one morning, instead of getting in at half past seven I got there at nine o'clock. The foreman was standing by the clock and he said to me, "Do you know what time this is?"

'I said, "Yer, just gone nine o'clock! Can't you tell the time?" An argument started and in the end I got him by the lapels and thrust him up against the wall! So after that they said I could go. The RAF were very short of aircrew at that time. They were beginning to disappear like flies on to a fly-paper.

'I joined the air force at the end of 1943, and the squadron just after D-Day. Twenty-four air gunners, people who came top of their courses, were rushed out to the squadron with no OTU or anything. They were so desperate. We joined crews that had already formed up but they were on the point of mutiny because of their losses.

'The squadron belonged to Second TAF, and I suppose all our operations were done under the army's direction. If they wanted to know where there were troop reinforcements and things like that, it was our job to go out and find them, where they were moving to, or if there was anything else. We used to take photographs and bring them back. Quite often the army would decide to call in the medium and heavy bombers to clobber the place before the troops moved in. I believe the squadron was originally part of Coastal Command. If you look at the squadron badge (*he shows me his log-book: he has pasted the badge on to the front page*) it says "With Vigilance We Serve" and you can see there's a telescope and an anchor.

'We were slung in at the deep end, more or less. We thought we were going on a training flight. We were stationed at Northolt so I came home every night. When I got back one morning there was a jeep with two RAF policemen in it. They said, "Get in!"

'I thought, "Christ! What have I done now? I'm not late!" So I said, "What's this all about?"

'They said, "You'll see." We went flying out to the airfield and there was a Dakota at the end of the runway, warming up. They already had my kit on board.

'We took off and eventually we landed at this place. A couple of airmen came rushing up, ground mechanics, and they said, "Got any newspapers, mate?"

' "We haven't got any newspapers, what do you want a newspaper for?"

' "Christ!" they said, "we haven't had none for days!"

'Somebody said, "Well, where is this place?"

' "Melsbroek."

'We started thinking, where's Melsbroek, Devon, Cornwall? "Where's that then?"

' "Just outside Brussels!" That was the first we ever knew of it. "What have we come here for?"

' "You've come to join the old Wimpey squadron."

' "Thanks very much for telling us!" They'd never tell you anything, they'd no time to tell anybody.

'My first night-flight in actual fact was an operation. We went to the Dordrecht Canal and got hit (*checks with his log-book*), yeah, that's the time we had our port aileron blown off!

'At the Dordrecht Canal they had these flak towers. If I'd have been more experienced it would have been dodgy, but because I didn't know, all I could see was a sort of firework display. It didn't look particularly hostile. There were these twinkling lights coming up and every now and again these red balls, spaced out, that rose slowly from the ground like this, and suddenly flew past. I could never understand how these things seemed to rise so lazily, then as soon as they got near you they used to hurtle by – zoom! God! What was that? There's all these little twinkling lights which you never connected with bullets, they were tracers, zipping through everywhere. You're inclined to sit there and think that's pretty, that's pretty!

'It didn't look dangerous until suddenly there was a tremendous flash and a bang on your port wing and then you come to realize, they're actually shooting at us! When the port aileron is hanging

277

down, which obviously makes the aircraft fly one wing low, it's then you realize that these things are not so innocuous as they look.

'When we joined the squadron the tour of operations on the heavies, Lancasters and Halifaxes, was thirty trips. We were sent to join this squadron, 69 Squadron SD. We found our tour of operations was only twenty-five trips! We were all cock-a-hoop! You had to do five less! We said, "Christ, this is not bad!" Then a couple of days later one of the blokes said, "I wonder why we only have to do twenty-five as against thirty on the heavies?"

' "That's a good question! I wonder why it is only twenty-five?"

'Now I think it's because they wanted somebody actually to complete a tour so that they could boost the morale! At least somebody had finished their tour.'

*'Did anybody finish?'*

'All I can recall is my own pilot and about two others. I know one chap, Tinker, had completed his last trip. You could hear him over the intercom – we were at the flying control – "Right, that's it! That's me! Get my bacon and eggs ready!" We had an ack-ack battery at the edge of our drome manned by ATS and as he put his wheels down to make his approach they blew him out of the sky! We used to get these intruders coming in, you know. The German fighters used to wait. As you put your wheels down to come in where you couldn't manoeuvre the German fighter would come down – we'd had plenty of those.

'I didn't do many trips, only about a dozen. I was wounded on the third one and spent two or three months in hospital. That's possibly why I'm surviving today! During that time our squadron suffered the heaviest losses, mostly due to flak because we operated round about seven hundred to fifteen hundred feet. You had to do visual reconnaissance, drop flares, then come in underneath the flares and take pictures. Obviously there's a very big bonus for the ground gunners because the Wellington's not exactly a small plane, and not exactly quick!

278

'Once you tracked in on your photographic run there were two gadgets in the back called pistol dischargers, two little boxes at the back of the fuselage. The camera was running the whole time, timed to go off at intervals so that each photograph slightly overlapped. If you were photographing a road or a railway, once you were tracking on this run, you couldn't deviate or turn to one side. As you're only say a thousand feet up, the gunners had quite a good target. These films that portray the Germans as gullible idiots, they weren't at all, we found their ack-ack, particularly the light flak, very very accurate.

'The rear guns were all we had and from the rear turret to the nose was totally blind. We were losing so many aircraft because it didn't take the Germans long to cotton on to the fact that there was a huge blind spot. The air gunner had to be trained because of the combat manoeuvres. The little pop guns we had, four .303 Brownings, were hardly a deterrent – their effective range was only six hundred yards.

'In combat manoeuvres it depended on exactly when and where the attack came from. As the fighter got his range, he would tilt his wings like this – he was just going to press his guns. At that instant you had to dive because once he'd turned like that (*tilting his left wing down*) he couldn't follow you. Once his wings had tilted you slipped away and he had to go up –'

'*It calls for very fine judgement!*'

'Well, it's split second really. When his wings tipped his finger was on the firing button!'

'*Were you ever in that position?*'

'Fortunately, no, although I say no, I'm not really sure. We saw something one night which I think was a 163 – the first rocket-fired thing. We'd never seen anything like this. Fighters had come to investigate us and we'd also done combat man-oeuvres with Spitfires in training: you expect the fighter to come at a certain speed, to close, but then you got this thing, I suppose it was twice or three times as fast as we were. You see it

279

as a dot and all of a sudden it whistles past you! You're sat there just stunned, what the hell was that!

'We found the worst thing was the radar-controlled search-lights, the blue searchlights. As soon as they switched on you were in the middle of them, and then all the others round about would cone you. That happened quite a few times. There's only one way out, get down as low as you can, because you'll never get out otherwise. If you were operating over occupied territory, France or Holland, and Holland particularly is a mass of pylons and cables, you had to take a chance on crashing into the pylons and God knows what. It was a matter of get your head down and go for broke!

'Birds were bloody dangerous. You go over a hedge and a huge flock of birds smash through the windscreen! We did lose a couple of aircraft like that. Where one came through the windscreen and smashed right in the pilot's face. There was no room for error at two hundred miles an hour, twenty feet up. You're gone.

'Another dodgy thing was flying over the sea, where there's no boats. The altimeter is little use at that sort of height but if there's a ship you can judge roughly how high you are. If the sea is empty, you could be at two hundred feet, you could be at twenty – there's nothing to tell you. You can see the size of the waves but you don't know if they're little ripples or fair-sized waves. It doesn't really tell you anything. The one thing we had to do was steer clear of the Royal Navy! Oh they were trigger happy! They really did like to pull their triggers! You had the colours of the day, but they'd shoot you down before you could fire them off.'

'*You got shot at by the navy?*'

'Yes, several times. We learned to steer well clear of them because they were more dangerous than the German ships. They didn't allow aircraft anywhere near them.

'Going out to the target, there was a corridor about five miles wide. You had to fly in this corridor, because anything outside, it doesn't matter who you were or what you were, our own ack-ack gunners would fire! We did actually lose blokes who had strayed outside the corridor and the ack-ack was on to 'em – it was another hazard, so the navigator had to be spot on! We flew so low they had to be good. They had to pin-point the target and as we went out just one aircraft to each target there was no bomber stream you could follow.

'We flew in khaki uniform because the German field grey was very much like the RAF blue, and we were at great risk of getting shot down and picked up. The Dutch Resistance in particular were the sort of people who shot you first and then came over and found out who you were afterwards. They had one or two mishaps so they gave us khaki uniforms to wear.

'We went out every day and practised low flying. Sometimes it was fun. I don't think people know how much you can see up there when you're low flying. They used to say during the black-out if you're smoking a cigarette, shield it, and people used to laugh, but you really can see it, particularly in the black-out where it's pitch dark. You can also see a couple making love in a field. You stick your wing down and just circle and suddenly this couple realize you're watching them!

'Every now and again we were given bombs – certain crews were selected – it was a sort of good-boy present. We were always there just to be shot at, without being able to retaliate. Every now and again they gave us bombs and said, "This is only if you're operating over Germany, you can't do it in occupied territory, just drop 'em wherever you like. Get a nice little sleepy town or village and unload 'em."

'One night we had some incendiaries and they fell on this farmhouse, only on the ground. The yard was lit up by these incendiaries. This old boy and his wife came out in their night-shirts with these long-handled hoes, trying to shovel these things away. We were in hysterics!

'We were all very young. I was eighteen and most of the other chaps were nineteen or twenty, little more than boys. There was a chap on our squadron called Johnny Hardy. I suppose he was a legend. He'd been an instructor on Wellingtons and was probably one of the most experienced Wimpey pilots in the RAF.

He could handle a Wimpey like a fighter pilot handles a Spitfire. He had a big rear gunner called – well, we called him Jack Shepherd after the highwayman – he was a big florid-faced bloke from the East End. When they used to go out to the aircraft you'd see Dick sitting on the tail-board. He was never drunk but he always had half a bottle of beer in his hand swigging away and singing at the top of his voice. They became the indestructible.

'Everybody expected Johnny to come back, which he did time and time again. Then one time he didn't and a tremendous shock went through the squadron. It made everybody feel that much more vulnerable – if he could go then we could all go!

'We lost a hell of a lot of people. They had a board in the crew-room with the names of pilots who'd gone out that night, maybe six or seven, with the take-off times and the landing times. The chaps would come in, then we'd get the old NYR up, not yet returned. After another hour or so they'd come in, rub the NYR out and write missing up there. Everybody had mates in the other aircraft.'

*'You wonder how they kept morale up when that was happening.'*

'Well, yeah, I think in a lot of cases – we did have one bloke who – well, we had two really. One was an officer but he was bunged off to England and given a flying job at a desk. The other was a flight sergeant air gunner, I forget his name, only a little feller. He had a DFM – he'd done a previous tour on Lancasters. He came to our squadron and half-way through his tour he got the old shakes, you know, when he picked up a cup and saucer, the cup rattled in the saucer. Everybody said he's got the old screaming ad-dabs and eventually he said he couldn't fly any more. In those days – it's not like now, they recognize the fact that people's nerve goes – but then he was marked LMF. He was stripped in front of the squadron. The officer was allowed to come back to England and have a desk job but this poor little bugger had to suffer that indignity.

'Once you get back to England with your papers stamped LMF your fate is to clean out the latrines and do all the filthiest jobs. There was no recognition of the fact that you couldn't help it. Most blokes would have rather died than gone LMF, it was their biggest fear. When they stamped your papers it was right across in big letters, and then, you know, ho-ho! LMF eh? We've got just the job for you, matey! Very unfair because the people that stamped your papers weren't the ones that had to go and do the job!'

'*What was the attitude of the people watching this fellow stripped?*'

'They just dropped their heads – there was nothing you could do about it. There was a few mutterings in the ranks but if you'd done anything that would have been classed as mutiny so you just had to stand there. I don't think anybody watched. An officer came out from England to make the humiliation complete. I think he was an air commodore, or something like that. He was the only one *I* knew who went LMF, though quite a few *wanted* to. But the stigma was so much they would rather have got killed.

'I suppose I had a good war really. But the flying wasn't the glamour job that you see on the films, these carefree young men who were willing to risk all with a smile on their lips, it wasn't like that in real life. It was like every other aspect of war, a dirty thing, and blokes – well, I never met anybody who wasn't scared. There was none of this off-we-go-into-the-wide-blue-yonder. You'd go to briefing, then from the time of briefing to when you took off you'd see a lot of miserable faces sitting around and cigarettes being chain-smoked and the old nerves were beginning to – nearly everyone was like that.'

'*Did people get superstitious?*'

'Oh yes, very. I had a little plaster angel that my mother gave me which I used to hang up in the turret, and funnily enough the night I got wounded I didn't have it. Every other time on the night-flying tests and the first two operations I hung this little angel up and on the night I got wounded I just forgot it.'

'*Did that make you worried, when you found you hadn't got it?*'

'No, I didn't even know I didn't have it! When they hauled me off the aircraft I asked somebody to get it for me and they said it's not there. It was in my kit.

'One of the big superstitions was that once you took off on operations you didn't whistle or sing. Most pilots would clamp down on that. As not being anything other than bringing bad luck.

'We were all round about eighteen, nineteen or twenty, even our wing commander was only twenty-four. There were a lot of spare bods hanging round the crew-room because of injuries to their pilots so you'd got enough to form a crew. They sent this pilot out from England, he wasn't a bad pilot. He tried to get a crew, but the thing was, he was *twenty-seven* years old! They all recoiled – they said, twenty-seven! God! Can he see? They all crowded in to have a look at this old geezer. As I say, our Wingco, our CO, was only twenty-four, and this bloke was three years older than him. So they were all nipping and hiding, hoping not to be assigned to his crew.

'What made it worse, on his first trip – and it was nothing to do with him – his aircraft was so badly damaged he pranged it on the runway! Unfortunately the aircraft belonged – I say belonged because we largely flew the same aircraft as long as we could – belonged to a bloke called Pilot Officer Cornwell. He'd been drinking and he immediately rushed to his billet and got his revolver – we all carried side-arms – and went round hunting for this bloke. He said, "I've flown that bloody thing for the last twenty trips, and this berk has gone and pranged it the first time he's taken it out!" He was beside himself with rage. Everybody's trying to hold him and they finally got him under control and disarmed him, but he meant it! He would have shot this bloke. Oh, there was some real clots there, there's no doubt about that! First-class idiots!

'There were two totally different classes. Pilots and their crews regarded themselves more or less as equals – we used to wake our pilot up by chucking a jug of cold water over his head while he was in bed. We played as many practical jokes on him as on anybody else. There was only one proviso – once you got into that aircraft, he was the skipper and his word was law! He'd have you court-martialled as soon as look at you, and it had to be that way, because it was the only way you could survive. The crew can't sit there arguing with the pilot, whether he's right or wrong in his decision, you'd get a Tower of Babel! The pilot's word was law.

'But the difference between the officers and the other ranks, well, it was a different world. They had all the privileges, and really we'd got nothing. We were just dogsbodies to do as we were told. Apart from me my first crew were all officers. We went out to Brussels one night and I was going to a bistro and find a bit of skirt somewhere, but Jack, our pilot, said, "Come on, we'll take you in the club!" They virtually forced me into this club and you should see the looks I got because I had a sergeant's stripes!

'The naval commander came up, a sort of a steward, and said to my pilot, "I'm afraid you'll have to ask the NCO to leave." Jack started to get very stroppy but they knew that being aircrew there was nothing they could do. All they could do was send a report to our CO and he would merely tear it up and throw it in the waste-paper basket, because he couldn't chuck half the aircrew in clink. You need 'em for flying.

'You can get killed with an officer but you can't drink with him, it's at odds, isn't it? You can die together but you can't drink together. What harm is there? I'm only human, the same as they are. But it's this class, this privilege thing.

'I remember when we got to one station, a non-operational place which only saw an aeroplane once every blue moon, the sergeants' mess was nice and comfortable. Each sergeant had his own chair and his own newspaper. If you went in, there was a counter with all the newspapers. When we arrived we used to walk in, grab any paper and sit down in the nearest chair. These blokes were outraged! One old boy, an old flight sergeant, was very bitter. He said, "I don't know," he said, "times have changed. The air force was a wonderful place, until you get all these bloody aircrew coming in with their aeroplanes!"

'This was their attitude. We were just interlopers. Another big bitch they had was the fact that once you passed out and got your wings or air gunner's brevet or whatever, you became a sergeant, whereas some of these blokes had been in for twenty-odd years before they made sergeant. They were bitterly resentful. But if they said anything to us we'd say, "All right then, mate, you do my job and I'll do yours. See how you like that!" That usually shut 'em up. Most of them were what we called penguins, you know, non-employed airmen.

'There was always this bitterness between the ground staff and the aircrews, but strangely enough not the ground staff that worked on the aircraft, the mechanics and flight engineers. Quite often we came back from an op and they were there waiting – they'd no need to. "Everything all right, skip?" In actual fact there was a great rapport between us. The *other* ground staff were the sit-wallahs and those that worked in the postal room and orderlies.

'I don't know why they should have been so resentful. After all, if we hadn't been doing the job they might have had to do it. They could see we were comparatively raw, hadn't been in the air force all that long, but because of our rank they couldn't order us about and this also rankled. Let me say, this was on stations in England, rather than on the squadron. *There* they had a sympathy and a rapport because they were on the spot – they saw blokes that didn't come back and blokes who came back shot up and all the rest of it, whereas these idiots over in England had never seen anything. They were very uptight about it all. In actual fact you'd have thought we were fighting them instead of the Germans! It was like two forces within a force, if you know what I mean.'

*'Did you think you'd survive?'*

'The blokes I flew with, their view was they were going to get killed. Where or when was the question. It was just when, where, how soon. This is why, as soon as you got paid, you blew your money on booze, or women, or gambling or whatever because you thought, well, I might not be here tomorrow! I'm not going to let anybody else have it so I'll spend it. So there were blokes going round borrowing all the time because they'd spent up and found to their surprise they were still alive and didn't have any money! (*Laughs.*)

'The favourite song in our mess was the one they had in the film with Errol Flynn. If one of the crew who was flying that night came in for a quick double whisky before he went, they would sit him on the bar, all stand round and sing, "Here's a toast to the men dead already, here's a toast to the next man to die!" With this poor little sod sitting up there with his whisky! (*Laughs.*) Particularly Australians, because on our squadron we had a hell of a lot of Australians, most of them from the outback. Tough as whipcord and no feelings whatsoever, completely devoid of any feelings like sympathy. They regarded that as some sort of a weakness. If you felt sorry for anybody, they used to look upon this with derision. But they lived hard and they played hard and they died hard. It was probably the sort of life they led before they joined the air force. Not an easy life in the outback, it made 'em used to the body blows of life.'

*'Had you any idea before you went in how high the casualty rates were?'*

'Oh no. All we knew was, oh yeah, one or two got shot down. It became a bit hard when you found your mates disappearing at a rate of knots and only on one small squadron. You never knew what was going to happen. My second pilot, Andy, was only twenty years old. When you're on your way back it all becomes jovial so when Andy called up and said, "I can't see!" there were gales of laughter.

'"Yeah, well we know that Andy! Some of your landings, we realized you can't see!"

'"No," he said, "I'm not joking! I can't see!" So, you know, all this banter went on, and we said, "Well, it don't matter, Andy! Your landing'll probably be better than it usually is!"

'And then the voice of the bomb-aimer came through and said, "Look, this is no joke, chaps, he can't see, he's gone blind," and we suddenly realized it was true! We only carried one pilot and

287

he couldn't see! (*Laughs.*) It wasn't until a few seconds had passed that it dawned on everybody that you're up there in an aircraft, stooging round the airfield with a pilot who can see nothing – oh Christ, what we gonna do? We knew we couldn't jump out and leave him in there. We all had to stay! We got in our crash positions. You had certain designated positions that you took if you thought you were going to crash. Andy said, "Well, don't panic! Ben's gonna talk me down!" Between 'em, as they approached what they called the funnels, that's the landing lights, he was saying, "How high am I? How am I positioned? Where's the funnels?" – they were in a descending order – "How high am I now, are the wheels locked?" And between 'em they got it down.

'Once it had rolled to a stop all the tension burst again, everybody was shouting, "It's the best landing you've ever made, Andy! Next time you want to wear dark glasses, you land better when you can't see!"'

'*Did his sight come back?*'

'Yeah. It was nerves. But it hadn't gone partially, it had gone completely. Total blindness. Scary for him because he just suddenly realized – everything's dark around you – he just suddenly realized he couldn't see anything. I suppose when he glanced at his instruments or where he thought they were.'

'*Did your parents know you were on bombers?*'

'Oh yeah, my parents knew but I don't think they thought there was any danger in what I was doing. I told 'em I was on a photographic unit and they seemed to think that was me rushing around on the ground with a camera snapping everything. I possibly survived because I got wounded. Our squadron's losses during that time were absolutely terrifying. They were disappearing two or three a night and there was only twenty-four crews. I think at one time they were down to three. They lost twenty-one of them and I thought, Christ, I could have been one of the twenty-one – it's a good job I'm lying here! My parents

288

had quite a nasty shock when they got the telegram that I was wounded. My nephew has it now, because my mother kept it.

'I'd only just gone back off leave. We'd had a bit of a party, laughing and joking and knocking back the old beers, and suddenly they get this telegram out of the blue. My mother had a miscarriage when I was wounded. I was twenty and she was something like thirty-seven, thirty-eight, and she was expecting a baby. She got the telegram and had a miscarriage.

'I got one right through my ankle there and it ripped all the flesh away from the top of the muscle which was all hanging out – it still does, if I tense my leg, the muscle still pokes out the hole. And then there was my hip and also right across the top of the thigh here. I can't see one bullet doing that, it must have been something that exploded. I think the worst part was the smell of – I don't know – cordite, and then you're aware of the cold. I suppose it's the shock. I could feel something strange happening in my flying boot, something warm and sticky which I thought somehow was hydraulic fluid until I realized it was bubbling out from inside my boot.'

'*How long were you in hospital?*'

'I went in in November and came out in March. The first trip when I returned was (*mimics wiping sweat off his face*) very shaky and at that time we were going nearly every day. The old nerves do get a bit tweaky. It doesn't matter if everything's dead quiet, no guns, no nothing, no searchlights, you're always waiting for that big bang, it's just suddenly going to come up and bang! bingo! You're never sure because it's already happened once!

'The big thing was the complete change. One night you were over enemy territory being shot at, a few hours later you're back to normality, in the mess having a drink or going to a dance, knowing that the next night it's all going to change again. There's this continual change from a normal ordinary life to gearing yourself up every night. Your nerves get tense – they're like bowstrings – and you want to go to somebody and say, "Look, I don't want to go, I can't go any more!" but you don't, you just sit there, and try and control your nerves. I found the worst part was when the aircraft was going round the perimeter track and it's stopped just short of the runway. The pilot would do his last check with the crew then the aircraft would turn on to the runway. Even at that time panic sets in and you start thinking, shall I leap out and say I've got a headache or I can't see or I've got the flu, or *anything*, but you just sort of get hold of your nerves and sit there. Then the pilot says, "Well OK lads, here we go!" The engines open up and you relax because you know it's too late, there's nothing you can do, once again this is it and away we go. But it's that feeling of panic, of wanting to –'

'*Has it had any long-term effects?*'

'Er, I don't think so much now. A few years afterwards I think it did, it changed me in a lot of ways. I suppose my wife could tell you more about that, because for quite a number of years I was jumpy, irritable, I couldn't stand firework night – used to bring me out in a cold sweat because some of these things sounded like how it was. But now I don't think it's had any real lasting effect, except I wonder what it was all for. I look back and think – being young and foolish is the phrase – we listened to the people who had no intentions of doing anything themselves, going out and fighting or anything. They said to us, "Right-oh lads, gird your loins and go out and fight for what you've got!" And us dopes said, "Cor, yeah! Terrific! Yeah! Go out and fight for what we've got!" and looking back I've thought well, what did I have? I had a suit and a broken-down old bike, and that's all I had! I didn't have anything else. All these big landowners, they had something to fight for, but most of us that did the fighting didn't have anything. All the blokes that I flew with were shop assistants, coal-miners, farmers, blokes who didn't have anything at all. Sometimes when I look back now I laugh to think how we were conned into swaggering off to war singing – with the brash thing of youth. That is the sort of thing now that makes me bitter, rather than the war itself, knowing that – we were told everybody is pulling together, everybody is making sacrifices, and you find out years later that that wasn't true. They weren't at all.

'I suppose looking back on it it's not something I would have missed. You can say that once it's all over and you've survived. I wouldn't like to say I enjoyed it but I suppose parts of it I did. I tell you what I did enjoy was wearing the wings and having all the girls flocking round, and people buying you free beer and the rest of it. The bits I didn't enjoy was having to go out and earn it! If I could have avoided that bit it would have been all milk and honey!'

*'Have you flown since the war?'*

'No. No, I resolved never to go up in an aircraft again. Don't like tempting fate. I got away with blowing out engines, ailerons hanging down – one day old Lady Luck might shake her head and say no, no more, mate. Probably how I'll die is one'll crash on me from the sky!'

# CONCLUSION

THE WAR OVER, DEMAND FOR THE PRODUCTS OF AIRCRAFT companies fell away and many of the smaller ones found themselves in difficulties. Westbourne Engineering was hard hit and within two years had all but collapsed. The great wartime firms survived longer, but one by one they fell victim to changing postwar circumstances and suffered bankruptcy or takeover. I found that my father's tendency to mourn the passing of the aircraft firm where he had worked during the war was an emotion widely shared:

'When you walk on de Havilland land you are walking on hallowed ground. All the most famous aviators in the world have walked over that ground. I used to go looking for mushrooms on it, if I had a tea-break. I used to go over and pick up a couple of mushrooms. I wrote to de Havilland's in 1939 and they took me on. During the war I thought it was a lovely place to work. You know, I worked there till five years ago. One thing that impressed me was when Hawker-Siddeley's took over. I'd worked for de Havilland's and I thought it was a lovely name, a lovely sounding name, but when Hawker-Siddeley took over and I saw them ripping DE HAVILLAND from the front of the factory I could have cried. They just ripped it off and that's it, chucked it on the ground, finished.' (*Mr Bowens*)

'I've got a pictorial record of Fairey's being demolished. We took photographs of it from outside the works and it looks as though it's been hit by an atomic bomb. They were bulldozing and this fellow was about to chuck all the records out. I said, "What's happening to this stuff?"

' "It'll be burnt!"

'I got a tea-chest, filled it with photographs, and it's out there in my conservatory today! A marvellous record that would have gone on the fire. I was one of the last six to leave the works. We literally handed the place over to the contractors, Slater Walker. They demolished it and rebuilt it. Two of the big companies that went in there straight away were Hitachi – Japanese, and the German Mercedes. And we'd been building aircraft there to oppose the Japanese and the Germans!' (*Mr Chinery*)

'I could see Handley Page's from here, from my home. I look back on the time and think it was a good firm. Put it this way – I made friends with people and they're still friends today. It was a great atmosphere in the place. And I watched it burn to the ground, what was left of it. I was at the top of the house painting one day and I saw a lot of smoke coming up there. I thought that looks like a fire and I actually saw the flames and heard the explosion – the roof fell in. You'd be amazed how you felt, here was your last link with your early days going up in flames. I felt most sad about it. I've spoken to other people who saw it and they felt the same way. There's not even a plaque on the wall to say, well, this was the site of Handley Page aircraft ...' (*Mr Handyside*)

The great figures of the aircraft industry are still affectionately remembered, blame for the harsher side of life in their factories often being attributed to managers or foremen:

'Sir Fred – Handley Page – was a very tall chap with a beak of a nose and he wanted a rushed job. Something for the Farnborough Air Show. He said, "Give me the bloody tools here!" He took off his coat, in his shirt-sleeves, and he's hacking and banging about on this aircraft! They've got the inspector and the foreman standing there – "Is that all right?" he said. "Yes, sir!" you know. No messing about. We were round the corner, kept having a look. The factory thought he was all right really. (*In a surprised voice*) They thought he was quite a decent bloke.' (*Mr Moreton*)

'Fairey's as a whole were a good firm. There's no getting away from it. I had no complaints. Young Dick Fairey who got torpedoed and had frost-bitten legs used to come waddling through the factory. He was one of us! He used to stand and talk to us. "Where's this going? What are you doing? How long have you been working on it?" and all that sort of thing. Have a chat with you. So did the old man, old Richard Fairey, oh they were people to work for! Never paid exorbitant wages but the job was always there whether you had the work or not. Most factories when you got short of work started putting men off, always have done. Fairey's didn't. Providing you behaved yourself and didn't cause them any trouble, they looked after you. I've got all the menus of the dinners that Fairey's put on for us. Over twenty-five years, servants every year, and when the bosses walked in, they used to bring the roof down.'

'*Applauding them?*'

'Yes. They were very fond of 'em. Because they got a fair deal from them. But do that with Parker's, where I worked before? Forgive me for being vulgar, but they would have chucked *shit* at them! They weren't popular. Fairey's was different. I was happy enough there – I stayed for thirty-two years. Of course, the factory now is all gone. Demolished.' (*Mr Randle*)

Class differences during the war seemed to be less than they had been before 1939, in particular to some of the people who served in the RAF:

'When you were an erk admin you just ran around and did everything, all sorts of odd jobs. I learnt to scrub a floor in the WAAF! I'd never had to scrub a floor before! Oh! We had servants to scrub floors when I was at home. They said, "Forbes, scrub that floor! Clean it up!" So I cleaned it up. That sort of thing. Very good for you. And I think great fun, too. It was a great leveller. It's a pity that after the war we thought everything would be – you know, the levelling would continue but it doesn't, does it? There's still so much snobbery about, so much difference.' (*Miss Forbes*)

'Discipline wasn't like the army, of course, but it worked. Everybody knew their job. There was informality in the crews, they were on Christian-name terms whether they were sergeants or officers, but nevertheless the captain's word is law in the air. But generally things were lax. A guards regiment would have been horrified. We had one or two ex-guards officers who had transferred to the RAF and they were quite amusing to us – when they were told to do something they stamped to attention, sah! disappeared and came back, sah!' (*Mr Gover*)

'Discipline in the air had to be good. As well as we knew one another we never used names, always trades. Pilot, navigator or whatever. And no chattering. Discipline on the ground was fairly lax even so far as one went out drinking with one's ground crew, which was accepted. You still paid compliments to Oxford, you didn't go out of anybody's office without saluting. The common courtesies were always observed. But for the war I might have finished as a clerk somewhere or office manager probably with a horizon about that wide. It was the war that made all the difference. When I got into the service we were marched into a barrack room in alphabetic order. There was a man called Petts on one side, myself, and on the other side was a man whose father was a judge in Nairobi. As the three of us were together we became friends, and we used to write letters to his wife for him because poor old Petts couldn't write.' (*Mr Power*)

'It was very relaxed. All sergeants, officers, CO, whatever. The CO was a Battle of Britain bloke who took over the squadron just before the *Scharnhorst* do, and he came in and introduced himself to us. We were all in the dispersal, and he said, "For your information, I'm Brian, no bullshit, but this doesn't mean if I happen to be talking to the AOC some sergeant pilot can walk up, whack me on the back and say, Wotcher, Brian!" And that was it. It was hello Brian, hello Fred, hello Charlie, or whatever. It was one big happy family. There was obviously always the odd one who wasn't madly popular, but generally speaking it was a cracking bunch.' (*Mr Robertson*)

Some, however, recall that the camaraderie of wartime faded soon after the war. Even during the war it had been difficult to persuade everyone that the British were now one community:

'We had women directed who came from the posh suburbs: they'd arrive for work in taxis wearing fur coats and with hands beautifully manicured. Some were very good, others were quite useless. They never did get the hang of things. You couldn't blame them. They'd not been brought up to it. They were the daughters of wealthy fathers who married wealthy husbands. They had servants and lived a life of ease. They just did the social round. They had no idea how the rest of the world lived and were not mentally capable of assimilating anything else. But they were drafted into the war effort and they had to do something. Some of them must have found it very hard. Engineering works are not very salubrious places, what with oily clothes and oily shoes and the reek of coupling oil. They didn't like the mixture of social classes in which they found themselves. In those days, much more so than now, the classes were separated. The middle classes couldn't rub shoulders – they couldn't even speak the same language. I don't think they even used the same words. They didn't understand each other. They were unhappy so we used to try and sort them out and put them somewhere where they'd do something useful. Everybody was rejecting them and so they went the round and everybody tried them out (*laughs*). Some of them eventually found life in the Salvation Army or running a soup kitchen more in tune with their life-style than working in a workshop.' (*Mr Toynbee*)

The mood in the aircraft industry after the war became more relaxed. Firms which previously had maintained strict discipline found that in conditions of full employment it was necessary to be less severe, as at Vickers of Weybridge:

'At Christmas time the clock stopped. People were bringing gramophone players in, setting up drinks, putting all the desks together and lining the drinks up, you name it, half-raping the tea girls. It was just after the war when things went absolutely mad, in the late '40s. There was an enormous amount of bribery and corruption among the subcontractors there. Oh yes. The Christmas trade in drinks was just horrific. And not only in drinks but in new motor cars. As they say, nice and easy. Winding up all the contracts at the end of the war, with the Ministry, was a game too, because there was such huge shortages, and so many things had gone astray. It was the same in a lot of firms. We lost hundreds of aircraft. They had to write off hundreds of thousands of pounds. They took the Ministry bloke out and filled him with drink and at the end of that he'd have signed anything.' (*Mr Phillips*)

In the air force too the mood relaxed as soon as the war was over:

'Everybody was organizing parties and flying over to Southern Ireland to pick up legs of pork, and butter, and all this kind of thing. They used to send a Dakota over probably once a week and it would come back loaded with all the goodies. The sergeants' mess used to throw a big party once a week where everybody went, CO included, the lot. This was an unheard-of thing before, though things during the war had slowly been getting more and more informal. You were racketed around and you ate and drank and had a wonderful time, felt terrible the next morning.

'The CO was really hard put to think how to keep the troops occupied. I remember being summoned every day to the group captain's office to play games! He used to demand that myself and the adjutant and one other guy come in and play this crossword-puzzle game. We had a whole stock of aircraft receivers which could be converted to ordinary radios so we used to put new power units in them, trim them up a bit and give or flog them to people for civilian radios which were in short supply. When the war finished everybody kind of threw their hats up in the air and a good time was had by all for a couple of years or so until the firm guidelines were introduced, and then of course it went along much as before.' (*Mr Dale*)

The long hours worked during the war and the fatigue many people felt at the end of it are still vividly recalled:

'At one time they asked for a special effort. We worked four months from eight till eight on weekdays, eight till four on Saturdays, and eight till four on Sundays, four months we did that! Coo, dear me! We were cheesed off at the end of that time! We were! It was mechanical, you know. You went in and they had all the stuff there – we didn't get any hold-ups – we made the stuff and turned it out – we had a target to do and we did it. This was during the war at one period when we were losing so much stuff. Sometimes you had raids on the way home and the trains were pretty shaky and some of the fellows never got home. They got to the middle of London, stopped on the station and came back in the morning!' (*Mr Herrington, Vickers*)

'I was fire-watching as well. In snow, wind, rain. I was up all night, then going off to work at six or seven in the morning. I was sixteen! Lots of people have laughed at me when I've told them I was working all day and all night. How the hell did you do that? Well, it's wartime! You had to do something. I worked Saturdays and Sundays, but when I came home at night-time it was nothing for us to dive under the table on the mattress because he (*the Luftwaffe*) was up above.'

'*When did you get any sleep?*'

'You used to have to take it when you could! It was long hours for little pay, put it that way.' (*Mrs Brown, Hawker's*)

'At the end of the war we were all so tired! We'd worked so hard. It was the last straw. I was exhausted – we all were – I can't describe it to you. What with food shortages and the dull diet, I was tired out. I needed a long rest. I was only eighteen or twenty but the war had really taken it out of me.' (*Audrey Groom, secretary*)

Others found that their health had been affected by conditions in wartime factories:

'All the time that you were working these machines you had a milky substance falling through – the slurry. You were asked to go to the foreman's desk where there was a pink barrier cream to protect your hands. But sometimes it sprayed on your face and like myself, you end up with a slurry skin infection which was your face covered in a rash. Then you had to go off sick for a couple of weeks to clear that up. So you were a little bit wary of the stuff.'

*'Did you get any compensation for that?'*

'Well, no.' (*Mrs East, Miles Aircraft*)

'I'd been bad for some time – bringing up my food – I never seemed to keep it down. The doctor said, "I'll get you into Windsor for X-ray," and do you know what it was? The appendix was full of fine metal!'

*'From the factory?'*

'It was through doing all that drilling! You inhaled it. Some of it was so fine, you wouldn't believe it. It depended on what you were drilling. The appendix was full and they said they couldn't wait. This was a big job! I'd got about forty stitches. The nurse came up to take the stitches out and she said, "Oh Miss McVicar, would you like to keep these as a souvenir?" Well, I could have hit her! I said, "What are you on about, souvenirs!"' (*Miss McVicar made components for the Spitfire.*)

'When I first went to Hawker's I used to have blisters on my fingers like nobody's business, they were absolutely red raw sometimes. I used to come home and put some cream and bandage on and bandage them up. When I did leave I had eczema metal poisoning in my hands. I had to leave the job. I asked for compensation and they said no, I couldn't, it's wartime. Sixteen weeks I was off and no pay. Some of the men used to get eczema all up their arm.' (*Mrs Brown*)

Many aircrew had great difficulty settling down to civilian life after the war, even if they came out of the air force without a scratch. Returning to the world of work after flying a Spitfire or Lancaster seemed a big come-down. Not every employer, particularly one who had spent the war at home, wanted a DFC and bar in the office or round the works, while eight hours' routine at a desk could be a grim contrast to life on the squadron. Demobbed pilots who had gone into the RAF as teenagers found themselves competing with young men five or six years their junior, who often had better qualifications. From being in charge as wing commander or squadron leader of large numbers of people, one might have to join a civilian firm at the bottom. One alternative was to stay in the RAF or transfer your skills to civil aviation:

'If you wanted to apply for a commission, they'd said, "You stay on for four years and we'll see how you go." Well, it's not much because at the end of four years, if they throw you out, you're four years behind everybody else! I did think seriously about going into BOAC but you've got this twice-a-year rigorous medical – I'm all right for a few years now, but if I fail the medical what's my position? And I was a qualified solicitor. I didn't find it easy to settle down in civilian life. I had the urge to go back. If I hadn't been qualified I would have gone back.' (*Mr Gover*)

Many found it very difficult to decide whether to stay in or leave the RAF. There is a tendency now for them to regret whichever choice they made:

'When the war finished they came round with their little pink form, will you sign up now for four years? Which is understandable if they were going to carry on training us. It wasn't worth their while if we were going to come out as soon as we finished training. I'd just done four and a half years and I was sick to the death of living out of a kitbag, so I said not likely. I was taken off flying, came out and went back to the old firm. I bitterly regretted it afterwards because I should have stayed in, finished my training and carried on flying. I was half-way through and even in those days it cost five thousand pounds to train a pilot. I should have stayed in because I loved it, very much.' (*Mr Waite*)

Others felt that they had used up all their luck during the war, and decided to settle down to a ground-based job:

'The CO said, "Look, we want fellows like you, ex-regulars, to stay in." I said, "No, I'm married now, I'm going out." My wife said, "No more flying, that's it," and I had to respect her views because we had a child and responsibilities. I reverted to ground engineering, and went to work at Vickers Armstrong.' (*Mr Thackray*)

Fear of flying is to be expected among former aircrew, but it is surprising to meet it among the factory workers:

'Funny thing that. What put me off, even though I done a lot in the aircraft, was, I worked right up in the nose and the nose cone was open. The bloody aircraft moved and it nearly pushed me out of the top there, and looking down, cor! That put the fear of God up me and I said I'd never fly and I never did. Till me daughter went to America and I've flown there five times! I didn't go there till I was sixty-five!' (*Mr Hawkins*)

'We had a leaking tank on a Mosquito. We took the tank door down and the bolts just sprang out! The door nearly dropped on our heads! That was the stressed part. Well, that was terrible. Bonus comes into it again. It's all a question of money. Some bright chaps in one of the factories had found out that if they put a taper on these bolts, they put 'em in, just turned 'em once and they were in. Just on one thread. Oh, about seven blokes got sacked straight away. God knows what happened to them. Straight in the army, I suppose. A lot of machines failed to return and it wasn't necessarily enemy action, but something like that! It's one of the reasons why I don't like flying now and I never will. I know the things that *can* go wrong and you can never get it out of your mind.' (*Mr A. Taylor*)

*Mrs York*: 'I always remember when I wanted to fly for the first time, Len said, "I'm not going to fly!"

' "Well," I said, "I'm not going on the water!"

'He said, "I couldn't fly, not the way I know they make planes. I'm not going on a plane. I've seen how they're made!" ' (*Mr York worked for thirty years at de Havilland's.*)

The camaraderie of wartime still continues. Aircraft firms like Handley Page which went bankrupt nearly twenty years ago are still commemorated by active works' associations. Although de Havilland's merged with Hawker-Siddeley almost thirty years ago, the enamelled silver medals given to long-service employees, with their names and the year they joined the company inscribed on them, are proudly produced, and DH ties worn. 'The damn good parties' the firm gave them are still recalled.

Squadron associations, specialized clubs like the Caterpillar Club for those who baled out and the Guinea Pig club for aircrew who were badly burned flourish and keep up a vigorous social life. Crews are often still in touch with one another nearly fifty years later:

'You had to be young. You couldn't stand it if you were over forty. It was slaughter really, when you sit and think about it, that's why there's such comradeship between ex-aircrew, particularly in Bomber Command. Ten Squadron now, we've got a marvellous association. We have a couple of reunions each year, one with the squadron which is still flying, and one in York in September. We go back to our old airfield. We have a Ten Squadron lounge in a pub which is really the Blacksmith's Arms

302

but ever since the war has been called the Bomber's Arms. The airfield is now owned by a farmer who is very very good to us. He said, "This place is as much yours as mine!" We've built a memorial at the entrance, he gave us the ground to put it on, and one lady puts flowers on there every week. It's a tremendous spirit which is nice to see.' (*Mr Thackray*)

The RAF included large numbers of personnel from overseas. Canadians, Australians, New Zealanders, South Africans, West Indians and Rhodesians flew and worked alongside Britons during the war. One senior officer thought that the fact that 'the war was the last time the Empire fought as a unit' was one of the most remarkable things about it. But the RAF also included Poles, Czechs, French and Americans, and the national diversity of squadrons and crews is fondly and vividly remembered:

'I happened to be with a New Zealand crew, so I was very very fortunate. Each of the crews had four NZ boys, the pilot, navigator, wireless-operator and bomb-aimer, and the two gunners and myself were English boys, and we all got on extremely well together. Their association in New Zealand was formed in 1948 and in 1978 they decided to have their annual reunion over here instead of in New Zealand. We had a marvellous reunion at Cambridge, oh fabulous! Wonderful weekend, well, even my wife loved it. Up until about three years ago all our crew were still alive and in touch with each other.' (*Mr Waite*)

Sometimes surprising contacts are made from the wartime past:

'About seven years ago I got a letter through the Air Ministry from a chap in Holland. This lad was fourteen years old at the time we crashed and he witnessed the plane blowing up in mid-air. A group of Dutch people have been going into all the planes that came down in Holland, finding out the details of who was flying, where they were going, and what happened to them. He latched on to the one he saw, and how he did it I don't know, but he traced my name and the names of one or two of the others.

This is forty years afterwards! After we'd all sent him our stories he came up with this – '

*It is a meticulously drawn map of the area where the plane crashed, pin-pointing the spots where the various members of the crew landed, and the houses that were damaged by bits of the aircraft.*

'I wrote and told him the names of the Dutch nurses who looked after me when I was in hospital, and he traced one, she's still alive, she still remembers me. In fact she produced a letter that I wrote to her in the hospital. He sent me a copy and I looked at it – it took me right back to the time that I actually wrote it.' (*Mr Towers*)

'That (*a photo*) is the little house I stayed in after I baled out over Belgium. That's Gaston – he's still alive. Fantastic man. I went straight back as soon as I could after the war. We keep in touch with them all, have done since I came back, seen them many times over the years. Their families have been over here, ours have been there. We've got the son of one of the helpers staying with us now. He's at Farnborough at the moment because he's an air correspondent. Our crew are buried in two different cemeteries for some reason. When we were at one of them we were introduced to a young man, a sergeant in the Belgian Air Force. He proved to be a very good friend and even found where my aircraft went down, took these pictures of it. I went back and laid a wreath on behalf of the Air Force Escaping Society. Even the boot that came off when I baled out turned up! They sent it back to me. That was in '48.' (*Mr Barton*)

RAF personnel and aircraft industry workers had lived with death for over five years. Aircrew friends and comrades had been killed, airmen and Waaf killed and injured on the ground, and factory workers had been attacked, especially in 1940. Some aircrew, shot down over Germany, actually experienced what it was like to be on the receiving end of a Bomber Command raid:

'When we got down to Frankfurt the RAF were bombing it! I'd been in the air raids in this country, but I've never heard anything like that in all my life! The RAF used to concentrate their raids and drop everything within about twenty minutes to half an hour. These cookies were coming down – the four-thousand-pound bomb's got no streamlining on it, it's just a straight cylinder of TNT and it comes down like an express train. We were stuck in a shelter with sandbags with an open top. One RAF officer ran out into the street shouting for his mother! Scared to death. Really it was terrifying. Frightened the life out of me!' (*Mr Poulter*)

Others joined parties of air personnel to be flown on 'Baedeker's' tours to see the damage the RAF and USAAF had done to Germany:

'They ran a sight-seeing trip after the war, to let the people on the stations know what the RAF had done in Germany, and it was absolutely horrifying. We flew over Hamburg and there wasn't – this enormous great city – there wasn't a roof to be seen! You wondered where people lived. They said, "Look what our boys have done, how clever!" Oh! Awful. It really was dreary. And Düsseldorf, that was another place we flattened. It was awful to see it – a great city devastated like that.' (*Miss Forbes, WAAF*)

Many RAF personnel who had flown over Germany during the war found they were stationed in the country after it:

'I never went to Hamburg on ops. I don't know if you've seen photographs of Hamburg? Oh dear oh dear! You could walk into our Luton town and stand near the town hall and as far as the eye could see not one building would be standing, just shells – there used to be these big black crosses on the walls to indicate dead people were still underneath. It used to reek horrible. If you were on a train travelling through Germany every siding we used to pull into hundreds and hundreds of German kiddies and women would be screaming out, "*Haben sie eine Zigarette für meine Mutter!*" or "*Haben sie eine Schokolade!*" And skinny! Dear oh dear.' (*Mr Emery*)

During the war 70,253 men were killed or went missing on operations. Over fifteen hundred ground crew, men and women, were also killed. Everyone I spoke to had friends and colleagues who are among the number of the dead, and who still recall them faithfully today. The RAF memorial at Runnymede, and the British cemeteries on the continent of Europe, continue to be places of pilgrimage. Even when men survived, their wives, fiancées and families often waited long years for them to return from the war:

'He came home exactly five years to the day!'

'*Had he changed a lot?*'

'Yes. Mind you, they built him up.'

'*He got into a very bad physical condition?*'

'I expect so. Because he wasn't demobbed until 1946. I waited for him five years, I did. Now there was lots of his mates, prisoners of war, their girls met other fellers and married them. My hubby could never do enough for me when we were married. Because I waited for him that five years. He said, "I've got a lot to repay you for."

'I said, "You haven't."

'He said, "All these girls were supposed to marry their blokes when they came back from the war, they never did, they got married." He said some of them committed suicide in the camp.' (*Mrs Brown*)

'If you said to me, was it worth it, I would say it had to be done, but it wasn't worth it, for what we have now. And a lot of other pilots feel the same way. I think, in all honesty, we deserved a better deal than we got. I should explain, I've been in intensive care three times! I'm approaching seventy-six and nowadays pilots don't last much longer than seventy. They've nearly all died off. It was a penalty of this particular commission. This applies to all aircrew. The normal life expectancy was about seventy. I've just got lucky.' (*Mr Landels*)